Daddy Grace

Religion, Race, and Ethnicity
General Editor: Peter J. Paris

Daddy Grace

A Celebrity Preacher and
His House of Prayer

Marie W. Dallam

NEW YORK UNIVERSITY PRESS
New York and London

NEW YORK UNIVERSITY PRESS
New York and London
www.nyupress.org

© 2007 by New York University

Library of Congress Cataloging-in-Publication Data
Dallam, Marie W.
Daddy Grace : a celebrity preacher and his house of prayer /
Marie W. Dallam.
p.   cm.
Includes bibliographical references and index.
ISBN-13: 978-0-8147-2010-3 (cloth : alk. paper)
ISBN-10: 0-8147-2010-2 (cloth : alk. paper)
1. United House of Prayer for All People. 2. Grace, Daddy,
1882?–1960. I. Title.
BX8777.6.A4D35 2007
289.9'4—dc22   2007023496

New York University Press books are printed on acid-free paper,
and their binding materials are chosen for strength and durability.

Manufactured in the United States of America
10 9 8 7 6 5 4 3 2 1

Contents

Acknowledgments

In the spring of 1998, my friend Sharron Jackson asked me what I was studying in graduate school. I told her about a course called "The Black Church and the Urban Challenge," and about the book I was then reading: Jill Watts's text on Father Divine. "Yes," Sharron said, "I remember him from when I was a little girl. Father Divine, Daddy Grace, all of them. We used to see them up in Harlem." I did not admit it at the time, but I had never heard of Daddy Grace. My friend's name-dropping propelled me to the library in search of an answer about who this religious leader was, and the lack of any satisfactory information is what caused me to begin this project. My research on Grace became not only a term paper for that class, but also the axis around which the rest of my graduate education revolved. Foremost, then, I thank Sharron for opening an important new door in my life.

Second, I must thank Lenwood Davis, whose annotated bibliography on Daddy Grace provided my initial starting point. Without his book I would never have known where to begin with the work.

Numerous professors guided and encouraged my research and writing, and for this I thank them immensely. Primary among them is Rebecca Alpert, my dissertation advisor, whose patience and careful attention was greater than I could possibly thank her for. I am also indebted to John Raines, David H. Watt, Evelyn Brooks Higginbotham, Robert Schneider, Katie Geneva Cannon, Wilbert Jenkins, Herbert Ershkowitz, and Bettye Collier-Thomas, each of whom worked with me on some part of the project.

Many thanks go to New York University Press, especially editor Jennifer Hammer, who believed in the value of my project long before most of the words made it onto the page, and to series editor Peter Paris for his careful reading and thoughtful suggestions for improvement. I also thank Despina Papazoglou Gimbel and Emily Park for their work on the manuscript.

I offer my gratitude to librarians who took time to help me with pieces of the puzzle. Among those who were especially helpful were Andre Elizee of the Schomburg Center for Research in Black Culture, New York Public Library; Randall K. Burkett, curator of the African American Collections at Woodruff Library, Emory University; the staff of the New Bedford Free Public Library, especially Paul Cyr of the Special Collections Department; Marion Paynter and the library staff at the *Charlotte Observer*; the library of the *New Bedford Standard-Times,* especially Gail Couture; Cathy Meaney, formerly of Paley Library at Temple University; Gloria Korsman at Andover-Harvard Theological Library at Harvard Divinity School; and the staff in numerous departments of the Free Library of Philadelphia.

I am thankful for those who generously assisted me with photographs for this work: the Sargeant Memorial Room of Kirn Library in Norfolk, Virginia, and Robert Hitchings in particular; historian Milledge Murray, who donated photographs from his private collection; and the *Charlotte Observer.*

Along the way, I have appreciated both input and moral support offered by many colleagues and friends whom I met at Temple University, including Simon Wood, Randall Pabich, Pam Detrixhe, Darren Trippell, Rebekah Buchanan, and Janice Anthony. My gratitude especially extends to Dan Gallagher for his heroic readings and re-readings of portions of this text, and to Rachael Swierzewski for her research assistance. Each of the following colleagues discussed sections of this work with me and provided pivotal advice, and so I offer particularly special thanks to Julie Sheetz-Willard, Deborah Glanzberg-Krainin, Joseph Fitzgerald, Kevin J. Christiano, David Hollenberg, and Lori Salem.

I am grateful to the associations that funded segments of my research and writing: the Temple University Society of Fellows in the Humanities, and the Temple University Graduate Board/University Fellowship Committee.

Finally, though it is barely enough in the way of gratitude, I thank my sister Rebecca Dallam for the twenty years' worth of encouragement that helped get me to this place. I thank Richard Gore for always being the captain of my personal cheerleading team. And most of all, I thank Jean Longo for love, support, food, and shelter, and for patiently listening to me drone on about Daddy Grace day after day, year after year. Everything is sweeter because of you.

Introduction

The reporter on assignment for the Associated Negro Press described the scene he witnessed in Philadelphia:

> A week-long shouting meeting was climaxed Sunday by the United House of Prayer as Daddy ("He's So Sweet") Grace baptized thirty white-clad converts with a fire hose at 16th and Christian Streets. With three bands on hand to assure jumping dance music, Grace first made a 20-minute speech. He reminded them that he flew to the South Pacific, stopped the Japanese-American war in 1945, and flew right back. This he did overnight. And his followers, who were spotted throughout the huge crowd, said, "Yes he did." As Grace raised his hands, with finger-nails from one to three inches, and fingers graced with diamonds and sapphires, local firemen turned on the hose. . . . As soon as the water struck them, the converts began dancing, shivering, twisting, prancing. . . . They screamed into the water, praising the sweet name of Daddy while Daddy stood safely under an umbrella and said, "Ain't I pretty?"[1]

Decades after it was written, this record of a United House of Prayer baptismal event stands as a timeless description of Bishop Grace, the founder of the United House of Prayer for All People who became a minor American celebrity. It is timeless because it captures so many of the pervasive mythological themes about both Grace and his church members: the leader's extravagance, his claims to fantastic power, his constant focus on himself, and the worshippers who were not afraid of being a public spectacle with their vibrant praise of "Sweet Daddy." The word "mythological" refers not to the truth value in these themes, but to their dominance of public perceptions about Grace and his church both during his lifetime and in the collective memory of American religious history.[2]

During the four decades of Grace's religious leadership, the United

House of Prayer frequently attracted mockery from those outside of its ranks. Observers ridiculed distinctive features of the church including the exuberant style of worship, the extensive line of goods for sale named after Daddy Grace, the pomp of annual convocation ceremonies, members' passionate devotion to the church and to the bishop, and the intricate network of church clubs, each with its own uniform. Grace himself received national exposure in both academic and tabloid form. At times he courted this publicity, while on other occasions it was unwelcome. In addition to attention-getting maneuvers such as wearing flamboyant clothing and jewelry, purchasing high profile real estate, and conducting baptisms in city streets with a fire hose, Grace reputedly accepted massive donations from poverty-stricken followers and used the money to live lavishly. From scholars to newspaper reporters, few hesitated to judge both Grace and his followers negatively. In an early academic example, anthropologist Arthur Huff Fauset characterized House of Prayer members as "gullible" and suggested outsiders should take pity on them and "smile at these manifestations and ascribe them to the child-like nature of the Negro which is attracted to these uniforms, and other baubles."[3] Popular writers crafted descriptions of Grace as "a brown-skinned P. T. Barnum who cracked the whip in a circus of gaudy costumes, wildly gyrating acrobats and brass bands that played as if God were a Cosmic Hipster."[4] More recently, in his study of messianic myth among African Americans Wilson Jeremiah Jones compared Grace with Father Divine and Prophet Jones, saying they were all "opportunistic, egotistical charlatans, who elevated themselves for purposes of self-aggrandizement."[5] Even a former member, in his apostate text, declared: "The House of Prayer still stands as a constant reminder of the gullible nature of mankind."[6] These examples demonstrate that the House of Prayer was often perceived as an illegitimate religious institution, and this mischaracterization was not without consequence. Grace was rebuffed by other pastors when he made ecumenical overtures, he and his followers were sometimes hounded by news reporters who wanted to substantiate outrageous headlines, and the church was usually designated a "cult" in the most pejorative sense of the word.

It was assumed by many that Grace was the charismatic glue that held his church together, and that once he was gone it would disintegrate. After his death in early 1960, some predicted that followers would be lured away by any new leader who came along. Never having taken the church seriously to begin with, outside observers underestimated its structural integrity and the commitment of its members to the faith, and they also overestimated the importance of Daddy Grace's role.[7] Church members ignored these predictions and were optimistic about their future despite sadness over the bishop's death. As Melvin Adams, a Charlotte pastor, told congregants: "Satan is just waiting for us to stop working, then he will say the House of Prayer is going down. . . . The House of Prayer is not going down. It's going higher and higher than ever before."[8] Adams proved correct. Though there were many legal and organizational hurdles in the years following Grace's death, the church restructured, streamlined, and continued to expand. Today the House of Prayer remains an active church with a national membership in the tens, if not hundreds, of thousands.

To date, neither the United House of Prayer nor its founding bishop have received sufficient scholarly attention. Because nonmembers tended to view Daddy Grace as a caricature, few scholars have bothered to examine the intentionality of his actions, the things that influenced his decisions, or the integrity of his religious leadership. This book is the first to make a serious examination of the religious nature of the House of Prayer, the dimensions of Grace's leadership strategies, and the connections between his often-ostentatious acts and the intentional infrastructure of the House of Prayer. This book is both a religious history of the first forty years of the institution (1920–60) and an intellectual history of its founder. I am particularly interested in some of the unique and unexpected directions Grace took in his leadership, and herein I attempt to discern what inspired him to make some of these decisions as well as how they affected the institution in the long term. Ultimately, this book helps to fill in the gaps of our knowledge about a man who was well known in African-American communities from the 1930s through the 1960s, but who is now noticeably absent from scholarly literature. Grace's leadership was exceptionally innovative, and there is much to be gained from reexamining his unique style of decision making. An understanding of each aspect of the church must begin with Daddy Grace but must also include the people, their beliefs, and their practices. In other words, I tell the story of Grace in order to tell also the story of the people who co-created a new American church with him. In the end, the details of this story demonstrate that Grace should be considered among the most distinctive religious leaders of twentieth-century America.

Behind Grace's Façade

One question that remains to this day is who the real man was behind the façade of Daddy Grace. What was Marcelino Manuel da Graca, the human being, like? Was the existence of his church the result of hidden motives—perhaps desires for riches or fame—or was he a sincere, God-fearing man whose every action was a response to a religious call? Very little information is available to answer these kinds of questions, as Grace left almost no writings and even fewer of his spoken words were recorded. After Grace's death, reporter Phil Casey summed up the way many people had experienced him, writing, "It sometimes seemed it must be easier to strangle eels than to pin Daddy down on points of fact."[9] Certainly, Casey's words aptly describe the challenge of uncovering the "real" Marcelino Manuel da Graca who spent decades camouflaged by Daddy Grace, founder and bishop. Now, half a century after his death, only Grace's church remains as a testament to his intellect, abilities, and achievement. Though the church was once a truly unusual piece of twentieth-century American religious history, today it is a much more mainstream form of Christianity, not readily identifiable with its ostentatious roots. To understand the developmental trajectory of this church, one must inevitably begin with a profile of its founder.

Marcelino Manuel da Graca, most probably the second of five children, was born in approximately 1881 and raised in the Cape Verdean archipelago, off the coast of northwestern Africa.[10] His youngest sister, Louise, remembered that their mother always proudly said Marcelino was "different" from the other children.[11] The da Graca siblings were raised in the Catholic church, which was the only established religion on the islands at that time, but when Grace came to the United States as an adult he had the freedom to pursue different kinds of Christian belief and practice. However Catholicism always remained influential in his life, and even in the 1930s when his own church was well established, Grace admitted that technically he was still Catholic.[12]

Grace always preferred to keep his background cloaked in mystery, saying things such as, "I came from the land beyond the sea."[13] Occasionally he claimed his parents were from Lisbon, but in fact Gertrude and Manuel had been born and raised on the island of Brava, just as his grandparents, Augusto and Constantina on his maternal side and Louis and Rose on his paternal side, had been. It appears that Marcelino Manuel had great respect for his father, Manuel. As the eldest son, he was his father's namesake, and though he toyed with his own name over the years he always kept the "Manuel" present in his experiments: Charles Manuel Grace; Charles Imanuel Grace; Emmanuel Grace. Grace also appears to have been close with his mother, expressing particular regret when she passed away in July 1933. As he wrote in a letter to one of his assistants later that summer, "I am feelling bad over Mother's death besides other trobles [*sic*]."[14]

Grace's native tongue was Crioulo, the language of the archipelago. Immigration records list him as literate in Portuguese and English, but various associates had conflicting opinions on how literate he actually was.[15] In court on one occasion, he was handed a newspaper and forced to prove he could read English.[16] His tidy, careful handwriting may suggest that he had to put great effort into the act of writing his name; on the other hand, it may suggest that he had a formal education. Such an education would most likely have been in a Catholic school where he was taught in Portuguese and which could have been located either in the archipelago or in Portugal. The da Graca family appears not to have been poor despite the fact that their father primarily worked as a mason, so it is possible that they would have found the money to educate their eldest son. Had they been poor, it also would have been out of the question for them to emigrate en masse to the United States, which was a very expensive venture undertaken only by families of means.[17]

Between the time Grace arrived in the United States, somewhere around 1900, and when he started his church in 1921, he was "studying and working and traveling. I traveled almost all my days. . . . I studied on the train, in the street car, in the homes and in the classes."[18] When asked how he earned a living during that time, he said, "I worked on a farm, I worked in the restaurant, everywhere I had to, I did not want to be idle anywhere I am, and wanted to do something, and I got in anything I chose and worked."[19] In addition to work and study, he married and fathered two children. His first wife, Jennie, was Cape Verdean. She claimed that she had met Grace at a social event at the South Harwich Methodist Church when she was 16 years old. At the time, Grace was employed at the Snow Inn. He used to ride a bike to Harwichport so that they could attend church together, and Jennie remembered that his favorite hymn was "Shall We Gather By the River?" Her father did not approve of their marriage, possibly because of the eleven-year age difference. Jennie said Grace had left her in approximately 1912 after they argued about the attention he was giving to another woman, although his niece always claimed the marriage had ended because Jennie "didn't want a spiritual life."[20] Grace was never vocal about the existence of his first wife, but he must not have had acrimonious feelings toward her, since her picture hung on the wall in his Charlotte home for decades.[21]

Grace's second wife, Angelina, was from Mexico.[22] One church member described Angelina as "a light skinned woman with light brown hair, and she had a mole on her face, a large mole, and she had curls."[23] After their 1932 marriage in Arizona, when Angelina was 19, she moved with Grace to Washington, DC. It seems that they did not really live together, however, because Grace's primary residence in Washington was on Logan Circle and Angelina lived elsewhere in the city.[24] Nonetheless, she bore him a son in 1935. Like his marriage to Jennie, Grace's marriage to Angelina lasted only a few years, and their divorce was finalized in 1937. Over the years, many other women claimed to have had sexual relationships or children or both with Grace, but none of these claims were ever confirmed by the courts.

Although Grace was only five feet eight inches tall, he made certain he stood apart from other men by adorning himself with nothing less than flamboyance.[25] His clothes were unpredictable, but usually flashy. He often wore tailor-made suits of lush fabrics, sometimes in vibrant colors and decorated with gold piping or shiny buttons. He paired the suits with brightly striped vests and hand-painted neckties. For less formal occasions Grace might wear a kimono or his red and silver cowboy shirt or his long, northern fur seal coat. His fingers and wrists invariably clanged with gold bracelets and rings containing precious stones. The fingernails of his left hand, which he allowed to grow several inches, were often painted in red, white, and blue. Grace kept his hair at shoulder length, and in early years he had a mustache and goatee, while later on he often simply drew his mustache on with an eye pencil. Though he mostly maintained a stoic countenance, when he was in the mood to have his picture taken he would smile broadly and stop to offer a variety of poses.[26] To the right of his nose Grace had a small scar or birthmark; this mark makes it possible to confirm the legitimacy of pictures of him, which is helpful because his facial appearance changed significantly as he aged.

Just as he dressed with great forethought, Grace also lived and traveled in style. He always had at least one luxury car for travel, such as a Packard, a Cadillac, or a Pierce-Arrow, and he sometimes had an entourage including a chauffeur, a body guard, invited guests, and any number of other assistants, such as elders, lawyers, or secretaries. His long-time chauffeur John Hero said that Grace usually kept the separation window in the car open, and when the two were alone they had friendly conversation. He added that Grace's "customary seat [was] the extreme right corner of the car."[27]

Grace's various homes, once he began collecting them, were often mansions much larger than anything needed by a single man, and he filled them with antiques and artwork. In his New Bedford home on County Street he had a collection of photographs that included one of Franklin Delano Roosevelt, whom he admired and for whom he had once campaigned. Another photo was of Dean Martin; Grace's niece said he was unfamiliar with Martin but kept it because it had been a gift. Grace also seemed to collect bits of memorabilia: in a Charlotte safe opened after his death, for example, Grace had placed letters reportedly written to him by people asking for help, blessings, and to become members of his church.[28]

Despite his extravagant taste in homes and clothing, for entertainment Grace enjoyed more simple pleasures. For example, at his County Street home he often sat on the lawn, just looking at the view. To relax in the evenings he played piano. He said he never watched television or listened to the radio, but he kept light fiction around the house that he sometimes asked others to read to him. Grace said he did not read the newspapers because he did not understand them. However, it is clear that he kept abreast of current events, particularly international ones, because occasionally he spoke about them to followers. Therefore, it seems likely that he either read the newspaper or listened to the radio, even if only irregularly.[29]

Grace believed that travel was one of the best forms of education, and so during his lifetime he went to Africa, Europe, the Middle East, and the Caribbean, in addition to traveling all over the United States. He avoided airplanes, preferring trains and cars for cross-country travel, and ships to go abroad. In 1936 he bought a vacation home in Cuba, twelve miles outside Havana. It was a somewhat unusual choice because it was located in a beach town known only for its casinos, yet Grace eschewed gambling.[30] For entertainment, therefore, he probably spent time on the beach and kept company with his traveling companions. Returning home from Cuba he once said, "I just returned from the land of sunshine and flowers. If I am able to take a trip for recreation, for a good time and to be among courteous people, I never miss the land of Cuba. I regret that I had to leave there so soon."[31]

Aside from lavish living, Grace had few identifiable vices. He neither smoked nor drank. His favorite foods were coffee, which he purportedly drank constantly, and various types of toast, including cheese toast, raisin toast, and cinnamon toast. As one visitor recalled, "Of all the foods served during the hours-long breakfast, Daddy seemed to mostly eat cinnamon toast. The more toast Daddy downed, the more he was served." Grace then insisted his guest have some too, though she was not really interested.[32] Grace preferred to sleep in the mid-morning hours, from 5 a.m. to 10 a.m., which put him on a slightly unusual schedule.[33] But in most other ways, Grace's personal habits did not distinguish him from other men.

Possibly because he was a target for accusations of impropriety, Grace's lifestyle vacillated between complete privacy and intense publicity, and this fact contributes to the difficulty of reconstructing his life and work. Grace had hundreds of associates but very few close friends. Aside from several long-term House of Prayer assistants whom he counted as friends, such as *Grace Magazine* editor Ernest Mitchell, chauffeur John Hero, and assistant Melvin Spencer, his social circle was small. Notable friendships with people outside of the church that he maintained over several decades included those with Edward Rogall, a Jewish businessman in New York who assisted him with real estate; J. S. Nathaniel Tross, a Guyanese pastor of a Methodist church in Charlotte; Samuel Keets, a white real estate speculator from Washington, DC, whose nickname for Grace was "bishops"; and Ernesto Balla, a Catholic Portuguese doctor who lived in New Bedford and was named in Grace's will as an executor of his estate. What is observable is that Grace liked educated people of all races. When he had the opportunity, he invited people for dinner in his home. He enjoyed just sitting and talking; friends attested that in addition to knowing a lot about the Bible, Grace spoke intelligently about history, and he had a sense of humor. Afterwards, Grace might sit down at the piano and "tear it up" to entertain his company, as Keets described.[34] Grace was also quite close with several of the females in his family, particularly his younger sisters Sylvia and Louise, and niece Marie Miller, the daughter of his sister Jennie. Curiously, he demonstrated only minimal interest in his two sons, Norman and Marcelino, and he had an on-again/off-again relationship with his daughter, Irene.

One on one, it seems that Grace used speech as much to say nothing as to say something. Reporters often noted that the bishop deflected any questions he did not want to answer by offering refreshments or talking at length on a completely different subject.[35] House of Prayer members who sought help from Daddy Grace found that when his response to a question was silence, it meant "no" or disapproval.[36] His friend Dr. Balla commented that despite his intelligence, when Grace spoke in parables he was difficult to understand.[37] Keets added that he was honest, but hard to pin down. "His word was one hundred per cent, if you could ever get him to commit himself," he said after Grace's death.[38]

What remains most elusive about Daddy Grace is how he felt about his life. Did he experience a tension between his public persona and his "real" self? Or was the "real" Grace exactly what everyone saw, what he presented to the world? Most of his life was spent living as a celebrity. Even in the solitude of his own homes, where he was attended to by followers who worked as caretakers, he was on public display. This meant he was left little room for personal weakness. I suspect that in order to navigate that kind of complicated existence, deep down he must have been a truly private person, a loner. His intense privacy made it possible for him to appear as a captivating leader with his human needs and feelings always concealed from public view. The moments when a more personal Grace shone through were fleeting, and so in the end we do not really know who and what moved him. Who, for example, caught Grace's attention one night during a service in New Bedford, prompting a reporter to note that "a look of casual recognition came over his face as he sighted a familiar figure in the audience"?[39] And who or what was it that provoked the rare, completely genuine smile captured by a photographer visiting with Grace in Norfolk?[40] All of these things are unknown, and what Grace thought about in his private time, what worried him, and what gave him the most pleasure will always remain his secrets.

Overall Themes of Investigation

In my interpretation of Grace's leadership of the United House of Prayer I raise numerous questions about the relationship of action to belief, the relationship of followers to leader, the relationship of church to context, and the relationship of self-identity to institutional identity. My explorations of the answers has resulted in several themes' being woven throughout the text, most of which are not limited to one section, but rather recur as pieces of the church story bring them to the fore.

One theme is the myriad influences on Grace's leadership choices. Grace's cultural heritage surely affected his understanding of race and class, his ideas about religious rituals and festival traditions, and his concepts about church hierarchy, as they all bear the marks of his Cape Verdean background. Other influences that were key in particular moments include both his friends and his rivals. Exploring each of these elements helps reveal both Grace the religious leader and Grace the man, and in turn helps us to learn about the followers and the institution.

In fact, an understanding of the people who followed Grace is a theme very closely tied with an understanding of Grace himself. We do not have the demographic data to know much about Grace's flock, but some aspects can be gleaned from considering characteristics of the leader whom followers built and supported, and characteristics of the church in which members channeled their energies. Is Grace in some sense a collective representation of the House of Prayer membership? Is his role a projection of their needs, constructed by their desires? To a degree the answer is yes, and therefore we can learn about the church members by learning about his role. However, Grace was not solely shaped by the followers, but also by his own creative energies, and therefore in considering his personal influences we in turn learn about his institution.

Another theme is the group identity of the House of Prayer, ranging from what it was like at various moments in time to the ways it was created through ritual. The construction of sacred space and time in the church seems to have occurred in ways unlike what most people would expect and understand. Therefore, I consider distinctive facets of the House of Prayer, such as the meaning of money and goods, which sometimes bordered on totemic; the ritual aspects of fund-raising and donation; iconography within the church; and the symbolic function of property and wealth. I am also intrigued by the way in which a group of people organizes and shapes itself into a religious institution; thus, I continually ask what the component parts of a religious institution are, and how they all came together in this particular instance. Not surprisingly, some of the House of Prayer's pitfalls are as helpful in exploring the theme of institution-building as are its successes.

Although it is certainly a relevant path of investigation, in general I am less concerned with white racism, white oppression, and white perspectives on the church than I am with the view from the inside. Therefore, I continually ask what everyday life was like for the African American church member, and therefore, what the church meant to him or her. How did the church fit into his or her worldview and experiences, and how did it subsequently shape them? As much as possible, I approach my questions about institution-building and identity from an inside view, using followers' words to express that for themselves. I am hampered by the fact that I am, by every definition, an outsider. Nonetheless, I believe that my work comes much closer to a sympathetic portrait than any prior study has, and therefore my work represents a step forward.

Situating the Study of Daddy Grace

Very little academic work has focused on Daddy Grace and the United House of Prayer, and the corpus of published pieces primarily consists of decades-old essays by social scientists who conducted site visits and interviewed members. Foremost among these works is Arthur Huff Fauset's *Black Gods of the Metropolis,* the book version of his dissertation in anthropology.[41] Fauset's pioneering project, mostly based on fieldwork done in Philadelphia in 1940–41, examines several forms of urban African American religion that were newly emergent at that time. The United House of Prayer was among the groups he studied. Partly because Fauset's study was broad, considering the history and organization of the church as well as its beliefs and practices, and partly because it was one of the earliest published pieces, his work on the House of Prayer became definitive. That is unfortunate, because in my estimation Fauset had a clear bias against the House of Prayer, which prevented him from evaluating the church fairly.[42] As a result, subsequent work on Grace and the church not only draws on his research but also recycles his bias. Particular manifestations of this are examined in chapters 3 and 4.

Beyond the work of Fauset are several notable essays published on the House of Prayer. G. Norman Eddy's preliminary attempt at typologizing "storefront" religions included a section on the House of Prayer, based on observations that seem to have been conducted in Boston.[43] As part of graduate work in anthropology at Yale, Alexander Alland was one among a group who analyzed religious trance in the church in 1959–60.[44] John Robinson's 1974 history essay on the church was intended as an update to Fauset's work, and he added interesting evaluations of the House of Prayer in the post-Grace years.[45] In 1977, Arthur Carl Piepkorn used unique sources to put together a brief portrait of the House of Prayer in a survey of Pentecostalism.[46] As part of a 1989 collection on religious leaders, John O. Hodges wrote a short, pithy entry about the history of the House of Prayer and Grace's role in the church.[47] And finally, Danielle Brune Sigler has recently reopened the field for study with two essays on Grace that question previous assumptions and raise many issues worthy of fresh exploration.[48]

Daddy Grace and the House of Prayer were also examined in a handful of unpublished dissertations and theses. The earliest significant piece is that by James Daniel Tyms, who visited churches in the Washington, DC, area and included a chapter on Grace's leadership in his 1938 master's thesis in religion.[49] Chancellor Williams's dissertation on economic endeavors in several religious groups included a chapter on the House of Prayer, partly based on written surveys and partly based on visits he made to East Coast churches from 1942–46.[50] Albert Whiting's 1952 sociology dissertation was the first work to focus solely on the House of Prayer. He conducted fieldwork in Augusta, Georgia, over several months in an effort to create a psychological profile of typical church members.[51] Some unique biographical work on Grace was included in Jean E. Barker's 1993 master's thesis on Cape Verdean immigrants.[52] And finally, Danielle Brune's (Sigler's) 2002 dissertation, a cultural biography of Daddy Grace, offers particularly good treatment of the early years of the House of Prayer, as well as compelling analyses of popular misconceptions about Grace's leadership.[53]

Survey texts in both American religion and African American religious history regularly mention Daddy Grace, but rarely go beyond that. Specific books are discussed in detail in chapter 4; however, the overall trend is that Grace and his church are treated as interesting but insignificant, and they receive decreasing attention in these works as the decades pass. An example is Catherine Albanese's highly regarded textbook on American religion. In the first edition, from 1981, one paragraph describes Grace and his church, and it is written in the past tense without giving any indication that the church still exists. By the third edition of this book, in 1999, Grace and the church had been completely written out of the text, no longer an important enough piece of American religious history to remember.[54] This dismissal is not uncommon in the history books and is at least preferable to the church's treatment in those books that continue to malign and mischaracterize Grace and the House of Prayer. Another trend in the history texts is that Grace is always paired with a discussion of Father Divine, another religious leader with whom he is typically confused. Often, the men are elided into a single "type" of which each is purportedly representative; sometimes the "type" describes their leadership, their theology, their organization, and/or their followers. The history books in particular show that the two men have become so closely identified with each other that scholars seemingly cannot mention one without mentioning the other. R. Marie Griffith articulately summarizes the problem this way:

> When Divine has been analyzed as a religious leader, he has most often been viewed (at least until very recently) through the narrow and often racialized lens of a "cult leader," indistinguishable from Bishop Charles M. "Sweet Daddy" Grace and other so-called "black gods of the metropolis." This lumping together of disparate figures has meant that their substantive teachings have been deemphasized, if not neglected altogether.[55]

I examine the issue of the collapse of Grace and Divine in chapter 4, including the history of this trend and how it has affected research.

Among books focused on African American religious history, the lone standout worthy of praise is Hans A. Baer and Merrill Singer's *African-American Religion in the Twentieth Century: Varieties of Protest and Accommodation*.[56] This text is concerned with sociological categories of Black religion and how particular groups have acted to accommodate or challenge American social norms. As an example of a group that does not clearly fit into one category of their typology, Baer and Singer discuss the House of Prayer at some length. Their work is unique because it implicitly recognizes the church as an institution distinct from its founding father, and because it considers it an alive and evolving organization.

Although the House of Prayer, at least in its first several decades, could certainly be counted among American New Religious Movements (NRMs), it has not been examined by scholars trained in this field of study. This may be due to the fact that after Grace's death the church began a process of internal transformation that moved it toward socio-religious legitimacy, and therefore by the time the NRM field began to flourish in the 1970s, the church was beyond the bounds of its purview. Additionally, since the trend in the NRM field has been toward the study of new religions populated by white and/or Asian peoples, the neglect of the House of Prayer is not especially unusual.[57] However, it is somewhat surprising that scholars have not reconsidered Daddy Grace or his church even within broad historical studies of NRMs in the United States, as many of the typical questions posed in this area are relevant to House of Prayer development.

Daddy Grace has also been written about in more "popular" types of publications, though these were usually more concerned with the leader than with the church. Numerous magazines profiled Grace over the years including *Time, Newsweek, Ebony,* and *Jet.* Biographer Gordon Langley Hall included a chapter on Grace in his 1964 work *The Sawdust Trail: The Story of American Evangelism.*[58] And former church member Paul Hunter published a monograph in which he used his perspective as a House of Prayer apostate to evaluate its beliefs and practices and to compare it with other religious bodies.[59] But even taken together, the majority of these sources—from unpublished manuscripts to well-regarded essays and everything in between—merely repaint a one-dimensional picture of Daddy Grace and the people who followed him. Ultimately, there is a dearth of academic work on Grace and the House of Prayer that both treats them seriously and evaluates them critically.

Source Challenges

While all of the early social science studies are problematic in some way, they are also valuable because they contain firsthand observations and interviews from the Grace years. My work draws on many of them, but I have been careful to interrogate the material presented and to consider the time, place, and motives of each author. In some cases this was easier than others; for example, an appendix to Whiting's dissertation includes transcripts of the personal history interviews he conducted with House of Prayer members. As a result, the members' words can be read independently from the interpretation Whiting provides throughout the text of his dissertation. Such benefits were not available in all cases, however, and so I have made many judgment calls about what should be read as fair or truthful reporting and what should be read with a grain of salt.

The slant of the early studies is just one among many hurdles I have experienced in my research process. Another issue is the lack of primary source material available. I have made the best out of what I could find, but research on Grace and the church would be tremendously enhanced by more data from the *Grace Magazine* and other church publications. The few copies of the house organs that are available—four and a half issues of the *Grace Magazine,* and seven issues of the *House of Prayer Quarterly*—offer a wealth of insight, and additional issues would only add to our understanding of the church. Both of these publications are discussed in more detail both in chapter 5 and the essay on sources, as are the collections of other church publications and ephemera that aided this study.

I regret that the church itself played no part in assisting me with my research. Historically the House of Prayer has been maligned by academic writers, even when the church welcomed such researchers initially. It is therefore no surprise that the church developed an institutional reluctance to speak with outsiders. As part of interpreting Mark 3:22–29, the House of Prayer taught that writers were troublemakers because they asked too many questions: "The scribes ask contrary things thinking that they will get a false answer and that they may be able to write a false statement concerning Jesus. . . . We have Pharisees today among the children of Grace."[60] The church urged everyone to stick together and be of one mind, which implied keeping church business private. "Speak only that which you know," seemed to be the Biblical lesson members have followed, though at one time Elder Mitchell specifically said that bylaws prevented members from speaking about the church without permission.[61] The House of Prayer leadership appears to believe that outside knowledge about their church might threaten it in some way. For example, as did Grace, the organization has continued to inflate its membership numbers grossly; this suggests it is aware that size is often translated as importance. The last membership statistic reported, in 1974, was four million; it seems that no information has been offered since then because the same number continues to be reprinted.[62] Based on my own research, I believe a current rough estimate of twenty-five thousand to seventy-five thousand is more likely; however, I do not have enough information to suggest this number is anything more than speculative on my part.[63] Had the church been responsive to assisting my research, I would have hoped to clarify details such as this one.

Another source challenge is the fact that parts of this work are heavily dependent on newspaper articles. The use of newspapers as source material is quite problematic. Every paper targets a particular audience, and many have particular agendas, and for these reasons the reporting is often skewed to serve an internal purpose (or purposes).[64] Additionally, the stress on publishing an accurate story versus a story that will sell varies from paper to paper and from year to year. I have taken great care in evaluating the stories I have used, cross-referencing information whenever possible and looking for patterns of accuracy and fallacy in reporting so that I could get a sense of what information was trustworthy. I also tried to use a wide variety of newspapers in an effort to find different interpretations of the same events. It is my hope that I have successfully filtered out many of the exaggerations. As a tangential note, by using the morgue of the *New Bedford Standard-Times,* I saw how reporters borrowed heavily from previous work; many of the same catchy phrases and descriptions were used verbatim in their articles for decades. This trend was never far from my mind as I studied and evaluated newspapers of all sorts.[65]

As it happens, Daddy Grace's words were recorded in newspapers more often than anywhere else. By hunting down his statements, I have attempted to present a fuller picture of his person and his leadership than has previously been made. I frequently use quotes from House of Prayer leaders and members so that, as much as possible, they can describe themselves in their own words. This is especially true in sections related to religious belief. Granted, these quotes, usually culled from newspapers and secondary sources, are not as desirable as would be information obtained through individual interviews.[66] However, I have done my best to piece together the myriad voices within the House of Prayer to provide a fair and realistic portrait.

Structure of the Text

Four elements serve to organize this book: chronology, leadership lessons, geography, and religious history. First, because it is a history of the development of an organization, the account unfolds chronologically. Overall, the time frame begins with Grace's birth in 1881 and extends just beyond his 1960 death, with the majority of the text falling in the window of 1922–62. Occasionally there are instances in which the text jumps briefly forward or backward in time in order to raise an issue or highlight events relevant to the topic at hand.

Second, each chapter is driven by an argument about a leadership lesson that affected Grace, zooming in on moments when the nature of Grace's leadership changed or grew. I trace the causes and effects of these changes and posit the significance for his overall religious leadership and, in turn, for the institution as a whole. These aspects of Grace's leadership style are not all equal: some are more distinct than others, some are more readily observable than others, and ultimately, some are more important to the church in the long term than others. This imbalance is the natural by-product of retelling the history of a real person and a real church.

Third, geography provides the book's narrative framework. Each chapter examines the House of Prayer as it existed in a particular urban setting or, in some instances, two settings, and when appropriate I include information about the city itself to help contextualize aspects of the church being discussed. The cities chosen are relevant to particular moments of change in Grace's leadership. In some instances these places serve merely as backdrops to the story; in other instances, the nature or character of the city in question plays an important role. Certainly, one could look at the activities of the church and aspects of Grace's leadership without thinking about where and when they took place, but from a sociological perspective the geographic and socio-cultural context always adds much to our understanding of a religious group. This approach is in line with the broader theory of "religious economy," which acknowledges that a system of religiosity can best be understood in relation to the other social systems operating in the same environment.[67] Hence, we must consider what Grace dealt with in order to establish and maintain a church in any given place, as well as what prospective members encountered each day beyond the House of Prayer doors. Furthermore, in Grace's absence, the people leading that church and the faithful in the pews continued to be shaped by their cultural, political, and social environment. Therefore, understanding something about that place helps us to understand the character and significance of that region's Houses of Prayer.

The fourth and final element that governs the text's structure is a gradual unveiling of the history of this particular religious tradition. Because there are many interesting, sometimes unusual, aspects of Grace's church—such as theology, characteristics of the membership, music, rituals, and many others—I discuss these elements as they become relevant to particular moments in House of Prayer history, rather than all at once in a single spot. Thus each chapter contains sections that advance the details of the religious history by addressing the question of what the United House of Prayer for All People under Daddy Grace was all about.

Chapter Overview

The first chapter, "The Call of God Brought Him," introduces Grace's prebishopric life by examining the social, political, and cultural circumstances of the Cape Verde Islands during the time he lived there, and by considering the picture of early twentieth-century immigrant life in the New Bedford region. Grace first came to public attention in 1922 with the establishment of his second church, located in New Bedford. By examining the local culture and the social divisions of New Bedford, as well as the theological identity of the early United House of Prayer, I posit that with this church Grace intentionally used the principles of the market to compete with other local congregations for membership. His success with this early strategem became one of the hallmarks of his approach to Christian evangelism and repeated itself throughout his forty-year career as a religious leader.

Chapter 2, "The Usual Miracles," examines Grace's earliest efforts at beginning the southern wing of his church in the latter 1920s, particularly in Georgia. I examine his experimentation with methods of attracting potential converts, and as part of this I consider House of Prayer theology and rituals in more detail, most especially the role that healing played in the lives of members. Additionally, this chapter traces the first phases of Grace's evolution from a reactive, defensive man to a religious leader who always stayed above the fray, no matter who tried to attack him or how.

The third chapter, "Led By a Convicted Man," is concerned with several issues related to membership in the United House of Prayer. One significant piece of this is whether followers believed Grace was God and to what extent that idea influenced their commitment to the institution. Though rules for church members were stringent and uncompromising, Grace himself did not always live up to the standards he set. The most egregious early example of his deviance is demonstrated by the Mann Act trial, a case in which a follower accused Grace of rape. On one hand, details of the case serve to contrast the life of the bishop with that of his followers, especially in the realm of behavior. But the Mann Act trial was also a defining moment for the institution because of what it came to symbolize. Rather than causing members to lose trust in Grace, the perceived senseless persecution of the bishop strengthened member support for their leader. And, rather than the declension that might be expected following a scandalous trial, Grace learned that his member base thrived on the unity brought by defending his good name.

Chapter 4, "He Ousted God from Heaven," examines a 1938 incident that altered the course of Daddy Grace's institution-building strategy. In the spring of that year Grace bought the building that housed the Harlem headquarters of Father Divine's Peace Mission Movement, and then he evicted both the members and their leader. This chapter tells the story of that incident, situating it within the larger context of Depression-era Harlem society. An examination of the long-term effects of the Harlem purchase demonstrates that it inadvertently taught both Grace and Divine significant new lessons about ways to sustain their churches, though each man implemented his new ideas uniquely.

Chapter 5, "My Joy Is Completed in Charlotte," recounts the story of the church and its leader during the heyday of the 1940s and 1950s. In this period, the United House of Prayer for All People increasingly ran itself without needing Daddy Grace's constant attention. Regional and local leaders managed most day-to-day affairs, and Grace had the time and freedom to begin refining more peripheral aspects of his church. In some sense, during these two decades the church gained momentum as an institution while the bishop was releasing the reins of his directive leadership. The story of the church during this era is essentially the story of an institution in its prime, with the results of Grace's design finally flourishing on an observable grand scale; yet the story of the bishop during this period is that of an elderly man in the summertime of his leadership, rarely in any particular place or focused on any particular thing but nonetheless occupied with making appearances and experimenting with new ideas.

Chapter 6, "Chaotic Confusion," examines the House of Prayer in the aftermath of Grace's 1960 death. Skeptics publicly anticipated that the church would fall apart without Grace's charismatic leadership, and the initial tumult and confusion in the church only bolstered this opinion. Though Grace's managerial carelessness caused intense disorder, reconsideration of the events following his death allow us to understand what transpired as not merely random chaos and confusion, but as a new wave of leadership utilizing the foundations laid by Grace to bring about major church restructuring. Additionally, theoretical frameworks from the study of New Religious Movements allow us to see the path of the United House of Prayer mirroring that of other institutions whose founding leader has died.

Contribution to Scholarship

In an effort both to fill in the gaps of the historical records and to demonstrate the religious significance of this church, which has been sidelined for far too long, I use various subfields of religious studies to examine Daddy Grace and his church. American religious history, particularly theological family groups, aids me in placing the House of Prayer in a theological context. By considering religious developments contemporary with the church, particularly Pentecostal belief and practice, the House of Prayer emerges not as something wild and crazy but as something quite in line with the most vibrant religious strain of twentieth-century America. In this regard, the House of Prayer does not stand out as original. By using the more particular lens of African American religious history, the House of Prayer can be readily compared with other forms of religion created and/or led by African Americans. Certainly, the House of Prayer can be categorized with churches that fulfilled some of the social needs of African Americans when middle-class-oriented Black churches would not. The reason this aspect is not my primary focus, however, is that although this may help us understand the House of Prayer in a given moment, it does not help us understand the church as it has developed over time, because being a refuge church for those shut out of mainline denominations is not what defines it as an institution.

Today, the House of Prayer is most frequently studied in the context of African American religious history because its membership has predominantly been Black. However, several aspects of the church explain why it should also be considered within the New Religious Movement field. First, Daddy Grace fits the popular understanding of a "charismatic leader," an epithet often used to describe founders of new religions. Second, like other NRMs, the House of Prayer has tended toward insularity, which makes those on the outside suspicious of what happens on the inside and casts it as "other" to a degree that has at times been extreme. This leads readily to a third factor, which is that mainstream America, in its reception of the church, has consistently treated it as a marginal religious group. Such treatment can be seen in all forms of printed material about the church, from newspapers to academic evaluations.[68] These factors, plus the fact that it has long been referred to as a "cult," provide ample reason to consider the House of Prayer alongside other relatively new religious groups. By using frameworks from the study of NRMs, I add support to recent theories about the fate of religious groups after a founder's death, and I also participate in the ongoing debate about how to recognize when a new religion stops being "new."

The House of Prayer history as a whole also provides numerous points of support to the theory of religious economy. This theory posits that the free practice of religion in the United States operates in much the same way as an unregulated capitalist marketplace, and thus many terms from economics can be used metaphorically to describe parallel processes in American religious spheres, or the "religious economy."[69] The benefit of using this terminology is that it turns historic events and concrete data—like a particular tent meeting, a convocation parade, or the number of Houses of Prayer in a given neighborhood—into more abstract, depersonalized concepts. Hence, it is easier to evaluate that data in terms of qualities like success, dependency, influence, et cetera. Using this theory, members and potential members of churches become religious consumers, religious activities turn into products, and mediating between the two are proselytizers and ministers, or salespeople. The relationship of supply and demand also affects how people respond to a particular product, as do time, place, and other unique circumstances. In the case of the United House of Prayer, this terminology aids us in thinking about Grace's target audience, his use of various religious products to attract consumers, his particular strategy for manipulating supply and demand, and the reasons his buyers remained so committed to the Grace brand of religion.

Ultimately, this work contributes to scholarship by giving full-length treatment to a religious organization and leader that has been repeatedly dismissed in academia, and it both broadens our knowledge of African American religious history and addresses questions relevant to NRM studies. Academic interest in Pentecostalism is still growing, mirroring to some degree the explosion of the religion itself, and as a result this history of an early, independently organized Pentecostal church is also valuable for the field of Pentecostal and Apostolic studies. Lastly, because I consider Grace's work in half a dozen localized settings, portions of the text add to our knowledge of working-class religious life, and therefore the overall social history, in these cities. While I cannot claim the work is absolutely comprehensive, I have attempted to be as thorough as possible, both in the array of sources consulted and in the topics broached.

Just as I did when I began this work, I again ask myself, Why was Daddy Grace successful? Was he successful because people followed him? Maybe, as Wilson Jeremiah Jones wondered about Marcus Garvey, Grace merely stepped into a role that happened to be vacant at the time.[70] In other words, maybe he didn't lead people into something; maybe the people were there, ready to be organized and led, and he was the man who happened to be in the right place at the right time. Could it have been the same movement, more or less, if a different person had stepped up to lead? My work has led me to conclude that the answer to this question is a definitive no. The shape of the United House of Prayer for All People was absolutely dependent upon the vision of Daddy Grace, the leadership choices he made, his background and life experiences, and even on the strange tension between his intricate control of the church structure and his careless record keeping. He did not act alone, but he did act with distinction, and without him this particular institution never would have been born.

1

The Call of God Brought Him

At the turn of the twentieth century, Marcelino Manuel da Graca, the future Bishop Charles M. "Daddy" Grace, came to the United States from a tiny Afro-Lusophone island in the Atlantic Ocean. His complex experience as a colonized Catholic "white Portuguese" man of means in his home country did not prepare Grace for the American life. Like so many other immigrants before him, when he stepped off a packet ship in New England he was relegated to the American class of Negroes, whose rights were always negligible. Yet Grace, a keenly intelligent and creative man with a strong religious drive, did not allow himself to be marginalized. Building on the strength of character he developed in Cape Verde, and embracing the immigrant ideal of American opportunity, over time Grace re-created himself as a glamorous bishop whose lively religious services were not to be missed. By 1922 he had begun to transcend his humble background as outsiders took note of the unusual New Bedford, Massachusetts, congregation he had founded. In his first newspaper profile, Grace explained to the public that God had called him to America to spread religious teachings, and for that reason he had opened the small mission in New Bedford. Furthermore, God's "stamp of approval" for his work was apparent in the numerous spiritual gifts bestowed on House of Prayer attendees, from miracle healings to speaking in tongues. The House of Prayer, Grace confidently declared, would prove to be a gift from God, and he himself was merely the instrument brought from a small unknown island to transmit it to Americans.[1]

Life on the Island of Brava

God had sent Grace from the island of Brava, in the Cape Verdean archipelago. The twenty-one Cape Verde Islands, several hundred miles

Daddy Grace eating his favorite food, toast, at his Princess Anne
Road residence in Norfolk, Virginia, 1958. Courtesy of Sargeant
Memorial Room, Norfolk Public Library, Norfolk, Virginia.

off the northwestern coast of Africa, were first mapped by seamen
working for the Portuguese crown in approximately 1460.[2] Portugal
had begun exploration of Africa at least fifty years earlier in search of
gold, territory, and other spoils; by 1420 it had begun colonization and
slave taking in earnest. At first the tiny and empty islands, only nine of
which were potentially inhabitable, seemed of no value. The mother
country invested little in their cultivation, sending only exiles such as
criminals, the poor, and Jews to the archipelago. When Portugal realized Cape Verde was an ideal place for friendly trade and slave "domes-
tication," the islands became a unique resource in the worldwide slave
business. Slave buyers, who preferred to avoid the African continent for

fear of problems including disease and violent resistance, could save themselves several hundred miles of travel by making their purchases in Cape Verde. Prices were higher than on the continent but the Portuguese crown sweetened the deal by claiming its slaves had been domesticated, or broken, already. It seems this process entailed putting the enslaved people through small work projects, spending a short time teaching them basic Catholic catechism and some words in Portuguese, and occasionally performing a group baptism before making them available for sale.[3] The enslaved people who moved through the islands originated in places stretching from Sierra Leone all the way to Morocco, and they were predominantly sent to Brazil and lower New England.[4]

With the recognition of Cape Verde's strategic and economic value, the crown gave land grants and trading privileges to Portuguese people willing to settle there and cultivate the land. These grantees, mostly single Portuguese men, often had little knowledge of how to care for the land properly and directed it to be worked in ways that maximized profits in the short term rather than in ways that protected it in the long term. Initially the labor on the islands was almost exclusively provided by enslaved people, but importation for permanent residence did not last long, and the slave labor force was instead maintained through repopulation. On several islands, manumission was granted quite regularly because it was economically advantageous to the Portuguese power-holders. Formerly enslaved people continued to perform the same jobs, yet now they paid for their own living expenses. So it was that the free, African-descended population grew.[5]

On the southernmost island of the archipelago, called Brava, Marcelino Manuel da Graca—Daddy Grace—was born and raised. Brava is an ancient volcano whose dramatic cliffs rise half a mile out of the Atlantic Ocean. Travel writer Archibald Lyall described the island in the 1930s as "a high, hunched mass of land with an almost perpetual mist draped like a white woolen shawl about its shoulders. . . . The steep slopes [are] dotted with white houses, though the villages seem all to be high up just under the clouds."[6] Each crevice and ripple in Brava's mountains is home to another of its well-tended villages, which numbered thirty-one in the last decades of the 1800s, when Grace was a boy.[7] Some parts of the island are dry and rocky with a landscape that writer Augusto Casimiro described as "parched land, skeletons of lava, bronzed, burnt, like remnants from a fire."[8] However, the greater part of the island is naturally lush with flowers and fruit trees, making it appear more like a large garden that happens to contain a few houses. Flourishing red hibiscus bushes act as property dividing lines; orange, lemon, and peach trees weigh heavily with fruit; and short, thick-trunked trees like baobabs and dragontrees line common walkways. Mineral springs were surprise boons in certain parts of the island. It is no wonder that Casimiro remembered his first morning walking around Brava as being characterized by the "anxious joys of discovery."[9]

The legend of Brava reveals that its first inhabitants were a Portuguese aristocrat and the beautiful peasant woman with whom he had fallen in love. Forbidden by his parents to be together, they defied the order by hiring a ship and sailing from Portugal to the uninhabited Brava. There, like a cross between Adam and Eve and Romeo and Juliet, the couple lived freely and happily in the lush greenery of the southernmost island of the archipelago. Their white descendants were the only residents of Brava until darker-skinned refugees from other islands came during the drought of 1680.[10] This story's lack of historical truth is not relevant; what is important is its meaning for Bravas.[11] The tale contains two significant mythological ideas: first, that Brava was unaffected by the Portuguese feudal system that structured life on the other islands; and second, that the original ethnicity of the Brava people was "white" Portuguese and not African. From the start, then, people native to Brava have set themselves apart as a special group among Cape Verdeans; a people of a higher class and a better origin.

One could say that Brava has been the privileged island of the archipelago. It has always been home to a greater proportion of continental Portuguese people than have the other islands, and therefore has had more wealth per capita. It long served as a vacation spot for the wealthy inhabitants of other islands; some even considered it a health resort and fled there during times of illness.[12] Certainly, its residents were spared many of the epidemics that passed through the archipelago over the centuries, such as cholera, typhoid, and malaria; only in 1868 did Brava fall prey to one, yellow fever epidemic that came from Senegal.[13] And as the southernmost island, Brava often had just enough precipitation to spare it from the droughts and famines that debilitated the northern islands.[14] Beyond mere geographical advantages, the Bravas had a reputation among the islands for considering themselves better than other Cape Verdeans, and were stereotyped as "mild-mannered and pious."[15] Because Brava had a smaller population of enslaved people than the other islands, as well as more settlers from Madeira and the Azores, its descendants are generally lighter of color than other Cape Verdeans and more likely to have light eyes and straight hair.[16] These are many of the factors that have contributed to the reputation of Brava and her people as superior among Cape Verdeans.

Despite the island's status, the quality of life on Brava was no more advanced than that on any other island of the archipelago. In the last two decades of the 1800s Brava had no cafes, restaurants, or hotels. Its homes had no running water, nor gas or electric power. For those who could afford it, horseback was the best way to transport anything on the island, but more commonly, women carried heavy loads on their heads. The single-story houses of the poorer people were built from volcanic stones and roofed with thatch, with approximate openings left for doorways and ventilation—Casimiro has called them black, gloomy "castles of lava." Residents of greater means lived in homes made of smooth white stucco, roofed with red tiles or shingles, and outfitted with glass doors and windows. In the decades surrounding 1900, the infrastructure improved, and the number of nicer homes built increased due to the money being sent home from emigrants. Streets in the larger villages were paved with cobblestones, cisterns were built nearer to homes, and many "castles of lava" were torn down and replaced. Although emigrants' absence was painful for everyone involved, its rewards also brought joy to the island and her people.[17]

Cape Verdeans Immigrate

American immigration started more by chance than by deliberate decision. Beginning in the early 1800s, men were recruited from Cape Verde to work on New England whaling ships. They made attractive employees because they were willing to work for less pay than American citizens. Cape Verdean men took to the sea on ships for months at a time, sometimes making stopovers in New England, and usually returning with decent pay to invest in their homeland and family. This work on whaling ships, as well as subsequent work as crewmen on American transport boats, precipitated what eventually turned into mass Cape Verdean immigration in America. Between 1880 and 1900, over 2,900 Cape Verdeans moved to the United States; between 1900 and 1920, nearly 18,000 more came. This represented a large portion of the islands' population, which at that time was less than 150,000.[18] Many factors contributed to the surge in emigration from the Cape Verde Islands, including a severe drought and famine beginning around 1900 that affected even drought-resistant Brava. For some, leaving their home was the only way to reunite their families when the seamen decided to stay in New England. Increasingly, Cape Verdeans determined that the riches of the United States were the path to a better life back home. Thus emigration was often temporary, or at least intended to be so, and money was sent back to use for property purchases in the islands. However, as with other immigrant groups in the United States, many temporary moves became permanent, and the Cape Verdeans grew into Cape Verdean Americans.

The ships visiting Brava's busy port pulled in and out of Furna, a crater on the northwest side of the island whose depth, winds, and cliffs made it Brava's most accessible harbor. Winding roads led from the towns down to Furna; in the late nineteenth and early twentieth centuries, this was where tearful good-byes were said to departing emigrants.[19] Over time, the loss of so many people from this tiny island came to affect the mood of the Bravas who stayed. Eugenio Tavares, a Cape Verdean poet born in 1867, was one of several poets who reflected on this mood. He referred to his native Brava as the "land of sodade," which means a land of heartsickness and yearning for what is missing and lost.[20] In his *Morna de Despedida* (*Morna* of Farewell), Tavares described the feelings of Bravas on both sides of the Atlantic:

> Leave me to mourn
> The destiny of man;
> This grief
> Which has no name;
> The pain of love,
> The pain of remembering
> Someone I love
> And who loves me.[21]

Travel writer Lyall later wrote that "in Brava more than elsewhere, the fate of true lovers is to part and never see each other more."[22] In their increasingly empty homes on the island, extended family and friends congregated by whale-oil lamps to amuse themselves with music, singing, and the spoken word. The *mornas* were poetry and songs that appealed to Cape Verdeans of all social classes. Despite a condescending tone, Lyall's description of musical *mornas* is evocative for those not familiar with them: "They were hauntingly lovely melodies, soft, plangent things that expressed all the heartache of this little race of exiles, the poverty and danger of their simple lives, and the ancestral melancholy of the warring strains of their blood. . . . The pent-up sorrow of their sensitive natures finds an outlet only in this native art-form."[23] And when they tired of *mornas*, Cape Verdean children and adults alike turned to another typical form of entertainment, spoken tales of Lob and Pedr, the dim-witted wolf with human qualities and the clever nephew who constantly outsmarted him.[24]

A Modified Portuguese Culture

While Cape Verdean music and stories are unique cultural developments, many of the islands' characteristics are modifications of an inherited Portuguese culture. For example, since the earliest years of colonization the islands' religion has been dominated by Roman Catholicism, and people at all levels of Cape Verdean society have generally practiced the same religion and celebrated holidays and festivals together. Like several of the islands, Brava did not always have a church official present to administer rites, and as a result Bravas were comfortable with the idea that religious leadership could be led by laypersons.[25] Furthermore, this situation allowed a degree of syncretism as vestiges of African customs were maintained within the religion of the colonizers. In Monteiro's study of religion on the islands, he described the Cape Verdean situation as "a religious arrangement reminiscent of Haitian voudou, Brazilian candomble, or Cuban santeria, in its vision of the world of spirits, as well as in its ability to coexist with and freely borrow from the Iberian brand of Roman Catholicism."[26] Protestantism was a latecomer to the archipelago, arriving piecemeal in the late 1800s via converted emigrants who returned. Though many Cape Verdeans looked askance at the faith, on Brava, at least, it was not spurned. Monteiro suggests that this was partly because in the United States Protestantism appeared to be a measure of distinction—as an example, almost all political leaders were Protestant at that time—and therefore Bravas who sought an Americanized life may have considered Protestant religion one element of that ideal. In an official capacity, the Pentecostal Mission of Brava was the first Protestant church established on the island, though shortly after 1900 various mergers of churches transformed it into the Church of the Nazarene.[27] As an offspring of the Holiness Movement, the church in Brava would have emphasized divine healing and entire sanctification, in which the convert was believed to be fully freed from his or her sinful nature; certainly, these were dramatic shifts in perspective from the Roman Catholic theology that dominated the islands' belief system.

Another example of the modified Portuguese culture is found in the islands' language. The official language of Cape Verde is Portuguese, but Crioulo, a Portuguese-based tongue that incorporates vocabulary and grammatical structures from African languages, is used for social life. The isolation of the archipelago has meant that language on the islands has not evolved in the same ways as has the Portuguese of Portugal, therefore Crioulo includes terms that would be considered archaic to speakers of modern Portuguese. Additionally, due to the historical lack of communication among the Cape Verde Islands, Crioulo varies from island to island, in some cases significantly. Despite the fact that only a small portion of the population ever learned or used anything other than Crioulo, Portuguese language ability was usually a requirement for any job above manual-labor level on the islands. Those who were upwardly mobile certainly understood the need to be literate in the islands' language of domination. Like anything of Portuguese—rather than Cape Verdean—origin, the language was considered superior, and therefore to use it was to wrap oneself in what philosopher Pierre Bourdieu would call "symbolic power."[28] As anthropologist Meintel-Machado has insightfully written about the islands, "in an atmosphere where expressiveness in all visible forms regularly meets repression, the spoken language has become the prime area for manifestation and assertion of cultural identity."[29] While she refers, here, to the importance of using Crioulo to resist the Portuguese cultural hegemony, the reverse would also be true: those Cape Verdeans who perceived themselves as upper class or upwardly mobile asserted their identity through the use of Portuguese and the avoidance of Crioulo.

Complexities of Race and Class Labels in Cape Verde

The idea of "class" in Cape Verde is not a straightforward translation of the Western concept. In the first few decades of settlement, the class system was clear: Portuguese power-holders were at the top, the en-slaved people were at the bottom, and a tiny group of exiles and freed slaves lingered in between. In time, as this middle group grew, out of necessity the class system became more multitiered and complicated. Unlike American society, where "class" has often been simplistically equated with income, Cape Verde has a much more intricate system of social stratification that weighs many factors. Similar to what St. Clair Drake and Horace Cayton explained about social class among African Americans in 1930s Chicago, the "constellation of traits" that contrib-uted to one's perceived social level in Cape Verde included ethnic ances-try, island of origin, education, religion, job, and wealth, as well as phe-notypical signs such as skin shade, hair texture and nose shape.[30] But this system only developed over a long period of time in response to the unique and changing situation of the islands' people.

The development of the Cape Verdean system of social identity started from issues surrounding enslavement and manumission. Until the 1600s, when female criminals began being exiled from Portugal to Cape Verde, almost all women on the islands were African. Therefore, most people born there were of mixed Portuguese and African blood. Contrary to the United States, where children born of master-slave rela-tions were regarded as slaves by the master, in Cape Verde such children had a rather ambiguous status. It was clear that they were neither slave nor Portuguese, so they were a race and a class for which the initially two-level society had no structure; and because they were not treated as secrets, their existence created social conundrums. Sometimes the mas-ters treated them as slaves until they were teenagers, then gave them their freedom and a job. Other times they were freed right away and raised in the master's home alongside his Portuguese children, although their mothers remained enslaved. Either way, such children were usually included in the father's will and eventually inherited land or property. As it grew, this new race was given names—*mestico* or "Crioulo"—and the more of them who were born, the more the social ambiguities worked themselves into a system.

Meanwhile, social divisions among the enslaved also developed. Dis-tinctions were made between those born in Cape Verde and those born in Africa, and African birth implied a lower status. Additionally, Catho-lic baptism was a factor that could improve a slave's social standing. Ei-ther way, in relation to the *mestico* population, enslaved people were consistently at the bottom of society and called names meant to keep them there: *preto* or *negro* or "African." They were always associated with Africa, which was positioned as the cultural opposite of Portugal. To be Portuguese was to be powerful, upper class, and sophisticated. "Purebred" Portuguese, also called "white Portuguese," were at the top of Cape Verdean society, as far from Africans as anyone could imagine.

Despite the crown's ideal of the creation of a new Portuguese society in Cape Verde, the Crioulo population eventually outnumbered people whose heritage was solely Portuguese or solely African. Some Crioulo owned property; some had skilled jobs; some were sent to Lisbon for extensive education; many were part of "Portuguese" families; some were of lighter skin than others; and some were born with features more Portuguese than African. Many Crioulo considered themselves Portuguese, and, although this was in fact their citizenship, to the dismay of the "pure" Portuguese they also claimed it as their ethnicity. All of these things complicated easy categories of social status, and thus more and more labels were employed to distinguish people within the hierarchy. Joao Monteiro writes that although the words used to describe each other were often explicitly racialized, the "categories, as they are applied, are not solely racial."[31] For example, one might be called a kinky-haired mulatto, a blue-eyed mulatto, or a thin-lipped mulatto. Though they all designate mixed blood, the first term implies closeness with one's African heritage, while the latter two designate that the person has more Portuguese blood and hence higher status.[32] To contrast this way of categorizing, we might think of the difference between the terms "white" and "white trash" in the United States. The first term merely specifies color and tells us nothing about social class. The second, however, designates both color and class, and is used only as an insult.[33] In Cape Verde, all of the terms used have implications about both ethnicity and class, just as "white trash" does. The key difference is that because Cape Verdeans are used to categorizing in this way, their terms are considered descriptive rather than insulting.[34] Basil Davidson has written that the 1856 census in the archipelago listed seventeen choices for skin color, apparently understandable and visible to everyone. He concluded that " 'distinction by skin colour' seems in time to have reached an almost pathological condition," despite the fact that their society was quite homogenous in its culture.[35] While this "pathology" might appear true on the surface, what his comment fails to capture is the fact that Cape Verdean terms evolved to describe more than color. As an example, consider two categories of social status in

Cape Verde: *branco* and *branco de dinheiro*. The first term is used for a pale-skinned person of high status; the latter, which means "white by money," is a high-class designation for people of darker colors who have obtained power and wealth. What is pathological, then, is the extent to which anything good, educated, sophisticated, or wealthy became associated with Portugal—and by default, whiteness; while anything bad, ignorant, lowly, or poor became associated with Africa. One may lament that the entire system of race and class stratification in Cape Verde was born of the colonial mentality, but more pressing is understanding that the resultant system is drastically different from that of the United States. When Cape Verdeans migrated here en masse, they found that their basic precepts of social life were inconsistent with American precepts. Unlike all of the choices at home, in the United States the emigrants were uniformly demoted to "Negro" and "low class."[36] One way they found to escape the strange American caste system was to operate within a Portuguese social world as much as possible once they arrived in New England.

New Bedford Life

When the peak period of Cape Verdean immigration began at the turn of the twentieth century, New Bedford, Massachusetts, was a vibrant, thriving town. No longer based solely around whaling, the economy expanded as its textile industry boomed and its commercial fishing port increased in significance. The first two decades of the century saw the new construction of mills, small businesses, schools, and churches. The city, suddenly made more accessible by new bridges and electric trolley cars, attracted immigrants who poured in to settle and find work.[37] Its population of over sixty-two thousand included people of many colors, nationalities, and religious persuasions. The recent-immigrant communities were sizable, making up approximately 75 percent of the people in the small city. Yet they were largely concentrated in two neighborhoods. In the North End lived people of Greek, Albanian, and French-Canadian origin, while in the South End were people of English, Russian Jewish, Portuguese, and Cape Verdean origin. Because of the direct shipping line between the islands and New England, the Cape Verdean group, all deemed Bravas, was the only immigrant group in New Bedford that came directly from its home country without any other

American stops in between. By making a hard left onto South Water Street just beyond the ship docks and Customs offices, the Bravas' first impressions of America came as they walked the short distance to a neighborhood that brimmed with old friends and a familiar cultural attitude. The two to three thousand Cape Verdeans living in New Bedford at that time were more-or-less segregated from the other people of Portuguese origin, whose neighborhood was a distinct enclave west of South Water Street. The Bravas, to the east and north of this area, were mixed in with African Americans and a wide spectrum of immigrants from other countries.[38]

South Water Street was the center of action and social life for those in the South End. Belgian-block streets served those with horse-and-buggy, and wide, paved sidewalks contained the crowds who shopped in store after store.[39] Wayward children could amuse themselves in pool halls, while men could visit houses of "ill fame" that offered them professional women of various ages and ethnicities. The 1900 United States census reveals that not only was South Water Street a bustling business thoroughfare, but it was also densely residential. Above and between the businesses were rambling wooden structures that served as boarding houses and apartment buildings.[40] Though we cannot truly know how successful the social interaction among people was at that time, we can certainly see that they lived in close quarters. Three-story houses on Water Street, the first levels of which were typically businesses, often contained a dozen or more upstairs residents of varying ethnicities. On Cannon Street, just off of South Water, the residents hailed from countries such as Barbados, Russia, Germany, and Ireland; there were "Black" Portuguese and "white" Portuguese; and there were African Americans from the southern United States. Just around the corner were French-Canadians and Poles.[41] All of these people shared buildings, public spaces, and privies.

The da Gracas Arrive

In May 1902, the da Graca family arrived at the port of New Bedford aboard the *Freeman*. Manuel da Graca, the father and literate member of the group, told immigration officials he had been in New Bedford once before, for six months during the year 1893.[42] He was accompanied on the *Freeman* by his wife, Gertrude; his son Benventura, age 14;

and his daughters Eugenia (Jennie), age 20, Sylvia, age 12, and Louise, age 6. One other person was traveling with the party: a 16-year-old, literate female, whose illegible name obscures her identity except that she is listed as another daughter of Manuel da Graca. The entire group was headed for the supposed residence of Manuel and Gertrude's daughter Mary Roza and her husband, Mr. Gomes, at 343 South Water Street, located on the precise spot that only decades before had been New Bedford's Common Burial Ground.[43] City directories, as well as the 1900 census, do not reveal any record of the Roza-Gomes couple at that address, although 343 does appear to have been a boarding house where the tenant roster frequently changed. However, this destination may just have been a ruse. The passenger lists of the *Esperanca* from April 1904 list a single woman named Mariana Roza Senna, age 28, arriving in the United States for the very first time to join Aunt Adelaido da Roza at that same address, 343 South Water Street. Exactly who the Roza family was and how they were related to the da Graca family is a mystery, but perhaps "the Rozas of 343 South Water Street" was just a fabricated family that nervous immigrants knew to name as their own. A mere four days after Miss Roza Senna actually arrived in New Bedford, the schooner *Luiza* from Brava brought cabin passenger Marcelino Manuel da Graca, age 22, who had also been in the United States previously. Marcelino claimed he was joining his father at 323 South Water Street. Unlike nearby 343, the building numbered 323 at the corner of Cannon and South Water Streets had in fact been torn down several years earlier. Despite this, the 1904 city directory lists Manuel Gracia, a laborer, as living there. Not only is it unclear where Marcelino actually went when Customs excused him and he made the left into the crowd on South Water Street, but by 1905 the number of *Manuel Gracia*s listed in the directories multiplied so dramatically that it is impossible to determine exactly what became of this particular da Graca family.[44]

Their American living arrangements are merely the first of many confusing elements about Daddy Grace's family of origin. A second example is the birth year of his parents: on the *Freeman* passenger list, they both have one age listed, crossed off, and another age written in. The father was originally recorded as 48, but this was replaced by 57; for the mother, age 42 was crossed off, and 50 replaced it. None of these ship-recorded ages correspond with the birth years 1837 and 1847, which are found on their joint gravestone.[45] A second murky factor is the precise number of Manuel and Gertrude's children. Only five—

Jennie, Sylvia, Louise, Benventura, and Marcelino—are consistently recorded, yet some sources have listed the number as seven, others ten. Occasionally one runs across a solitary mention of another particular da Graca child. For example, the only mention of daughter Mary Roza to be found is in the *Freeman* manifest. Likewise, the name of the 16-year-old daughter who traveled with them on the ship has not arisen elsewhere. Other individual mentions include brothers named John and Joseph. Taken as a whole, the consistent data suggests that the actual children are those five listed above.[46] It is possible that other "children" were occasionally mentioned for purposes such as easing immigration. The 16-year-old, for example, may have been a niece or family friend who immigrated as a da Graca in order to pass through Customs with little trouble. In other cases, the surprise da Graca children might simply be errors or misunderstandings caused not only by the commonality of the Graca surname among Cape Verdeans, but also by the commonality of the father's first name; in fact, a Manuel da Graca in Cape Verde might be likened to a "Michael Jones" in the present-day United States.

Cape Verdeans in the New Bedford Region

The da Gracas would have witnessed the rapid changes of economy taking place in New Bedford in their first few years there, but despite all of the new business opportunities, most immigrants were relegated to jobs as unskilled or semi-skilled laborers. Some worked year-round in the mill industry, while others created pasticcio employment that changed each season. Picking cranberries on Cape Cod during the harvest time was one job that became dominated by immigrants from Brava. From approximately August until November, Bravas of all ages and both genders poured onto the Cape to live in nonwinterized cabins and find jobs as temporary pickers. Good pickers could earn approximately eighty dollars for the season, which was enough money to sustain them until spring. The cranberry-picking experience varied widely, depending on the bog one worked and what type of employer one had. In some, the housing was clean and acceptable, the pay was fair, and the pickers worked alongside owners and other managers in a harmonious fashion. They could joke with each other as they worked, sing songs, and even flirt with potential mates. In others, however, the bosses demanded strict subordination of pickers, who were watched closely using overseers; they skimmed pickers' pay; and only shabby overcrowded living quarters were provided. Regardless of the working environment, the job itself always required pickers to labor in a stooped position and spend full days hunched over with their weight on their knees. Later in life many suffered from arthritis, knee pain, and arm or shoulder problems. However, because of the ability to earn a large sum in a short period, and because of the desire of many Bravas to invest money in their home country, cranberry picking remained an enticing job for them.[47]

When they returned to town after the harvest and found new work, the Bravas' social life was much like that of any other New Bedford resident. At the end of the day, the city's largely working-class population relaxed in the bars, pool halls, and meeting places such as the Cape Verde Club.[48] Other local amusements for those who could afford the ten-to-fifty-cent entrance fees included clambakes, band concerts, vaudeville performances, and steamer excursions on the bay. Lectures by circuit speakers, occasional park concerts, and baseball games were free to those who sought them.[49] And of course, there was always church on Sunday, as well as on many weekday evenings.

Albeit a small city, New Bedford offered a plethora of Christian religious options including not only Catholicism and all brands of Protestantism but also faiths such as Christian Science, Spiritualism, the Reorganized Latter Day Saint Church, and a variety of small missions. The Portuguese-speaking communities had their own churches, like the Portuguese Baptist Church, the First Portuguese Methodist Episcopal Church, and St. John the Baptist.[50] However, just as certain measures of segregation would have existed in all areas of social life, racial and ethnic divisions were also found in the churches. Among those of Portuguese nationality, people of lighter skin color generally considered themselves to be of a different race and therefore on a different social plane, and so in formal settings they preferred to segregate themselves from Cape Verdeans.[51] Thus it became a public issue when the islanders took to attending a particular church whose membership was dominated by the lighter-skinned, continental Portuguese. In 1903, local papers reported that at the Roman Catholic Church for Portuguese speakers, St. John the Baptist, "Bravas allege that . . . when at church they frequently have to stand up, after paying to enter, and then are made fun of by the worshipers." One man from Brava articulated the problem that despite their common national heritage, non–Cape Verdean Portuguese citizens "hold that we are in a different caste and won't allow us to become

Daddy Grace, Bible in hand, July 1, 1952. Photographer: Charles Borjes. Courtesy of Sargeant Memorial Room, Norfolk Public Library, Norfolk, Virginia.

members of their societies. The distinctions made have become intolerable to us."[52] Our Lady of the Assumption was the constructive answer to the great shame the Cape Verdeans were made to feel. This church opened on Water Street in 1905 with a handful of new members under the governance of a Belgian priest named Stanislaus Bernard.[53] Meanwhile, other Cape Verdeans drifted away from Catholicism, finding new religious homes in local Protestant congregations.

All of these elements were part of immigrant life in southeastern Massachusetts, where the da Graca family was comfortably settling in. The eldest daughter, Jennie, was married to Philip Vieira and bore her first child, Marie, in 1905, followed by Annie in 1907.[54] The middle daughter, Sylvia, also married, staying in the New Bedford area. Benventura, called Benjamin, soon began working as a crewman on various ships that ran out of New Bedford, and lived intermittently in both Cape Verde and Hyannis, Massachusetts.[55] Louise, just a child, presumably attended local schools and became acculturated to American life. Never married, she was one of her brother's most loyal followers when he later became a bishop. And finally, Marcelino, the future bishop who was still just an indistinguishable immigrant from Brava, busied himself in a variety of ways.

Bishop Charles Grace in New Bedford

The stretch of fifteen to twenty years between Marcelino's immigration and the start of his first church is mostly a jigsaw puzzle with the majority of the pieces missing, but there are a few generally known, oft-repeated facts. The story goes that during this period Marcelino Manuel da Graca lived and worked primarily in the greater New Bedford region. He labored as a seasonal cranberry picker; he worked as a cook at the Snow Inn in Harwich; he sold patent medicines on Cape Cod; and he ran a small grocery business in Wareham. He traveled to a variety of places including Boston, Baltimore, Los Angeles, and Mexico, and he attended various churches, including Methodist and Nazarene. When he was 28 he married Jane Lombard, commonly called Jennie Lomba, who was of Cape Verdean descent and eleven years his junior. She bore him two children, Irene in 1910 and Norman Walter in 1912. Marcelino left Jennie after three years of marriage and was granted a divorce in 1920. And, somewhere in the midst of all of this, he started using the first name "Charles" rather than Marcelino, and he Americanized his surname. Thus did Charles M. Grace come into existence.[56]

And then, in January 1922, New Bedford declared that the "call of God [had] brought him," as a newspaper headline announced.[57] This soft-spoken man was transformed from a virtual "nobody" to a touted religious leader of a quickly growing local congregation. In later interviews, Grace claimed he had been ordained as a minister by the Church on the Rock of the Apostolic Faith, and elected bishop by the same in Boston in 1921. His charge was to travel, preach, and open new Houses of Prayer. Many sources assert that Grace had previously founded a church in West Wareham in 1919, but rather than return to it, his first order of business as bishop was to proselytize and missionize in New Bedford. There, Grace began meeting with his new converts in temporary locations that rotated based on the availability of space.[58]

Bishop Grace formally opened the New Bedford House of Prayer in December 1921 at 357 Kempton Street, a few doors west of Cottage Street in an area called the West End. Though it has long been referred to as a predominantly Black neighborhood, census records show that in 1920 it was racially mixed, with Irish, British, Chinese, Russian, and Albanian residents, as well as those labeled both "Black" and "white" whose nationalities were listed as Canadian, Portuguese, and American.[59] The majority of residents were renters, but most were stable and did not move from year to year. It would be difficult to characterize the socio-economic level of the neighbors, because while many worked as operators in the mills, a significant number of more desirable professions were also represented among them including nurses, foremen, plumbers, carpenters, firemen, and one police officer.[60] Later called the "three-decker" area, the buildings in the West End generally had shops on the first story, with the second and third stories rented as apartments.[61]

In the early 1920s, Kempton Street was lined with businesses including a tailor, a cotton shop, a pool hall, two barbers, and a number of food and dry goods retailers. But near the corner of Cottage, merchants had been less successful, and several empty single-story buildings were clustered together. These included a building recently vacated by a combination fish and grocery store; this was the precise spot into which Grace's first New Bedford congregation moved. It was conveniently located right next door to the only other occupied building in that stretch: the Church of the Nazarene at 359 Kempton, pastored by Reverend Brown. In addition, two other potential competitors were very close by: Bethel African Methodist Episcopal Church was less than one block east, and an AME Zion church was only two blocks south. It is likely that this choice of location was strategic; certainly, the theory of religious economy suggests that Grace, as a man who clearly gave much thought to his actions, saw an opportunity for success in this particular spot. As soon as the House of Prayer opened, Grace began testing the religious demands of local people by offering an overabundance of his product—lively religious services and a community to share them with—and learning how much people would consume. While the Nazarene, AME, and AME Zion churches all held two services each Sunday, in this instance Grace succeeded at netting potential converts by changing the product supply, holding services every night of the week and a single lengthy service on Sundays. In later years, the tendency to flood the market with his product emerged as Grace's evangelistic calling card. Though he never overtly claimed to compete with other faiths, he liked to attract attention to his church's activities and pique the interest of potential converts by simply placing his church in the middle of an already successful niche market and offering a slightly different, more plentiful option for religious consumers. Kempton Street was his first successful experience with such a maneuver.[62]

Because the church was active every night, neighbors were not necessarily pleased with what God's call had brought. In short order, the Church of the Nazarene vacated its space, moving to larger quarters around the corner on Cottage; perhaps they were chased away by the noise from their neighbors' tambourines, banjoes, and hearty singing. By August 1922 the West End police station, only half a block from the House of Prayer, received several complaints that the loud services went on late into the night and kept residents awake. One unhappy person was Mrs. Anna Harris, a white divorcee who lived with her little boy in a two-story apartment building, the backyard of which abutted the property on which the church rested. Her complaints prompted Grace to be called to the station, to which he brought his assistants Miss Hughes and Miss Rainey, and after cordial discussion with the lieutenant the bishop agreed to begin services at an earlier time. In other instances, parents complained that their daughters were too involved with the church, staying late into the evening and being overly tired for work the next day.[63] Though Grace tempered his behavior in this instance, late-night services remained a feature of the church as a whole for the next several decades, including special event services that sometimes lasted until daybreak.

Theological Context

It is necessary to situate the United House of Prayer theologically in the larger context of American religious history, or at least in one aspect of that history, not only so that we might recognize what it is, but also so that we might recognize what it is not.[64] In terms of its formation, the United House of Prayer arose independently rather than as a break from another church, and it never institutionally affiliated with any

Christian denomination. Its belief system represents a culling, rather than a genealogical descendency, though it might logically be placed in the Pentecostal family.[65] This outline of the House of Prayer's religious teachings is not, and cannot be, complete. Such a task is impossible due to the church's tendency toward congregationalism as well as its lack of printed material.[66] These beliefs are inferred from a variety of sources, but are drawn most heavily from interviews with Daddy Grace, his pastors, and church members during the era in which Grace served as bishop.

Theologically, Grace's church is comparable to both the Holiness and Pentecostal families due to its beliefs about salvation.[67] Protestant Christians have long striven for eternal salvation, and generally believe in two spiritual processes that will bring a person closer to this goal. The first process, or first work of God's grace, is called justification. In this event, the person enters into an earnest relationship with God and is forgiven for his or her sins. The second process, called the second blessing by some, is sanctification. In this, God causes an inward change so that a person's sinful nature is removed, and therefore empowers him or her to live a life in which his or her intentional actions will embody true godliness. Beyond agreement that these two steps exist, Christians have disagreed about exactly how they work. For example, some believe that justification and sanctification occur simultaneously, while others believe they are distinct steps. Furthermore, some believe sanctification is an instantaneous and entire change, while others consider it a gradual one that happens over the course of a person's lifetime. Many Protestants have tended to put their focus on justification, and consequently have minimized questions about sanctification; in critique, Wesleyan theology reversed this trend and put attention on the sanctification process.

One religious impulse that took a firm stance on the precise relationship of justification and sanctification was what eventually came to be called the Holiness Movement. In the nineteenth century, Holiness swept across the United States, with revivals bringing new converts to its theological position. Holiness people believed in the second blessing of instantaneous, entire sanctification. It was an optimistic theology, because it meant the sanctified person had truly come into living as God intended within his or her lifetime. Holiness people often saw justification and sanctification as one event that happened simultaneously, and understood this as the baptism of the Holy Spirit alluded to in the Bible.

Many Methodist leaders who converted to Holiness brought with them the emphasis of missionizing to those in spiritual need, and so as Holiness churches sprouted across the nation they also sent missionaries worldwide.

In the early years of the twentieth century, the Azusa Street revivals in Los Angeles complicated the theological picture promoted by the flourishing Holiness Movement. There, Christians experienced what they, too, understood as the baptism of the Holy Spirit: speaking in tongues, or glossolalia. Azusa Street begat Pentecostals, who believed there were three pieces to salvation: justification, sanctification, and perhaps the most important, baptism of the Holy Spirit as evidenced by glossolalia. Speaking in tongues was the evidence that a person was sanctified, and it was therefore the symbolic merit badge one needed to be recognized as truly saved. On the question of sanctification, Pentecostals considered it a gradual process that began unfolding the moment God effected a change in the believer. As a result, these theological requirements were not necessarily successive; a person who was still undergoing the process of sanctification could certainly receive the baptism of the Holy Spirit. As a broader phenomenon, Pentecostals also understood tongues as the sign that the end-time was near. No sooner did Pentecostalism begin to form as a recognizable religious strain than it began to splinter, and the primary divergence came from those who had been part of the Holiness Movement. Holiness people differed because they believed sanctification was instantaneous and complete; and while they felt tongues-speaking was a gift of the Holy Spirit akin to a third blessing, they did not consider it the only incontrovertible evidence that one had been sanctified. However, theologically distinguishing Holiness from Pentecostalism, especially during this period when each was still developing, is at best an approximate endeavor. There was extensive overlap in what the two groups believed and practiced, and arguments could be made that the greatest difference between them was the socioeconomic status and/or race of their membership bases.

Simultaneously with the early years of Pentecostal fervor, a smattering of Holiness churches that eschewed the tongue-speaking phenomenon broke away and institutionalized as a group, becoming what is today known as the Church of the Nazarene.[68] Nazarenes were Wesleyan in many of their beliefs and practices, including the instantaneous "entire sanctification," and they added divine healing and a stress on ministering to the urban poor. Because they believed God had removed their impulse to sin, pure forms of living were the natural result of entire sanctification. As they were for other Holiness people, lifestyle and behavioral expectations for Nazarenes who had received the second blessing were extremely conservative and strictly upheld, and they preferred to stay away from Christians who had not been inwardly perfected. However, Nazarenes differed from others in their belief in divine healing in combination with medical science, while most Pentecostals at that time tended toward a faith in divine healing alone.

The United House of Prayer arose within the matrix of Holiness, Pentecostalism, and Nazarenes, and its theology must therefore be placed in the context of these other religious developments. The theological framework of the House of Prayer is most similar to the Pentecostal faith, though on a few minor points it lies closer to Holiness belief.[69] Like Pentecostals, the House of Prayer considered tongues the sign of the end-time. Hence members were living in the last days.[70] Additionally, while they believed God could bestow spiritual gifts of all sorts, not merely glossolalia, tongues-speaking was understood as paramount among these gifts. This is because it was the evidence of a person's true salvation; it was *the* baptism of the Holy Spirit. Thus, on this point too, House of Prayer belief was very much in line with Pentecostalism. However, House of Prayer followers were closer to Holiness theology in their belief that the stages of salvation had to be successive and that therefore only those who had been sanctified were ever able to speak in tongues. Furthermore, because sanctification was gradual, episodes of backsliding were understood. This was contrary to faiths like the Nazarenes, who would have viewed blatant sins as evidence that a person was not yet sanctified. Lastly, similar to Nazarenes, House of Prayer members were strongly discouraged from mingling with anyone outside of their faith, because Grace emphasized that theirs was the only true church and anyone outside of it was beyond the realm of salvation.[71]

Pastors of the House of Prayer, usually called elders, served as moral examples for members to follow as they tried to uphold the many behavioral codes, including not drinking, gambling, smoking, dancing, or participating in public amusements. However, these men were human, examples only, and were not to be followed uncritically. Grace said that holy guidance needed to be the dominant theme for Christian living. "Many of the so called Christians belong to the church of Reverend Dr. Somebody rather than the church of God," he said, emphasizing the importance of religious substance over personal magnetism; in light of his later career, this early comment may seem ironic.[72] Nevertheless, Grace felt it was important to be guided by the Trinity—God the Father, God the Son, and the Holy Spirit—rather than ministers, both inside and outside of church. Additionally, he emphasized that individuals should read and study the Bible, rather than just listening to pastors preach about it.[73]

House of Prayer members believed in divine healing, and Grace's reputation as a healer was frequently a reason that people visited the church. He was known not only to "cast out devils" spiritually, but also to heal the sick, the blind, and the crippled physically. As he aged, Grace tried to put less emphasis on his own power to heal, and instead encouraged believers they would heal by faith. According to research done in the 1930s, many members believed in spiritual healing in lieu of medical care, though medical attention was not prohibited by the church.[74]

In toto, the above sketch demonstrates that the House of Prayer's theology corresponds most closely with Pentecostalism, though it also has points of crossover with Holiness groups, particularly the Nazarenes. Like other charismatics, their services emphasized praising God and fostering encounters with the Holy Spirit rather than rituals such as communion. Yet like noncharismatics, they also put attention on preaching quality and careful study of the Bible. Grace explained that services were guided by the spirit rather than humans, and thus, "If we are directed to sing we sing; if we are given the inspiration to testify we testify; and if we are called upon to exhort we exhort."[75] Therefore, though services may have followed a blueprint, God could call upon them to go in a new direction at any time.

House of Prayer theology and practices were still in their fetal stages during the New Bedford heyday of the early 1920s. Although the New Bedford church never dissolved, the fiery start that caused neighbors to complain could not remain consistent without Grace's presence. When he left the country for a long overseas trip in the autumn of 1923, the Kempton Street House of Prayer fell silent. There were still faithful followers, but services were not held without Grace in the early years; and though Grace returned to New Bedford periodically for the rest of his life, never again did a single House of Prayer receive his undivided attention.[76] God, it seems, called him to take what he had learned in New Bedford and go elsewhere.

2

The Usual Miracles

Daddy Grace's first major southern evangelizing tour took place in the spring and summer of 1926. Though the House of Prayer eventually grew into a large institution that appealed to many people, when it was first beginning Grace himself was the main attraction for those who visited his church. Through the 1920s and into the early 1930s, in order to gain a market share he had to be directly involved in the start-up process in every new town. Grace's pattern was to make a well-publicized arrival that generated widespread interest in his meetings, welcome all those who attended, dazzle them in services, and then leave town before people had a chance to tire of him. Understanding the importance of promotion, he often traveled in a car plastered with advertisements about his message, and when possible he sent a scouting group of assistants ahead of him to announce his impending arrival. One elder remembered driving around a town calling out over a loudspeaker, "Daddy Grace is in town. Come one and all, and listen to the man of God."[1] Another elder, a former church band member, said that they used to play music on street corners to attract attention and then invited listeners to attend services. Assistants passed out handbills advertising Grace's attributes and occasionally placed ads in the newspapers. Once in town, Grace stayed for two or three weeks holding frequent services in a temporary meeting space. He invited local reporters to the meetings, and if that failed, he paid for newspaper advertisements that were designed to look like articles. Sometimes he used other dramatic attention-getters to assist in drawing crowds, such as guests like Nora "the midget evangelist."[2]

One story about Grace's methods comes from the 1960s legal testimony of trumpet player Enoch Walker.[3] The motives for Walker's testimony were entirely suspect, as was the important role he claimed to have played in House of Prayer history; nonetheless he did seem to have knowledge of inner workings of the House of Prayer. Walker claimed to have been a member of the church's three-piece traveling band starting in the early 1930s. As he claimed in writing, "Some of our duties were to enter a town before Daddy Grace and play on the streets, alleys and corners, advertise when Daddy Grace would be in town and that our band would play the music for every service."[4] Of particular interest is his testimony that it was the band members who often took responsibility for renting or purchasing necessities for services, such as a meeting space, benches for seating, and pans to collect the offering. Then, members from other cities would visit and attend the services so that Grace was guaranteed a lively crowd. If Walker's testimony is to be believed, it appears that Grace managed to detach himself from logistical concerns very early on, and that people other than Grace had a vested interest in the success of each tent meeting. According to Walker, the band members were willing to take on so many responsibilities because they were treated with respect and admiration by the crowds. Music was at the heart of why new visitors came; not only did it draw people into the services, but the music "captured their minds" and held them there. Walker claimed, "The people came to hear the band as much as they came to hear [Grace] talk, or even more."[5] Though Walker may not have been speaking from his own experience, it is likely that his emphasis on music as an important attraction for newcomers is accurate.

Savannah

Grace launched his first southern tour in the spring of 1926. Two months before his visit to Charlotte, where he formally founded the House of Prayer, he began his first series of tent meetings in Savannah, Georgia. Rather than setting up camp in Yamacraw, the most populous Black neighborhood in Savannah, Grace sought to create his own niche-market in the more prestigious neighborhood of Brownville.[6] Targeting a newspaper-reading audience, Grace ran an advertisement in the *Savannah Tribune* for two weeks prior to the start of his meetings. The ad featured a large photograph of Grace, who was draped in fabric, and the text announced that he would be arriving from Jerusalem to preach "that Jesus is not dead but he is risen as he said and lives forevermore."[7] In addition to promoting Grace as an international religious figure, the ad suggested he had the power to heal, just as Jesus had. His tent meetings began on a Sunday afternoon in mid-April, and four days later the *Tribune* ran its first news piece about Grace's miracles. According to the article he was "attracting wide attention, in fact the people of the city are astonished to see the blind get their sight through prayer."[8] Member Eula Wright, who attended the Savannah meetings, recalled that Grace "began to preach and teach that the kingdom of heaven is at hand. He began to heal the sick, and clean the lepers, to give sight to the blind and made the lame to walk, and many sad hearts were made to rejoice in the God of their salvation."[9] After one man's vision was restored at the meetings, it was said that he ran through the streets of Savannah in joyous celebration followed by hundreds of people. The *Tribune* reported that thousands of attendees daily witnessed this and other miracles of healing by Grace. The paper also suggested that everyone desiring more information about Grace's work should continue to read the *Tribune,* which would be given out free of charge at the tent meetings.[10]

The *Tribune*'s positive reports were short-lived. Elder J. W. Manns, pastor of a Seventh Day Adventist church located three blocks from the tent meeting site, began preaching against Grace in sermons with titles such as "Is the Fake Healing of Bishop Grace of God, or the Devil?" and in written diatribes against him. Manns said that although divine healing did exist, Grace was nothing other than a fraud and a *camou-fleur.*[11] In reply, Grace publicly announced that Manns should attend a service before judging his work, but Manns apparently felt no need to see him in action and instead made various contradictory charges against the bishop. First Manns asserted that no one at Grace's meetings was actually being healed, because he had visited several of the people in question and found they were still afflicted. Then Manns used the Book of Revelation as support for his assertion that any superhuman feats Grace achieved were only the result of evil spirits working through him. At odds with both of these accusations, Manns also claimed that what people witnessed in Grace's meetings was the result of both their own ignorance and Grace's power of hypnotism. He publicly offered twenty-five dollars to anyone who could show him a person truly healed by Grace's powers.[12]

A few days later Grace, along with his manager Mr. Madden and Madden's wife, was arrested during a Wednesday night meeting. A local group of ministers led by Pastor Manns had pushed for charges against Grace of criminal libel and disorderly conduct. After posting bond Grace returned to the tent meeting, still going on without him, where he "held his forces together until long after midnight." The *Tribune,* which began to call Bishop Grace's credentials into question by using quotation marks around his title, predicted this would be the end of his stay in Savannah.[13] Yet the article about his arrest was Grace's first time on the front page of the newspaper, and it was accompanied by both an extra-large advertisement Grace had taken out in the same issue, and another editorial about him written by Elder Manns. Grace's advertisement pointed out the failure of those who tried to persecute him, and celebrated the double luck of all those who had been healed because they could now visit Elder Manns and receive a cash reward. In defense of his powers, the ad listed many of the healed by name and address, described their previous illnesses, and boldly said that Elder Manns should "either come up or shut up and if he don't give them their money that is the best evidence he has told a flat lie."[14] Manns's piece, on the other hand, warned that false prophets were a sign of the end-time and that "ministers of the gospel should take a very definite stand against frauds who operate using sorcery to lead away disciples."[15] Manns was firm in his stance that it was "Savannah's unlearned peoples" who were being preyed upon. Having done his research, he revealed that Grace was from Brava, not Jerusalem; that he was a divorced father rather than a virgin as he claimed; and that his parents were living on South Water Street in New Bedford, Massachusetts, rather than Palestine.[16] But the faithful of Savannah were not to be dissuaded by Elder Manns, and when Grace completed his meetings three days later the spirit was still strong. In less than a month, Grace had gone from being completely unknown in Savannah to being a widely discussed man of the Christian faith. As in business, so too with a religious economy: in this case the maxim "there is no such thing as bad publicity" certainly worked for Grace and his goal of religious growth.

Grace next landed in Charlotte, North Carolina, where he was nicknamed the "Black Christ."[17] Though he had established churches in a minimum of three places prior to the Charlotte trip—West Wareham, New Bedford, and Savannah—followers forevermore remembered the House of Prayer's founding as having happened on June 26, 1926, the first day of his Charlotte services.[18] His progress there mirrored the more successful aspects of the Savannah meetings with healings, people marching in the streets, and services running loudly and late into the night. Grace later recounted that on one occasion in Charlotte, "The trees began to shake, the hills trembled, and more than one hundred of my ardent followers jumped into the river when the power of God seized and moved them. . . . Believers jumped into the river to be baptized with their finest clothes on."[19] Though Charlotte newspapers evidenced a degree of suspicion about him, he faced no serious legal troubles there. This time he made ample use of his manager as a spokesman, and had little to say to reporters or ministers who questioned his work.[20] Grace left on a high note and continued his southern tour through the summer and into the autumn of 1926, with numerous stops in Virginia and the Carolinas.

Though Charlotte was a success story, Grace's 1926 efforts in the South were somewhat rocky overall. In addition to the conflicts in Savannah, charges were filed against him in several other cities. In Newport News, his mixed-race meetings upset local ministers, who attempted to get an injunction against him. The city was legally segregated in many arenas but neither municipal nor state law prohibited integrated religious meetings. Grace prevailed, but ignited the ire of white ministers. In another setback, a drowning accident occurred in Seversville, North Carolina, while Grace was conducting a mass baptism. Grace explained that he was baptizing followers when he realized a man was struggling in the water nearby. He tried to pull him up, twice, but could not. Exhausted, he swam to shore himself, and the man drowned. Grace then realized there were many more people still waiting to be baptized, so he returned to the water and took up his work again. Years later he commented, "I think it was good for the man. It was a beautiful way to die, don't you think so? He was working for the glory of heaven and he must have had a beautiful death."[21] Though not everyone thought Grace was to blame for the man's death, most newspapers spoke poorly of his subsequent actions. Grace left town almost immediately, apparently fleeing any aftermath from the drowning. In truth, Grace departed so quickly because he had received word that his father had just passed away, and thus he left to be with his mother and siblings in New Bedford.[22]

Despite such conflicts, the bishop returned to many of the same southern towns the following year, holding meetings and baptisms and continuing to grow his flock. He felt better about his autumn 1927 trip, on which he was accompanied by his sisters Sylvia and Louise as well as nieces Olive and Beatrice. Highlights from this trip included baptizing two hundred people in Washington, DC, and making his first visit to Norfolk, Virginia. Grace's new, consciously reserved approach was evident in a subsequent interview about the trip, in which he simultaneously demonstrated pride in and indifference to his work by telling a reporter, "I met with about 6000 members of my faith. The usual miracles were performed. Hundreds of the sick, blind, lame and crippled, who proved their faith in God, were cured."[23] This early example shows the nonchalance that eventually came to define Grace's public persona and that was one of the ethereal qualities that kept so many people intrigued by him. The fact that he had no need to tout his miracles demonstrated his status as a man who was closer to God than to ordinary humans. To many of his followers, Grace's characteristic indifference to his achievements was evidence of an intense focus and deep knowledge of himself, and, akin to a *deus otiosus*, it made them long to be closer to him. He was, after all, their "Daddy," and they were referred to as his "children" or "babies."

"Daddy"

Though unusual to American ears, the use of "Daddy" as a term of reverence was not without precedent. In some parts of Africa people have long referred to respected elders as "Daddy." WPA writers noted an 1861 study of Ethiopians in which this tendency was observed; it remains true today, as demonstrated by cases of African Christian ministers called by the same title.[24] In the case of Daddy Grace, it is unclear precisely how he first acquired the title and when it became the one most commonly used. As early as his 1926 tour he referred to himself as "Brother Grace" in advertisements, but during this same time he also used the title "Daddy." Greeting his followers upon entering a tent meeting, Grace asked them, "Are you glad to see me, children?" The audience replied in the affirmative. He then asked, "Who are my children? All my children hold up your hand! . . . Am I your daddy? . . . Ain't you all got a nice daddy?"[25] A woman who joined at this time explained that she had used the title "Daddy" to refer to Grace, "Ever since I met him in the House of Prayer at Savannah. . . . I do not call him Bishop Grace. I call him Daddy Grace."[26] When asked to explain his title, Grace said, "I consider them as my children according to the Bible that Paul wrote to his son Timothy. I felt that I am a father to them in the Gospel and they are my children. . . . No matter how old they are, whether they are men or women, it makes no difference, they are all my babies, that is the way I feel."[27] Furthermore, the *House of Prayer Quarterly* taught that, "The world thinks it is strange that the children of the House of Prayer should say Daddy Grace. But Paul called his ministers his sons because they were begotten by the words of his ministry."[28] Additional House of Prayer teaching cites the fourth book of Proverbs, in which the narrator speaks as a figurative father to his children and advises them about wisdom and understanding.[29]

In addition to the moniker "Daddy," Grace had also used the term "bishop" in referring to himself since his earliest days of preaching, and this title was one of the things that caused other religious leaders to bristle. Bishop Noah Williams of the AME Church, for example, spoke against Grace's use of the title at the 1934 Quadrennial Convention in Missouri, saying it "cheapened" what he considered the true office as found in the Roman Catholic, Episcopalian, and Methodist Episcopalian Churches. "The African Methodist Episcopalians should call on the editors of Negro papers and respectively ask them in the interest of the race . . . not to use the title of 'Bishop' in connection with persons of non-historical if not spurious bodies."[30] Having learned from his experiences, Bishop Grace responded, at best, indirectly to any challenges about his title, with comments such as, "I was Bishop when I was born, if I am one now."[31]

Grace's Racial Identification

Grace's answers to questions about his race were not quite as evasive as those about his title, but they functioned similarly because they further defined the boundaries between leader and followers. The House of Prayer members were primarily African American, and as Grace's self-understanding was dictated by his Cape Verdean heritage rather than by American categorization, he carefully drew a line between their race and his. We do not know precisely what Grace's social status was in his home country but several factors suggest an answer. He was from Brava, the most privileged of all the islands. His skin complexion was on the lighter end of the Cape Verdean spectrum, though he still was clearly of partial African descent. His eyes were a medium shade of brown, and as a young man his nose was slim, more European than African. Visually, he would have been seen by his fellow Cape Verdeans as having many Portuguese traits. Added to this are the facts that he spoke Portuguese, he had had at least a small degree of formal education, and his family of origin immigrated as a group to the United States. These things demonstrate that the da Graca family was not poor and that son Marcelino was being groomed to pass as Portuguese. In Brava, then, we can imagine that he was considered to be in a category like *moreno,* the person with European features but a darker complexion, or *mulato claro di cabeca seca,* a light mulatto with wiry hair, or possibly even *branco de dinheiro,* white by money.[32]

In the United States, this framework for understanding his place in the social strata did not translate because the categories were different. The fact that his skin was brown, regardless of the shade, meant Grace was perceived as a Negro, and thus neither money nor power could ever allow him to be counted among the elite. Nonetheless, he acted as though he were above American racial constraints. He insisted, "I have never suffered discrimination or Jim Crow in any form. I don't bother with these things. The white man loves me and so do colored people. I won't talk about prejudice or discrimination, because I am not political. I talk to God. I am God's child. And God is colorless."[33] Though it is impossible that Grace never experienced racism in the United States, his own version of his life suggests that he may have experienced some of the privileges Americans tend to accord those with a European-based accent, dark skin notwithstanding. It also suggests that his avoidance of race questions was less politically motivated than it was driven by the fact that he was at once comfortable with his own self-understanding and not particularly concerned with racial classification in general. When he deigned to comment on his race, Grace defined himself using Cape Verdean terms. He consistently said he was Portuguese by nationality and that he was of the white race.[34] Interestingly, he tended to gloss over the fact that he had been born and raised in Cape Verde. In a typical example he told one interviewer: "I am not a colored man. I am from the white race. I was born in Portugal."[35] Statements identical to this remained consistent throughout his four decades of religious leadership.[36]

Though it may not have been a primary concern, Grace certainly knew that racial categorization and power went hand in hand; this had been as true in Cape Verde as it was in the States, if not more so. It is evident that he felt his own social status was above that of most African

A convocation parade in Augusta, Georgia. Courtesy of Milledge Murray, private collection.

Americans. He pointed out: "These papers call me a 'Negro.' I am not a Negro, and no Negro in this country can do what I am doing."[37] He often said that God had sent him to help African Americans because of their oppression and low status in society, but he also made note of the fact that he was not one of them by referring to them as "you poor colored people."[38] Nonetheless, he said he wanted to "become acquainted with the better educated colored people of America" because they might be able to help him achieve the social uplifting of his followers.[39] Though his comments often stressed his separateness from African Americans, over the years he also emphasized that questions about race were irrelevant to religion. "I am a colorless man. I am a colorless bishop. Sometimes I am Black, sometimes I am white. I preach to all races."[40] In a 1934 court case when Grace was asked about his race, his lawyer tried to end the questioning by interjecting that "most of the Portuguese people are white." The opposing lawyer then asked Grace, "Do you consider yourself of negro extraction, Doctor?" Grace answered, "I do not consider myself anything but human." The lawyer persevered: "Do you consider yourself a white person?" Grace replied, "I say I do not consider myself either white, Black, blue or red. It is whatever you take me and say, I am satisfied." The lawyer, confused, said, "What do you say?" And Grace replied, "I do not say."[41] Grace did not want race to be part of how he, as a man trying to improve the

People standing outside of a House of Prayer in Augusta, Georgia. Courtesy of Milledge Murray, private collection.

religious lives of Americans, was evaluated, and he resented the suggestion that race had any significant impact on his work.

The Growing Church in Georgia

As the intricacies of Grace's persona grew, so too did his church, and
followers looked to him for guidance. He was careful to indicate that
one man could not be a church, and therefore he tried to inspire new
followers to organize themselves and keep the church alive after he was
gone. In his first years he often bought a plot of land for the group to
build on, and sometimes he left one or more assistants behind for a
short period to aid in the organizational process.[42] After the success of
Savannah's 1926 tent meetings, for example, Grace appointed a pastor
there and believers built a large church at 643 Bismarck Street in
Brownville. Though Brownville, located southwest of Forsyth Park, differed from many of the neighborhoods where the House of Prayer typically organized, the church flourished. It achieved a degree of social acceptability and, unlike in most other places, House of Prayer service announcements were often found in the local newspaper's weekly church
listings. By the mid-1930s the House of Prayer was the largest nontradi-
tional African American church in Savannah.[43] But while members continued to organize and proselytize, Grace himself had other cities to
visit and other followers to comfort. As he said, "I'm going all the time,
from the Atlantic to the Pacific looking over the churches. . . . [We are]
getting in where we can to preach the Gospel."[44]

Grace's missionary efforts also succeeded in nearby Augusta, Georgia, where a House of Prayer was located on Wrightsboro Road in a
neighborhood called "the Terry." A sign over the door read "Great Joy!
Come to the House of Prayer and forget your troubles." Though the
building was made of rough wood with sawdust on a dirt floor, members kept the interior looking cheery with bright colored crepe-paper
festoons for decorations.[45] Just down the road from the House of
Prayer in Augusta was another church, called the House of Faith, that
was started by dissatisfied Grace followers; by 1930 a second break, the
House of the Lord and Church on the Mount, had also occurred in Augusta. These churches were examples that even those who did not agree
with Grace learned something valuable from him about organization
and independence. Meanwhile, the Augusta House of Prayer grew to be

one of the largest congregations in Grace's domain and became the regional center for members of the eighth district.[46]

Beliefs and Practices in the House of Prayer

Though the church continued to grow in many cities, Daddy Grace remained independent from other denominations. At one time he described his group as "a Pentecostal religion" based on "the principles of Christ"; this was the closest he came to drawing comparisons between his church and others.[47] The full church name, the United House of Prayer for All People of the Church on the Rock of the Apostolic Faith, is Biblical in origin. The first portion refers to Isaiah 56 in the Hebrew Scriptures, in which God promises salvation to those who are faithful and obedient regardless of their social status. In verse 7 God specifically declares: "Mine house shall be called a house of prayer for all people." The second part of the name refers to both Acts 4:10–12 and Ephesians 2:20, which discuss Christian salvation as being built on a figurative cornerstone, or rock. Grace, raised in the Roman Catholic tradition, understood the cornerstone as representing the teachings of Jesus as carried forth by the apostle Peter, hence the phrase "on the Rock of the Apostolic Faith." Grace and his pastors often emphasized the openness of the church, putting stress on the words "for all people." For example, Grace said things such as, "It's not my little crowd against your little crowd. The House of Prayer is for *all* people!"[48] House of Prayer members considered their practices to be a return to those of early Christians, and thus they believed theirs was a religious community more free from human corruption than others were.[49]

Despite a welcoming attitude, Grace's literalist interpretation of Isaiah meant that only the House of Prayer could truly offer eternal salvation to those calling themselves Christians. To be outside of the House of Prayer was to be damned. Members used the words of Paul in Ephesians 4:5, "One Lord, one faith, one baptism," as their motto and prooftext for this belief.[50] As Grace wrote, "The House of Prayer is God's Kingdom and the gateway to Heaven. All people must enter into His gates. For inside is salvation, but outside, there is damnation and death."[51] There was no apparent hesitation or modesty in their religious righteousness; pastors taught this exclusivity as a definitive creed. An example was Elder Mitchell in Washington, who sermonized authoritatively: "There is no salvation outside of the House of Prayer. Nobody can be saved outside of the House of Prayer."[52] Grace derided non-members as "beasts," and House of Prayer art portrayed the church bathed in God's light, hovering over a pile of rubble made up of other "churches of the world."[53]

Grace believed in a kind of modern-day Apostolicity, also referred to as Apostolic Succession. Within Catholic tradition Apostolicity means that Christian leadership has been divinely chosen from Peter through the present day, with a single man selected at a time to lead under God's guidance.[54] Grace accepted the idea that there was one leader for each era, and he believed he was the leader for the modern day. Very early on he explained,

> The God who made Jesus knew why He did it. The Jesus who sent the preacher knew why He did it. When Jesus left this earth He left a commission to the preacher to carry His word to all the world, that the world might be saved. He sent me to preach the gospel—the old, old gospel—the gospel that has power to save men and women from their sins. He told me to go into all the world and preach the gospel, saying the Kingdom of God is at hand.[55]

Certainly, Grace's Catholic upbringing was influential in his understanding of leadership and mission, as his emphasis on Apostolic Succession demonstrates. On other occasions he explained his role as part of a more generalized Biblical lineage and said that he was another of God's chosen leaders, like Noah and Moses.[56] As National Evangelist J. J. Bailey wrote in a House of Prayer pamphlet, "God didn't have a man to bring it about in the last days, because Apostle Paul said it had to be revealed to a prophet and God declared his secret unto Grace the prophet from Jerusalem." Hence, Grace's leadership was also considered a fulfillment of Biblical prophecy.[57]

The Bible dictated many structural elements of the church, so just as House of Prayer members did not use the word "church" to describe themselves, Psalms 111:9 stipulated that they not address their leaders as "reverend."[58] Instead, these men were referred to as ministers, pastors, or, most often, elders. However, Grace did not always teach literal Bible reading. He acknowledged that many things found in the scriptures were not applicable to the present world because they were written so long ago in different social, cultural, and political contexts, and therefore should not all be taken at face value. Christians, then, needed apt interpreters of the Bible to teach them, rather than the many ministers of the world who did not understand God's word correctly.[59] House of Prayer elders were just such people. Nonetheless, members were also encouraged to read and study the Bible on their own time.[60] Members in Augusta specified that in their opinion, what distinguished House of Prayer elders from other pastors was that not only did they teach the Bible correctly, but they were also living examples of its principles. As one woman further explained, she had become more educated about the Bible since joining the House of Prayer because for the first time in her life she was being encouraged to read it.[61]

As a charismatic faith, the House of Prayer believed in the power of tongues, divine healing, ecstatic dancing, and prophecy, because they were "signs of Christ" as explained in the New Testament.[62] As Grace once explained, speaking in tongues was a sign of true communion with God. "God does not answer your prayers when you use your own language. God wants us to speak his language, not your language."[63] Grace called holy dancing "an expression of joy" and readily explained its precedents in the Biblical books of Psalms, Jeremiah, and Luke.[64] Those who had received the gifts of the Holy Spirit were considered to be part of God's "church" and therefore in line to be truly saved; as a sign posted outside a church clarified: "The church is not brick and wood, but people baptized with the Holy Ghost and Fire."[65] Spiritual gifts did create a certain degree of divide among members, and there were essentially two classes: those who had received the holy blessing already, and those who had not. Both groups were expected to refrain from sinful behavior consciously, and those who had been blessed with the gift of tongues were not guaranteed salvation because it was still possible to backslide.[66] An example is found in the testimony of a man from Scotia, South Carolina, who "joined the Sweet House of Prayer in 1939 and received the Holy Ghost and Fire the same year. . . . I went to Columbia, S.C. and there I strayed from Dad's teaching and Satan stole all my joy and I began to do wrong things." The man then returned to the House of Prayer where he was assisted in getting back on his feet, and he was accepted once again.[67] This belief, therefore, aligns House of Prayer theology with modern Pentecostals, and distinguishes their theology from Holiness belief in "entire sanctification."[68]

Furthermore, spiritual gifts were among the signs that the world was in its last days. Grace often referred to Isaiah 2:2 because it foreshadowed the formation of a true church prior to earthly destruction and the coming of the messianic kingdom. At various points in House of Prayer history the world's imminent end was emphasized in greater or lesser degrees, but during Grace's years it always provided at least the subtext for the church's function. Grace professed that the world was in poor condition due to humanity's "erring from the straight path. . . . With no outlet men will surely find trouble. They should look to God. In him they will find an outlet for their energy."[69] Grace, then, believed that the House of Prayer should be not only a spiritual home, but also the place where members would come together for social purposes, Christian in nature, to avoid the evils of a secular world in its last days.

Auxiliaries and Music

Joining the church provided people with the opportunity to participate in the hearty social life sustained by the House of Prayer's clubs, which were referred to as "auxiliaries." Auxiliaries were designed to involve everyone in the church, from toddlers to the elderly, and they were focused on a wide array of interests in order to provide at least one social group for every person. Most auxiliaries had their own uniforms, ranging from the members' simply wearing the same color, to formal tailor-made attire, and members wore these uniforms for all special events. Average-size Houses of Prayer usually offered two to three dozen auxiliaries, but beyond a few standard clubs the specific groups available varied somewhat from church to church. Regardless of which auxiliary one joined, much of the regular activity involved fund-raising, so in some sense the auxiliaries were not especially distinct. Early on, Daddy Grace specified that he wanted everyone in the church to work on the same things, and that what truly distinguished the auxiliaries were the uniforms. Groups were praised for upholding the auxiliary mission statement, which stipulated that everyone should "put their whole hearted cooperation in this work and put the program over for God and Grace."[70]

Some auxiliaries functioned essentially as a lay leader corps, such as the Elder Board and the Banking Committee, and so their meetings were largely business oriented. Others were more social in nature and united people who had common interests or lifestyles, such as the Home Lovers, the Literature Club, or the Willing Workers. Young people were kept busy with groups like the Junior Nurses, the Female Scouts, the Buds of Promise, and the Grace Juniors of Jerusalem. Other auxiliaries sustained aspects of the church services; every House of Prayer, for example, had male and female ushers, and every city had Grace Soldiers, who had the privilege of escorting Daddy Grace around town when he visited. The bishop also chose a small number of women in each place to serve as Grace Maids, who were single and assumed to be celibate. The maids acted as Grace's personal assistants when he was in town, and they were occasionally invited to travel with him for missionizing purposes. Among the unusual auxiliaries were the Grace Baby Band, a musical group of little boys and teenagers who traveled around the country playing at House of Prayer meetings, and the Soul Patrol, a drill team from the Bronx that incorporated acrobatics into their routines.[71]

In the earliest years of the church the auxiliaries were not tightly organized, but after 1936 everyone followed a general set of bylaws. The rules stipulated that each auxiliary was to have a president, elected for a period of ninety days, who was responsible for running the group, keeping its records, and attending a weekly meeting of other auxiliary leaders. If a president was caught drinking, smoking, or cursing, he or she could be penalized by the auxiliary "president of presidents." Churchgoers, who were restricted to membership in two auxiliaries only, were required to pay weekly dues and fines for any unexcused meeting absences as well as for poor behavior during meetings (such as talking out of turn or chewing gum). Those who failed to pay dues and fines were ultimately barred from participation in all auxiliaries, which meant a large part of church life was closed to them.[72]

Ultimately, Grace wanted church to be fun, or as he described it, different from "long-faced religion."[73] He wanted members to enjoy themselves and not to think of church as something that was separate from the good parts of their lives. In addition to auxiliaries, another way this value was manifest was in the music of the House of Prayer, which evolved and expanded over the years.[74] For his first churches Grace ordered a customized hymnal with his own picture on the cover, labeled "Evangelist C. M. Grace." The book contained a range of Christian music including standard hymns from the Evangelical tradition as well as gospel songs, with some written as early as the turn of the nineteenth century and others less than 10 years old.[75] The bishop made it clear that he didn't want religious music to be "morbid," and so the hymns were accompanied by lively piano, banjoes, and tambourines, and members were encouraged to be experimental with their arrangements. At an outdoor baptism in Savannah in 1928, the music involved singers, a piano, a cornet, and tambourine, and prompted one observer to comment that "such weird music had never before been heard hereabouts at such a service."[76] At that time African American gospel music was developing in a voice-led direction; that is, syncopation and the layering of vocal harmonies created its musical complexity. In the House of Prayer, however, musical complexity was being directed by unusual instrumentation, particularly the addition of brass horns, and by the emphasis on the band rather than the voice. By the early 1930s, the House or Prayer's music was taking small steps toward an entirely new genre that became known, decades later, as "shout."

Shout is a genre of lively religious music centered around the trombone, and it evolved over a long period. As early as the late 1920s, House of Prayer auxiliaries included tambourine bands and small string bands. As children increasingly learned to play wind instruments in school, these too were added to the instrumentation. The bands, which played in services, parades, and at special events, came in all sizes depending on the interest and abilities of church members. In time, two main band types developed in the House of Prayer: concert bands and shout bands. Concert bands included over a dozen instruments and also had nonplaying members such as flag-carriers and majorettes. Photos show that some of these bands included female players, and there were even a few all-female bands. The all-male shout bands had fewer members than concert bands. Their instruments included a sousaphone (also called a bass horn), drums, half a dozen or more trombones, and occasionally other horns, and they had a sound that was all their own. Shout's numerous musical influences include New Orleans and Dixieland jazz, Caribbean rhythms, Congo percussion, and Evangelical Christian hymns. Though the House of Prayer was by no means the only church with brass bands, the trombone-centered shout developed as a unique form and was therefore a new genre of religious music.[77]

Shout first emerged in Newport News, but part of its development stemmed from Charlotte. In the 1940s trombonist George Holland joined the church band in Newport News and changed its sound with his distinctive patterns of playing. Shortly thereafter, sousaphone player Robert Washington joined too, and the combination of the two horns gave the Newport News band a new style.[78] Grace liked their sound and urged members in other cities to form similar bands. One of those places was in Charlotte, where member Herman Coleman was performing lively marches and rhythm and blues with a small church gospel band that included horns.[79] Grace admired Coleman's style as well, particularly because of the wide array of music he played. In the mid-1940s he appointed Coleman to be the local bandleader and told him he wanted players to learn to read music, not just play by ear. Grace instructed Coleman: "When I come back here, I want to see a band organized." When he returned three months later, Coleman and the twenty-five members of the Grace Concert Band were ready to perform.[80] Though Coleman remained involved primarily with concert bands, his leadership expanded the musical repertoire of Houses of Prayer all over. During the 1950s the role of the trombones in many of the bands increased in importance, and eventually they became the lead instrument of shout.[81] Thus, the musical form of shout was an outgrowth of both Holland's work in the Newport News band and Coleman's diversification of the church music repertoire, and shout ultimately came to be the primary form of music found in the House of Prayer.

The theological basis of shout is found in Psalm 150, which calls on people to praise God with exuberant music. The specific name "shout" comes from the book of Joshua, in which God tells the Hebrews they can conquer Canaan by marching around the city, blowing horns. Joshua 6:16 reads: "And it came to pass at the seventh time, when the priests blew with the trumpets, Joshua said unto the people, Shout, for the Lord hath given you the city." Shout thus symbolizes victory of God and God's people, and so when the horns play, the congregation is exhorted to respond by glorifying God.[82] The music is God's music, intended not only to be heard and enjoyed but also to stimulate a spiritual experience: members' catching of the Holy Spirit. It was as important as, and sometimes more important than, any message an elder could preach, and it could sustain the spirit of followers when they were outside of church. One member summed it up by saying, "We live off of music like we live off of food. So we thrive on music in the House of Prayer."[83]

The House of Prayer Routine

Once any given House of Prayer was fully organized with a building, a group of leaders, a band, and a full slate of auxiliaries to engage the members, worshipping and socializing took place there seven days a week. Weekday evening services began at 7:30 or 8:00, and on Saturday nights they often ran so late that some people just slept in the church until it was time for Sunday School. Each night of the week was thematically different. The weekly schedule of an Augusta church serves as a rough example of Houses of Prayer all over: Monday was a regular worship service; Tuesday was Pastor's Night, and so the collection was solely for the pastor; Wednesday was called Home Builders Night, and the collection went to the national building fund; Thursday was the Young Peoples' service, which often functioned much like a talent show; on Friday nights the Mother House of the region held a Union service; Saturday was the Flood Gate Meeting, which focused heavily on prayer; and on Sunday there was Bible study in the morning followed by three services throughout the day.[84]

Despite the fact that Houses of Prayer ranged from old ramshackle structures to newly built or renovated ones, from place to place their interiors were quite similar. The deliberate arrangement and décor clearly expressed House of Prayer values: specifically, the privilege of being allowed up to the altar, the exalted role of the bishop, the symbolic nature of church property, and the promotion of American nationalism among members. As in most Protestant churches, wooden benches faced a raised platform at one end of the building. The platform, often called an altar by other Christians, is known to House of Prayer members as the "Holy Mountain," as found in the fourth chapter of the Biblical book of Micah.[85] Members believed that "holy men didn't pray in pulpits, but went to pray in the mountains."[86] Usually, some type of chancel rail surrounded the Mountain, such as picket fencing or a wooden banister. If approaching the Mountain, members did so from the side aisles of the sanctuary, because the center door and aisle were only used on special occasions, and even then they were usually restricted to church leaders and special assistants. Any obstructions near the Mountain were regularly tended to so that people would not hurt themselves in moments of religious ecstasy; for example, if there were building support posts nearby, they were kept padded, and fresh sawdust was regularly piled on hardwood floors.[87]

On the top level of the Mountain, a throne for Daddy Grace was covered in a plush, vibrant fabric and trimmed with a fringe or throw. Often the throne was flanked by lights, statues of angels, and life-size cardboard cutouts of the bishop. Grace's throne was kept under a protective sheeting unless he was in town; even in small missions that he was unlikely ever to visit, this pristine throne awaited him. Nearby was a podium, and at the sides of the Mountain were places for a choir and band to perform. On a lower tier was seating for elders and other service leaders; no one but the bishop and his maids and assistants were allowed on the top of the Holy Mountain. Often, as people entered the sanctuary, they would kneel for a moment at the base of the Mountain and say a prayer.[88]

Behind the Mountain pictures of significance adorned the walls. Some were portraits of Daddy Grace; others were photographs of buildings owned by the church or by Grace himself. Placards with the bishop's sayings were found on walls around the room. In several Houses of Prayer there were pictures of Grace "stripped like Atlas, holding up the universe with one hand."[89] The rooms were always decorated in the colors red, white, and blue, which Daddy Grace said were his favorites because they were the same colors as the American flag. One elder summed it up by saying: "We're united, just like the flag," and a newspaper commented that were it not for the throne and pulpit, a typical House of Prayer sanctuary could be "mistaken for a political convention hall."[90] A poster listing the House of Prayer auxiliaries and their recent fund-raising sums was usually posted toward the back of the sanctuary.[91]

The order of House of Prayer services tended toward informality, with much room for variation based on mood and Spirit.[92] The average service began with announcements, music, and intense prayer, followed by a long period of people's "coming to the Mountain," which essentially meant that the Spirit descended and caused some people to engage in ecstatic worship. Spiritual ecstasy could take many forms, such as dancing, speaking in tongues, falling down, crying, and even "walking the benches," in which people stood on their seats and jumped from one to another. Many were eased out of the rows and toward the Holy Mountain so that they had more room to move about. When women fell out, aides quickly threw a blanket over their legs to prevent any indecency. After people gradually calmed down, collections were taken in aluminum pans by assertive men who competed with each other to get the most money. Anything was acceptable, but Grace preferred bills to coins, saying that, "The sound of metal hurts my ears."[93] Sometimes the collectors walked up and down the aisles, and other times donors were invited to line up to give their money. Pleas for donations were often free from Biblical jargon; instead, the men forthrightly explained that they needed people's money simply because the church could not exist without it. Woven throughout the services were periods of singing, member testimonials, and preaching by the elder. On some nights they would also engage in marching, described as a "rhythmic half-step," and known as Daddy's March.[94] Time for the sale of Grace products was also worked in somewhere, and in some sense created a break during which people came and went. Each service ended gradually, with people kneeling on the floor in personal prayer and leaving when they were finished.

If Daddy Grace was attending a service, he arrived after it was well underway. Regardless of what had been happening prior to his arrival his entrance always caused waves of excitement among the crowd as the music kicked into high gear, people called out and rushed toward him, and others caught the Spirit. Preceded by a Grace Queen or Junior Maid, Daddy Grace walked down the center aisle protected by uniformed guards, his path carpeted and sometimes strewn with flowers. He knelt briefly at the base of the Holy Mountain before ascending to his throne. In his earliest years, he took an active part in services, preaching from the Bible and healing those in need. After a period of watching the congregation catch the Spirit, he would signal the band to stop playing and stand to speak. An outside observer once described Grace's process as "casually warming up the audience and finally becoming intimate and, at times, frolicsome."[95]

However, contrary to what might reasonably be expected from the flashy founder of a large church, preaching ability does not appear to have been one of Daddy Grace's greatest strengths. Many scholars noted his lack of dynamism in speaking, and the few recordings available demonstrate that his sermons came stylistically closer to the calm homilies of Catholicism than the lively "fire and brimstone" approach popular in both Pentecostal churches and African American Christianity more generally. Chancellor Williams politely said that Grace was an "able orator. His sermons, when he condescends to preach, lose none of their force by his concern with grammar and diction"; and a reporter for the *Afro-American* wrote: "Though not an orator, Bishop Grace was a persuasive speaker. He could charm an audience with his showmanship, personal magnetism and his sincere interest in the problems of his followers. . . . He had the knack of talking at length without saying anything."[96] Church literature even celebrated the fact that Daddy

Grace never spoke "above a common man's understanding. It is wisdom of the human family to speak the thing that everyone can understand."[97] Perhaps he was also less comfortable with lengthy public addresses because English was not his native language. Grace's prominent Cape Verdean accent did not diminish over the years, though through Americanization he learned many phrases common to southern dialect and they became part of his vernacular. Many noted that when he spoke he frequently gestured with his hands, and most of his physical movements in public were stylized and theatrical.[98]

Perhaps feeling that preaching was not his finest skill, Grace often left it to his elders; when the occasion demanded that he speak, he was more likely to give an informal talk about member behavior or national issues than he was to preach from the Bible. He sometimes came down from the Mountain and walked among the congregation as he spoke, posing rhetorical questions to the audience, and he did not hesitate to make little jokes or to take the time to think through a tangent aloud. When he did preach from the Bible, the format was generally that an assistant would read a passage aloud, and Grace would extemporaneously interpret it for listeners verse by verse.[99]

When Grace was not leading the service nor otherwise required to speak, he sat back on the Mountain, fanned by maids in attendance. In later years the bishop decreasingly took an active role in the services he attended, instead sitting quietly in his throne, blankly watching the proceedings. Just as he arrived in the middle of the action, so too did he always exit services prior to their end, putting on his hat and waving his handkerchief at the crowd as he departed. In keeping with his knack for leaving on a high note, he was always absent for the denouement during which followers fell into long periods of intense prayer.[100]

When Grace was not in attendance, members paid homage to him in other ways. For instance, letters he wrote to his congregations were read aloud in services over and over again. Some letters reminded followers of upcoming events, while in others Grace recounted his own recent activities. In some, he meditated briefly on spiritual subjects, such as the following:

> Have you ever stopped to think of your blessings? If you would try to count your blessings, you would find them numerous. Thank God for the sunshine and thank Him for the rain, thank Him for the beautiful trees and flowers and the things that He provided for us to enjoy

through nature. If you are sick, thank Him because you are still breathing the breath of Life. He didn't have to wake you up this morning nor keep you alive, but thank God, He did.[101]

These letters were considered just like those Paul wrote to various groups of Christians in the earliest years of Christendom, and they were reread and treasured for years.[102]

Healing through Faith and Grace (Products)

Though Grace seems to have had an indescribable charm that drew thousands of intensely devoted people to him, his renown was not the only reason the curious first came to visit; he offered a product religious consumers wanted: healing. It is clear that healing played a large role in attracting new members to the House of Prayer in its early years, though its significance as the initial draw diminished over time. There were different kinds of healing: healing that came from Daddy Grace himself, healing that came through items Daddy Grace had personally blessed, and healing that came through the use of Grace products—a line of items available for purchase at the church. Medical research shows that it is possible for psychosomatic illnesses to be eradicated by faith in a healer, but in the eyes of members it was equally true that the power of God was working through Daddy Grace to cure them.[103] Grace never claimed to be doing anything all by himself. He pointed out that, quite simply, faith healing necessitated the sick person's faith. "I pray over the clothes of sick believers without their presence and they are cured," he said, "if they have faith."[104] At one time he explained the reason that illness and death still existed. "The answer is simple. You all don't have the kind of faith that is necessary for healing. Without that, neither God nor Daddy can help you! I can heal only the strong in faith. . . . You doubters can never be healed."[105] On another occasion he told reporters in Charlotte that only about 1 percent of those who sought his help would be permanently cured, presumably due to flaws in their faith.[106]

In the earliest years, the possibility of being healed by Daddy Grace himself clearly attracted potential converts. Grace had no fear in asserting that he had been given the spiritual power to heal. In North Carolina he told the people: "I am come as the power of the Gospel to heal the sick, cleanse the lepers, raise the dead, cast out devils. . . . And don't you believe I can heal them? . . . If you do not believe me then you do not believe the Gospel. It teaches me to do these things in His name."[107] One of Grace's repeated claims in his first years in the South was that he had raised his own sister Jennie after a doctor declared her dead.[108] Many new believers likewise attested to his powers, recounting how they had personally experienced his healing touch, and it was not long before the followers did Grace's promotion for him by telling their stories to all who would listen. One man from Charlotte explained,

> All of a sudden I fell dead. I died, fell dead in the doorway. But Bishop Grace put his hand on my chest and right away it was like an electric shock passing through me. I quivered and shook all over and my right arm just rattled against the wall. I got up right then and there and I have never had a doctor since 1929.[109]

Mrs. S. explained to a researcher that prior to joining the church, she had been troubled by illness that doctors could not cure, and so she allowed friends to carry her to the House of Prayer one evening. There, Daddy Grace lay his hands on her abdomen and told her she must "catch faith." Mrs. S. was healed and became a faithful member.[110] And Sister Young from South Carolina wrote that, "Sweet Daddy Grace was in Columbia, SC, and I was in his presence and he saw what condition I had been in and wanted to know about my condition since he last saw me and bless God, he only gave me a peanut and I was healed immediately. It's wonderful to have faith in God's man."[111]

By the mid-1930s Grace was not able to respond to all the requests for healing, but members and potential members continued to clamor for his personal blessing. He used three strategies to solve the dilemma and keep the faithful satisfied. First, his public healings began to taper, and eventually he no longer performed them at all. Second, he allowed people to send him word of their conditions and ask for his prayers of healing. For example, Mr. Hall from Spartanburg, South Carolina, attested that when he fell ill with a type of paralysis in the spring of 1941 he sent a letter to Daddy Grace in New Bedford, explaining his situation. "Soon after the letter had reached him I was able to be up and to walk about. Oh! what a wonderful Saviour."[112] In another instance, an Augusta woman explained that a "nervous attack" had debilitated her. "My burdens looked like they was getting so heavy and so hard I couldn't stand no more. I asked Sister 'F' to write a letter to Dad for me. She never got to finish the letter, before she got halfway through I began speaking in tongues—the spirit done hit me."[113] The third way the bishop kept his followers satisfied was by introducing a full line of Grace products, which were modeled on the early success of his blessed handkerchiefs. Many of the products contained healing energy that could be utilized independently. Therefore they filled followers' insatiable need to access Grace's perceived spiritual power.

The impetus for Grace products dates to the 1926 tent meetings, when Grace realized he had neither the time nor the opportunity to heal personally all those who sought his help. He attempted a numbering system, in which people arrived early to receive a number and then were called forth during the evening meeting for a turn at healing. However, this was not enough to placate the crowds. In Savannah, an eyewitness explained that Grace prayed over a handkerchief "as Paul did in the days of old and a man who got one of these handkerchiefs who had rheumatism could not straighten his back nor his limbs was healed through the anointed handkerchiefs."[114] The Biblical reference was to Acts 19:11–12: "And God wrought special miracles by the hands of Paul, so that from his body were brought handkerchiefs or aprons, and the diseases departed from them, and the evil spirits went out of them." This strategy for healing was successful, and believers then clamored to get the "miracle-working handkerchiefs," paying between one and five dollars apiece.[115]

The success of the handkerchiefs was subsequently parlayed into the Grace product line. Most of the items sold, all of which carried Daddy Grace's picture, were not made by church-owned companies, and their manufacture did not provide jobs for members. In fact, it is unclear whether the sale of these products earned much of a profit or if they merely covered the costs of their own production. Grace products were sold at intervals during regular services, and, just like the clear reason for donating money to the church, there was little masking of the concept that buying the products helped to support the church financially. While some members were attracted to the advertised attributes of the products, others purchased them out of a sense of duty.[116]

Some Grace products, such as cookies, creams, powders, and shoe polish, held no specific powers, although hawkers came up with snappy phrases to advertise them. Daddy Grace coffee beans brewed "the best" cup of coffee; Daddy Grace Allwater Soap was "good for babies"; and one could use Grace toothpaste to achieve "a brighter Christian smile!"[117] However, Grace explained that he blessed all of the products. He elaborated, "People can even be cured by touching a piece of paper I throw away."[118] Other items were used for more specific purposes, like the Grace writing paper. The stationery, which sold for five cents for two pieces with envelopes, had Grace's picture at the top, labeled "A friend who sticketh closer than a brother," and numerous Bible verses listed down the left side of the page. The stationery was said to be able to improve any letters written upon it.[119] The most valuable of the products were those that specifically held preventative and curative powers, such as the healing cloth, a small square of fabric blessed by Grace, which cost only a quarter and had been available for sale since his early days of preaching.[120] Most significant among the healing products was the *Grace Magazine,* the existence of which predated most other Grace products by several years. The magazine could be worn or carried on the body to promote physical healing, and it could be read and studied for wisdom about healing.[121] As taught in House of Prayer Bible study, with reference to healing in Acts 19:11–12, members should "try *Grace Magazine* or the anointed cloth; if they were good enough in the days of Paul and others they are good enough now."[122] Many wrote in to the magazine attesting to its powers. Rosa Waters of Philadelphia provided a typical testimony when she explained: "For five years I suffered with the agonizing pains of the rheumatism. I tried different remedies but they did not help me. At last when all hopes were gone, Elder Bush, a minister of the House of Prayer gave me a *Magazine* and I applied it to my body and was healed."[123] Another woman soaked a piece of the magazine in water and drank the solution any time she had an ailment. A member from Raleigh, North Carolina explained that the healing power of the magazine was foretold in Ezekiel 47:12 and Revelation 22:2, both of which refer to a leaf that serves as medicine. "The *Grace Magazine* is from the leaf," she said, "that's why it can heal."[124]

Followers continued to testify in services and in the magazine about their experiences of cures that came through Grace and Grace products. However, the bishop rarely spoke in detail about healing after his early stumbles in Savannah, when he had tried to prove his God-given abilities by allowing the paper to print the names and addresses of some of those healed:

Mrs. Mary Donalds . . . who was on crutches for 15 years and was bent double was healed she threw her crutches away and came back to the meeting to testify . . . [and] Mrs. Harris . . . had indigestion for 11 years and had not ate one single meal in peace and was instantly healed now she enjoys anything she eats . . . [and] Mrs. Martha Snipes . . . was healed of trouble in her head which she had for two months.[125]

Descriptions of the Savannah miracles only heightened persecution, rather than alleviating it. One Savannah pastor said his visits with the "healed" revealed the people were no better, and this led to the local ministers' uniting to get libel charges brought against Grace. The consequences of his actions in Savannah taught the bishop not to discuss healings in interviews and not to use particular cases as advertisement for his religious meetings. His answers during a New Bedford interview in 1927 were typical of this new approach, in which he avoided giving details while acknowledging healing occurred. Describing his travels, he noted that he had been arrested for "treating human ailments without a license when I freed many of disease" and summarized his actions in the passive voice, saying, "The usual miracles were performed."[126]

In fact, after Savannah, Grace remained largely disengaged from people who spoke against him for any reason. Though he would defend himself in sermons and other talks with followers, he no longer made public statements that showed disdain for his attackers, such as that demonstrated in a 1926 Savannah advertisement he placed: "Anybody that follows Manns or any other of these men who had their names signed to this [libel complaint] will surely go to hell."[127] Grace stopped lowering himself to a reactive level, and thus ceased hurling words unbecoming to a religious leader. Though both Elder Michaux of the Church of God and Bishop Johnson of the Church of the Lord Jesus Christ of the Apostolic Faith regularly spoke against Grace on the radio, he made no retort.[128] When various New York City clergy spoke out against Grace, calling him things such as "a novelty," "a disgrace to all decent-minded communities," and "just another of the long line of imposters," Grace simply ignored them.[129] Even in more serious instances of provocation Grace managed to turn the public gaze onto his own good deeds rather than disputing accusations with inflammatory remarks. For instance, when Bishop R. C. Lawson of the Refuge Church of Christ accused Grace of pretending to be God, it was a highly offensive insult that compelled Grace to respond. He called a press conference and spoke at length about his most recent accomplishments and his new plans for building, then declared: "Instead of filling my own pockets as has Bishop Lawson, I have invested money entrusted to me in valuable real estate holdings. This property belongs to the members of the House of Prayer. I am not surprised nor do I blame Lawson for his jealousy. However, I would expect a man of his reputed stature to deal in facts, not fiction."[130] When reporters prodded him further, he advised them, "I haven't got time to take care of the spiritual needs of my members and answer unfounded, ridiculous charges from this so-called Bishop Lawson."[131] This was clearly a different Grace from the man who lashed out at Elder Manns in the Savannah newspapers and provided lists of his healings to prove his merit. Grace had simply become more politic.

Grace's switch to an imperturbable persona affected the tone of the House of Prayer during its formative years. The institutional leaders, always eager to please, as well as the church body emulated Grace's behavior by avoiding speaking to outsiders about the church, and the members became increasingly insular about their socio-religious world. Followers were suspicious of potential intrusion and manipulation by outside researchers, because experience showed that such people usually worked against them.[132] Grace's tendency toward restraint also meant that he did not necessarily make himself accessible within the church, and therefore his presence was craved by followers. In other words, Grace's coolness affected the culture of the House of Prayer because it shaped the role of the bishop within the organization—both his role as he played it, and the way in which followers perceived it, experienced it, and brought it to life.

What is known about Daddy Grace throughout the majority of his bishopric is markedly different from some of the earliest examples of his behavior as a religious leader. Today, he is sometimes described as a wealthy and notorious leader who was treated with abundant devotion by his followers. But in the late 1920s he was a relatively unknown, itinerant preacher, funding his travels through donations, frequently distracted from ministering because people sought to interrupt him with suspicion of his motives. At the same time that Grace was growing into the members' "Daddy," the role he appeared to encourage, he also began to grow into the shoes of the leader on a pedestal, which the job seemed to require. The result was a man of mixed demeanor: reserved with the press, intensely private about his personal life, rarely speaking informally with anyone, yet also at home with the adoring followers who bestowed exuberant love on him. Perhaps Grace's church was not officially founded in Savannah because his leadership had not yet crystallized. It was only after he began transforming into the composed bishop, at once both a reserved man and the peoples' Daddy, that he found the way to lead that was comfortable for him, and so the United House of Prayer for All People was born from his moment of insight.

3

Led by a Convicted Man

The growing strength of Daddy Grace's membership base sustained him not only during the rocky and unpredictable early years of his ministry, but also in times of crisis. This loyalty was best exemplified by House of Prayer members in Hampton Roads in the early 1930s. Hampton Roads, a region comprised of several towns and cities in Virginia, lies in the southeast part of the state where the James, Elizabeth, and Nansemond Rivers coalesce and the Chesapeake Bay meets the Atlantic Ocean. The region was first settled in the early years of American colonization and came to revolve around facets of a maritime economy. With ebbs and flows of employment, many African Americans migrated in and out of the region during the 1920s and 1930s. During these years Daddy Grace spent considerable time in Hampton Roads, first in the city of Newport News and later in other parts of the area, increasing his membership base. At that time Newport News occupied only a tiny portion of the geographical area it encompasses today, but it was nestled among the numerous thriving communities lining the northern part of the coast. The city's economic value to the area was growing because it had become both a railroad hub and a center for shipbuilding. The approximately thirty-five thousand residents of Newport News were racially and religiously varied, but the town was strictly segregated and African Americans were ghettoized on the south side of the railroad tracks. Without a serious business district of their own, Black residents had little economic independence; even for news, they depended on the *Journal and Guide,* an African American newspaper from Norfolk, which at that time gave scant coverage to their side of the bay. Despite these obstacles, Newport News was the only part of the region that experienced an overall increase in its African American population during the 1930s, and as a result that decade saw the Black community becoming stronger both socially and economically. Eventually, even the *Journal and Guide* saw fit to print a weekly "Peninsula" edition of the paper, which was dedicated to the cities of Newport News and Hampton. However, when Daddy Grace was first starting to proselytize, Newport News was still only a blossoming small town without the apparatus of a full-fledged city.[1]

Meanwhile, across Hampton Roads Bay and a few miles down the Elizabeth River, Norfolk already had several thriving African American neighborhoods. With one hundred thirty thousand people, Norfolk was a significantly larger city with a multitude of industries that attracted job seekers. African American residents, who made up 34 percent of the population, worked mostly as unskilled laborers. A small group of merchants and professionals fostered a Black business district on Church Street that was sometimes called the "Harlem of the South." A busy thoroughfare, Church Street was lined with stores, banks, places of worship of every kind, and entertainment houses ranging from proper theaters to clandestine gambling rooms. Though economically Norfolk experienced more fluctuations than Newport News, partly due to haphazard infrastructures, the size of the city meant it offered opportunities to African Americans that did not yet exist for residents across the bay.[2]

Daddy Grace first went to Hampton Roads in 1926, and he attempted to launch a revival in Newport News. He said that although many people in the city were interested in his work, because he held mixed-race meetings, he faced strong opposition and could not establish a church there. Nonetheless, he added Newport News to his traveling route, returning each year to further his work. In 1927 he began preparations to build a church on 17th Street between Jefferson and Madison Avenues, a short walk from Pinkett's Beach where he later conducted baptisms.[3] In the autumn of that year Grace added Norfolk to his southern circuit. Right away he opened a House of Prayer referred to as "Tents Hall" on Elmwood Avenue just off of Church Street, thus planting himself in the hub of Black Norfolk life. The following summer he tried to add a third Hampton Roads congregation, this time setting up a tent on Mallory Avenue in the nearby city of Hampton. However, within days of its assembly, three young men committed arson and burned it to the ground. Their motives were unclear, but newspapers reported that it was because they opposed Grace's arrival. Although he did not try to establish a church in Hampton again, Grace refused to let the incident be a major setback. Less than three months later he held a giant baptismal event, with between seven hundred and one thousand people baptized in the Bay and an estimated crowd of twenty-five

Daddy Grace in his Princess Anne Road residence in Norfolk, Virginia, 1958. Photographer: Orby C. Kelly, Jr. Courtesy of Sargeant Memorial Room, Norfolk Public Library, Norfolk, Virginia.

thousand looking on. Afterwards, people attended services at the newly opened Ivy Avenue House of Prayer, a brand new building in Newport News with a capacity of several thousand.[4]

In these early years of the Newport News church, local resident Joseph James Bailey was a House of Prayer member in training to become an elder. In an autobiography by his daughter, renowned singer Pearl Bailey, she recalled the excitement of members whenever Daddy Grace came for a visit. Some of them lived upstairs from the church, and they became zealous about cleaning, decorating, and selecting their very best outfits for the occasion of his arrival. She also remembered that when people caught the spirit during services, money sometimes fell out of their pockets onto the floor. She and other children would then pretend to shout as well, falling on top of the money and slipping it into their own pockets. "Look at Elder Bailey's girl!" she remembered people doting. "So happy, isn't that wonderful!"[5] Elder Bailey, who was half Creek Indian, later moved to Washington, DC, to be closer to church headquarters, and eventually became a traveling minister with the title of "National Evangelist."[6]

Hampton Roads over Time

While membership in Hampton Roads grew, Grace's work was hampered by the fact that he could not get publicity. In December 1930 the *Journal and Guide* printed a survey of African American churches in Norfolk. The article individually praised churches that had "developed a strong feeling of responsibility for others," as evidenced by their contributions to schools and missionary work. As a church that did not make these kinds of charitable donations, the House of Prayer was not among the many singled out, though its existence was noted.[7] In fact, Grace rarely received coverage in the conservative newspaper at all, and when he did the stories were often about scandals in other cities rather than reports of his local activities and progress. Retrospectively it is clear that this was mainly caused by the strict conservatism of the newspaper under the direction of its owner and editor, P. B. Young. But Grace may have thought that a strong community showing in the Hampton Roads region would help him, and therefore he made overtures there unlike the noninvolvement he practiced in most other communities. In 1934, for example, he held a "city officials night," to which he invited members of the Newport News City Council to discuss "the upbuilding of Newport News."[8] Specifically, Grace had ideas about building an elderly home and a hospital. Officials were unresponsive to his invitation, as were pastors in Norfolk when, the following year, he announced a desire to work ecumenically toward ending the economic slump. Though the House of Prayer was never invited to participate in Norfolk's annual Emancipation Day parade and speaking events, the church held public parades of its own in Newport News every Easter and in Norfolk each Independence Day. Sometimes, Grace visited elderly homes to minister to residents.[9] In 1949 he hosted a luncheon for the City Council at his newly constructed Newport News apartment building, and a reporter who attended explained that, "Bishop Grace

House of Prayer parade on Freemason Street, Norfolk, Virginia, July 1958. Courtesy of Sargeant Memorial Room, Norfolk Public Library, Norfolk, Virginia.

says his church is endeavoring to help provide more and better housing for colored people throughout the country."[10] Grace echoed this mark of progress in Norfolk three years later, completing the Grace Village apartment building on East Princess Anne Road, not far from the primary House of Prayer in the city. He said in an interview, "Grace Village in Norfolk was my own idea. It's kind of cute, a little bit foreignish . . . the prettiest [apartment building] in America."[11] When he was in town, Grace lived on the top floor of the Grace Village, where he had a balcony and windows on all sides.[12]

Beyond these grand gestures, Grace did his usual training of ministers, building of churches, and regular visiting, all in an effort to strengthen House of Prayer membership and improve his reputation in Hampton Roads. He even sent his sister Louise to Newport News, where she lived for many years providing administrative leadership for the Houses of Prayer in the region. In terms of membership, his efforts did seem to result in success: by the mid-1930s, WPA workers observed that Grace's Newport News following alone was approximately two thousand people.[13] Such a number would have made his church a very serious contender within religious circles, as well as in the community at large. Assuming that Newport News had approximately the same proportion of African American residents as Norfolk, the two thousand members of the Newport News House of Prayer represented an unusually large proportion of the Black community at approximately 16 percent.[14] Even if the membership number was greatly exaggerated, Grace clearly drew a significant audience. In other words, despite his lack of press there, by the mid-1930s the multiple Houses of Prayer in Hampton Roads had become an undeniably important membership base for Bishop Grace. As he learned firsthand in the early 1930s, this large membership was something to be concerned about in times of trouble, and depended upon in times of need.

Who Joined the House of Prayer

Who, then, were these members? One of the questions researchers have frequently asked is, What kinds of people were attracted to a religious leader like Daddy Grace? Many have addressed the question by giving Grace primacy, surmising that because he promoted himself as a stylish and ostentatiously wealthy man, the kind of people attracted to him are likely to have had particular characteristics.[15] However, I believe that a top-down approach such as this cannot reveal much about followers. No leader is solely a "personality type" who attracts followers defined by a particular personality type, economic status, or educational level. Additionally, membership in the House of Prayer meant far more than merely following Daddy Grace; it meant being an active part of a distinct religious community. Inevitably one must examine aspects of that community's life to begin to understand what attracted people to it and held them there.

In ideal circumstances, demographics for the House of Prayer would provide a broad portrait of the religious community as well as elucidating the relationship of the members to the leader. Statistics could help us understand the contours of House of Prayer membership in different time frames, in different regions, and from a variety of other sociological angles. Unfortunately, there is almost no demographic data to support such an analysis. Though observers maintained that the House of Prayer membership during the Daddy Grace years was predominantly made up of poverty-stricken, poorly educated African Americans, this assertion is based on very thin statistical evidence combined with assumptions about the kind of people attracted to charismatic worship.[16] In fact, we will never know for certain who the members were during the Grace years, because even the House of Prayer kept scant membership records. Thus, despite decades' worth of assumptions, very little is actually known.

A handful of scholars, mostly graduate students in the social sciences, visited and wrote about Houses of Prayer during the years of Grace's bishopric. Their observations were often supplemented by interviews of members. Though they did not offer viable statistical data to support their claims, their findings tended to contribute to the negative generalizations made about House of Prayer membership. For example, based on his visits to Houses of Prayer in the Washington, DC, area in the late 1930s, James Daniel Tyms described members as "outcasts" from the "slums" who were typically unwelcome in other churches.[17] In the late 1940s historian Elmer Clark's visit to the Augusta House of Prayer caused him to evaluate members as "nervously unstable Negroes."[18] In the late 1950s, after conducting participant observation in several East Coast locations, Norman Eddy characterized House of Prayer members as poor people who used worship to "regress" and "vent their aggressive drives."[19] Shortly thereafter, anthropologist Alexander Alland assessed the House of Prayer by saying, "Middle-class Negroes do not join this kind of church."[20] Last but not least, in the early 1940s an assistant to Arthur Fauset collected numeric information at a single weekday meeting of a North Philadelphia House of Prayer. Of the eighteen members present, everyone was originally from the South, and the majority had previously been Baptists.[21] Fauset then used this data in conjunction with other groups he studied to substantiate a claim that the perplexing experience of northward migration resulted in many African Americans' seeking less traditional forms of religion in the North.[22]

Because all of these House of Prayer studies were small in scale and based primarily on observation, none should be regarded as anything more than an anecdotal assessment.

A slightly more valuable study was made by Albert Whiting, who provided potentially interesting statistics but failed to explain enough about his measurement parameters. From 1949–50 Whiting surveyed fifty adult members of a House of Prayer in Augusta, Georgia, conducted general psychological studies of nineteen of them, and obtained more detailed biographies of ten from that group. He also engaged in participant observation in the Augusta church. He concluded that House of Prayer members came from broken homes more often than average, that they had lower than average educational levels, and that they had worse than average housing. What renders these observations unhelpful is that Whiting does not explain precisely what "average" group(s) he was comparing the members to, be it Americans, Georgians, African Americans, southerners, churchgoers, or some other particular demographic. He did specify, however, that relative to other nonwhite southerners, House of Prayer members had lower than average income, though not without exception. As Fauset's work had, Whiting's also found that a majority had previously been Baptists, and like African American churches in general, the most devout included more women than men.[23] Overall, Whiting said that members' faces and clothes showed "obvious poverty," and his psychological tests showed that they were often "poorly oriented to reality" and "intellectually dull or culturally deprived."[24] However, it must be remembered that his study sample, especially for the psychological evaluations, was quite small and would not count as statistically significant under current social science standards.

One final study worth noting comes from the work of Chancellor Williams, who, along with five assistants, studied House of Prayer members in several East Coast cities from 1942–46. Williams did not offer hard statistics, but he provided a voice of reason about a murky picture. Yes, he said, he had found many members who were limited in education and income, but he had also met intelligent and educated members who earned a middle-class salary. Williams noted that only 14 percent of Americans had as much as a high school diploma at that time, and he expressed doubt that a careful profile of House of Prayer members would be disproportionate to the American public at large.[25] Williams's work stands out from that of other scholars because he refrained from making sweeping negative assessments without statistical support, and because he questioned the assumptions commonly made.

A profile of the "typical" House of Prayer member, then, is not known. It is likely that thorough studies, had they been conducted, would have shown regional distinctions of membership that would complicate the oft-held assumptions about House of Prayer members. Though we do not know exactly what the real membership looked like, surprisingly there are more substantial answers available to the question of why people joined. Journalists and academics frequently asked this question of members, and issues of the *Grace Magazine* and other church-related publications often included testimony about how and why people had joined. Thus, the question of why people joined has been addressed far more often and in a wider variety of sources than the question of who members were.

Why People Joined the House of Prayer

The range of answers to the question of why people joined, which were often interlaced, includes such factors as the vibrant social life of the church, the honor of being associated with a powerful organization, a life-altering spiritual experience within the church, and the appeal of Daddy Grace himself. And in addition to the direct answers supplied by followers, researchers themselves often provided their own interpretations of subconscious causes. In an instance of the latter, Eddy assessed the psychology of House of Prayer membership by saying that the emotional release experienced in services fulfilled a need for the downtrodden members. In his opinion, the freedom to act "like a child, without fear of censure" in services compensated for the turmoil of their daily lives.[26] In another example, although he saw that people usually gave very specific reasons for why they chose to join, Whiting believed that House of Prayer membership was intrinsically linked with a history of coming from a "broken family."[27] There may be truth in any or all of these answers but due to the flaws in the studies themselves, as mentioned earlier, it is not possible to determine the relative merits of these alleged underlying reasons for membership.

It is clear that some people were drawn to the House of Prayer by the regularity of its socio-religious community. The close, consistent social circles within the church were strong attractions for potential members.

One interviewee told Whiting, "The thing I like about the House of Prayer is that it lets you keep renewing religion. By going more often you feel strong and the more you serve Him, the stronger you feel. In the Baptist Church you just go once a week."[28] This comment provides evidence for sociological theory about exclusive firms, or the "strict church thesis," which suggests that religions like the House of Prayer thrive precisely because their commitment demand is higher than that of the average church. While this member perceived that the House of Prayer allowed her to worship more frequently, it was also true that the church required she do so. Furthermore, had her Baptist church increased the supply of services and increased the expectation that she attend them all, such theory would conclude that she would not have changed her religious affiliation.[29] The high value of the intensity of membership in the House of Prayer was also echoed by a man from Detroit, who explained that the church would be a safety net no matter what ailed a person. In a letter to the *Grace Magazine,* he wrote: "This faith will make you glad when you are sad, lift you up when you are burdened down, regulate your mind when it is wavering, establish your heart with Grace."[30] In addition to the regularity of attending services, auxiliaries built around avocational interests provided social connections. The large number of auxiliaries, each of which needed officers, provided many opportunities for leadership that might not be available anywhere else. One member pinpointed a key difference between leadership in mainline churches and in the House of Prayer, saying, "You don't have to be no big doctor or lawyer to be somebody in the House of Prayer. Even if you can't read or write, you got a voice in our church."[31] Holding these positions of authority and responsibility enhanced self-respect and heightened peoples' perception of their own social status.[32] While such opportunities existed within most denominations, the sheer number of positions available in House of Prayer auxiliaries meant that a greater percentage of members gained access to lay leadership experience, and as a result these opportunities created a stronger pull factor compared to other denominations. The significance of the social network in the House of Prayer is also supported by the theory of religious economy. Using metaphors of investment, this theory explains that social connections are comparable to capital that has been invested. Research has shown that preserving and protecting one's valuable social connections, or social capital, is one of the most important factors in a person's decision to affiliate with a given religious group—

often more important than doctrine.[33] Thus, whether people joined the House of Prayer because others in their social network had already done so, or if they joined because they wanted to become part of a social group, the stability of the House of Prayer services and the regularity the auxiliaries certainly guaranteed fulfillment in the social realm. The House of Prayer, then, had much to offer in terms of social and community life.

As discussed in chapter 2, healing was also a reason that some people attended the church, particularly in its early years. In Whiting's survey of fifty Augusta members, healing and attraction to the teachings were the two reasons most frequently given for why people had joined. He also found that most people seemed to have experienced healing in the church whether or not it was the reason they had initially come. Among churchgoers of any type, a degree of dissatisfaction and/or complacency normally occurs after years of involvement in the organization, but formative experiences in the House of Prayer were often strong enough that they sustained peoples' commitment even if they subsequently felt less engaged. As one woman expressed, although she had been a House of Prayer member for about twenty years, she had reservations about the kinds of programs and events the church held, and she also thought the church attracted some "peculiar" people. Nonetheless, she remained loyal because of her original spiritual experiences there.[34] This member's comment is one example of the idea that people remain in a religious group because it "satisfices" them: that is, it satisfies them more than the other obvious choices available, but in other ways it is merely sufficient. Nonetheless, incomplete fulfillment is deemed preferable to leaving and trying to find something more completely satisfying, so people will stay in a religion despite not being fully content.[35] In this woman's case, her conversion narrative acted as the strongest part of her satisfaction, and it would be unlikely to be challenged unless she deliberately sought out a new religious experience.

Certainly, another reason people joined was that they felt a close identification with Daddy Grace, and so belonging to his church was like being a part of his family. This point was exemplified by a Georgia woman who, when her boyfriend mocked Grace for being foolish, scolded him and explained, "When you talks about 'Daddy' you talks about me."[36] Another member's description of Grace, made after the bishop's death, made him sound like the patriarch of the man's own family: "He made my life mean something. He made it possible for me to look forward to tomorrow. He taught me how to be happy because Sunday was coming. He made me look forward to Christmas time. He showed me that I was somebody too."[37] In a similar vein yet one step removed, other members felt personal prestige by being associated with the church that had the glamorous leader and which ultimately came to own a vast empire of real estate. A member in Columbia, South Carolina, wrote about her local House of Prayer, noting that among the attractions in the church were photos of other buildings that "belong to Sweet Daddy and his children."[38] In fact, this kind of close identification with Grace's wealth seems to have been fostered by church leadership; numerous writers observed the curious tradition of photos of church real estate framed and hung on the sanctuary walls. This was especially true of the El Dorado, a building that received so much attention that it was nearly fetishized.[39] Even on basic missionary trips, traveling members made a point to visit not only other Houses of Prayer but also apartment buildings owned by the church.[40] As Norman Eddy told a reporter upon Grace's death, "They might live in slums, but Daddy was rich, and they could feel like big shots."[41]

Salvation Is by Grace Only

However, above and beyond each of these reasons for belonging to the church, writers have often insisted that it was the appeal of Daddy Grace himself that primarily buoyed membership and that this was because people believed Grace was God. The evidence most frequently used to support this stance is a statement that Grace allegedly made in the early 1940s, reported by Arthur Fauset and reprinted countless times, in which Grace seemed to say that he was God incarnate. The quote, as found in Fauset's book *Black Gods of the Metropolis*, reads: "Never mind about God. Salvation is by Grace only. . . . Grace has given God a vacation, and since God is on vacation, don't worry Him. . . . If you sin against God, Grace can save you, but if you sin against Grace, God cannot save you."[42] It is not clear if Fauset or one of his research assistants actually heard Grace himself speak the words in question or if the speaker was a church member summarizing beliefs. In an early draft of Fauset's work an ambiguous comment precedes the quote, and it indicates only that the words represent something followers believed.[43] Nonetheless, Fauset's interpretation of this point—that Grace claimed he himself was God—has been almost completely definitive in both academic and popular literature, and only a handful of writers have ever questioned it, usually as an aside.[44] Danielle Brune Sigler's research, which has treated Fauset's interpretation more comprehensively than any other extant work, uses a more lengthy version of the original quote to show that Fauset selectively quoted in a way that significantly changed the meaning of the statement. Her excellent analysis ultimately concludes that, based on this and other information, Grace's role for the church was not that of God himself but merely an "intermediary" and "the path to salvation."[45] Regardless of whether Grace actually spoke the words about "grace" and "salvation" that Fauset attributed to him, Sigler is certainly correct in her position that the full text of this particular statement does not suggest that Grace was God, either in his own eyes or in the eyes of his followers.

However, the answer to the question of whether his followers did actually believe Grace was God is not absolutely clear. Aside from the long history of problematic assumptions based on Fauset's work, the fact is that most writers have attempted to give a definitive answer to a question that actually demands something more contoured. We must not assume that all followers thought or believed the same thing about who and what Grace was. Furthermore, we cannot equate followers' beliefs with Grace's own self-conception. The evidence makes it appear that Grace, and most of his followers, believed he was a human with a special connection to God, but that in some instances followers projected a greater divine significance onto him, and neither elders nor church publications ever definitively clarified the precise relationship. Added to this is the fact that some of Grace's own statements alluded to a divine heritage, and he did not go out of his way to enlighten those who inquired directly. Hence, there is a range of conflicting evidence about whether followers believed Grace was God.

Some members of the church indicated that they believed Daddy Grace was God, or at least had hope that he was, and while they were probably few in number their existence should not be ignored, though it may be an uncomfortable fact. There is evidence that members called on Grace in prayers, testified about his supernatural powers, and gave thanks to God for bringing them a savior. As one woman effused in a letter, "[Daddy Grace] is my life, health, strength, and my salvation. . . . The more Satan oppresses me the more Daddy blesses me."[46] In Eddy's research, a member explained in an interview that since Jesus was long deceased, it was "easier to call on Daddy Grace," and therefore prayers were often addressed to Grace and thanks was given to him, rather than for him.[47] And, when the *House of Prayer Quarterly* marked North Carolina's Grace Emmanuel Day with a lesson on Romans 5:15–21, the Bible teaching referred to their bishop as, "Sweet Daddy Grace Emmanuel, the present God."[48]

Elder Mitchell, one of the top leaders under Grace, was one of those who often implied a nearly indistinct connection between Grace and God, and he frequently took the word "grace" as found in Biblical texts and rhetorically spun it to say that the reference was to Daddy Grace. For example, in a prayer at the Washington, DC, Mother House, Mitchell said:

> Heavenly Father, we thank thee for Daddy. We thank thee for sending him into the world at this critical hour to lead us from darkness to light. For when we were lost as wandering sheep, Daddy came upon the scene and saved our souls. And we know for a truth that today Daddy holds the entire world in the hollow of his hand. We know that if we only trust in Daddy everything will be all right. Even from the beginning of time our sweet Daddy had us in his mind. We know that we have found the true way at last and that we shall be saved, O Heavenly Father, for thou said in thy holy word that by Grace are ye saved."[49]

In a *Grace Magazine* article, Mitchell retold the story of the Samaritan woman's meeting Jesus as found in John 4, then concluded: "Be it known to you and the entire world that the same Christ is here again in the flesh in the person of Sweet Daddy Grace."[50] The influence of Mitchell, who was an elder at the House of Prayer headquarters and the editor of the *Grace Magazine,* would certainly have been significant.

Helping to clarify this picture, at least in terms of member belief, are the words of a learned elder who explained to researcher Chancellor Williams that there are always those members who "create unofficial dogmas. They make claims for the leader and give to him attributes which were never declared to be the official doctrine of the church. Thus, when the bishop said in the emotional height of a sermon some years ago that he was 'present at the crucifixion,' he meant only that he was 'spiritually present.' But the members took the statement literally and spread it abroad."[51] In other words, this elder felt that beliefs about Grace's really being God himself were akin to folk beliefs, anomalies within the church that could not be easily squelched and not important enough to worry over. His goal as an elder was to teach what was true, rather than to try to combat every rumor or misunderstanding.

Despite those who believed and suggested that Grace was God incarnate, the majority of the evidence suggests that most people considered Grace a kind of intermediary, with a somewhat heightened status, between average humans and God. Since the House of Prayer was the only door to salvation, it logically followed that the founder, Daddy Grace, must have a special role under God. That role was often thought of as akin to Jesus' role in that Grace was a teacher who brought new understanding to the world about God, but he was distinct from Jesus because he was not divine by nature. As one follower wrote in the *Grace Magazine,* "God has always had a man to carry out His plan in behalf of the souls of men. That man is not God, but a servant of God."[52] The *House of Prayer Quarterly,* explicating Isaiah 40:13–16, explained that Daddy Grace had been sent by God to teach that the gospel could enrich and sustain a person in life. It further explicated, "Every one carries his own cross but Daddy Grace gives you power to bear it."[53] Similarly, the *Quarterly* used the eighth chapter of Proverbs to suggest that Daddy Grace was a vehicle for the wisdom of God, and it taught that his good works were the evidence that he had been sent by God.[54] A Norfolk elder, asked about the nature of Daddy Grace, eloquently explained: "Some people in the world have a misconception about the House of Prayer. They think we are fanatics, that we don't know what we're doing, that it is all based on his personality. Of course we honor the man but we are worshipping God. The Christian God. The man was just God's servant. We know that."[55]

Grace himself never went out of his way to clarify the picture with either followers or the public. On many occasions he made statements to indicate his subservient relationship to God. He said that Christian scripture taught him to heal and spread the good word "in His name"; he referred to himself as a "servant of God" and "God's child"; and he wrote to followers that he would "pray many Blessings upon you from my Father in Heaven."[56] In 1938 he corrected a reporter's suggestion, saying, "Do I look like God? I don't regard myself as God. . . . I am a servant of man"; and when he won a 1950s court case, he cried out in joy, "There's a God up there!"[57]

However, at other times Daddy Grace gave vague answers and allowed people to make their own assumptions, and he sometimes echoed

Jesus' words in the New Testament books of Mark and Matthew. When asked directly if he were God, Grace might reply, "Some people say that I am."[58] As member Ed Black recalled, "I know he seemed different from any man so one day I ask him, 'Ain't you Jesus?' And he said, 'Look upon me and what you see then that is what I am.'" The man interpreted that Grace's answer meant that, "while Jesus was dead, [Grace] was carrying Christ in him and he was the last prophet."[59] Occasionally Grace implied that he had special powers, such as in a letter to followers that said although he could not physically be in every place, if there was "peace, love, and joy among you, you know that I am there" in spirit.[60] Statements like these, which were evasive and yet suggestive, contributed to the ongoing confusion about the precise nature of Daddy Grace.

Expectations for Member Behavior

Whether followers believed Daddy Grace was God, quasi-God, or merely a very important human, most regarded him as a living example of God's moral code. The House of Prayer was open to all seekers regardless of color, class, or gender, but to belong one had to commit to principles of Christian behavior as prescribed by Daddy Grace. The bishop taught that evil lurked in the world, ready to ensnare careless Christians, and it was manifest in both human inventions and behaviors. He urged followers to be good people so that God would care about them. As he wrote to them in a letter, "My children, I warn you to be careful as you walk day by day. I have warned you time and time again to watch your step because when you disobey me, you will find trouble at your door. When you disobey me, how can you expect Jesus and God to help you?"[61] Grace believed the body should be kept clean and pure, so church members were forbidden to drink or smoke. On the question of alcohol Grace paraphrased the New Testament, saying: "The man who drinks shall not inherit the kingdom of Heaven," and he disliked cigarettes so much that he would not allow them to be smoked even outside of his churches or his home.[62] Other prohibitions for members included dancing, swearing, and adultery, and interfaith marriages were strongly advised against. Grace claimed never to have seen television, and he specified that followers were not to see movies. As an elder in Charlotte explained it, "television is connected with hell, and I am working for heaven."[63] Other forms of modern life that Grace frowned upon included airplanes and the radio.[64] He sometimes claimed he did not read newspapers, but there were occasions when it was evident that he did. Nonetheless, he specifically told his followers, "I don't want you to read colored papers because they print only trash."[65]

Though Grace spoke about political concerns only infrequently, he did consistently preach the importance of world peace and he made it known that Christians should be ethically opposed to war. For this position, he referred to the second chapter of Isaiah, which teaches that ideally "nation shall not lift up sword against nation, neither shall they learn war any more."[66] Although Grace was against war as a concept, he did voice support for those serving in the military. In the 1930s he encouraged followers to pray for the end of the war in Ethiopia. During World War II, the church bought ten thousand dollars' worth of war bonds, and Grace told members to buy more as they were able. He explained that despite his stance against war, "the present conflict is of primary concern to Christian peoples."[67] Followers believed world peace could come if people heeded Grace's call. As one elder wrote, "If the people of our day would see the man whom God has anointed with the Holy Spirit and power, peace would reign instead of trouble. . . .War will stop."[68] In 1945, Grace commanded that all Houses of Prayer have a nightly time of prayer for every person being affected by the war, and in 1947 he instituted an annual service in each church that would focus on world peace efforts. Grace remained outspoken during the Korean War as well. In 1951, for example, he made a public call to New Bedford clergy to meet with him and discuss methods for ending the war, though it does not appear that any responded to his proposition.[69]

Through both their behavior and their beliefs, Grace wanted House of Prayer members to be known for their ethical nature, and to be fair people who were accountable for their actions. They were taught to question the causes and effects behind sleek concepts so that they might become better people. For example, in a prayer printed in the *Grace Magazine,* they asked for divine help with "the world's true problems: the problem of lying, which is called propaganda; the problem of self-ishness, which is called self-interest; the problem of greed, which is often called profit; the problem of license, disguising itself as liberty; the problem of lust, masquerading as love; the problem of materialism, the hook which is baited with security."[70] Grace also taught people to speak carefully and with forethought. As one church publication further explained, "He also tells us it is not expedient to speak the truth at all times although he did not mean for the children to lie. But if the truth does harm hold your peace and then you are using wisdom."[71] Grace expected House of Prayer members to be upstanding American citizens not only within the church walls, but, even more importantly, in the rest of their lives. Grace said, "We teach our people to respect and obey the laws, all the laws."[72] In many cases, broken church rules and backsliding were overlooked because it was acknowledged that sanctification was a gradual process. As Grace explained with compound metaphors in a 1955 letter: "I am a shepherd who has many sheep. Yet I am not contented for some have strayed away from my pastures, you must help me to bring those back, where they might be fed the bread of life so that they might live again."[73] However, in the case of extreme or egregious infractions, members could be tried in the House of Prayer church court and punished or expelled.

Behavior and Roles of Women

On top of the many prohibitions already described, there were additional expectations for women in the House of Prayer. One was the frequent admonishment to be virtuous. Grace told females not to be drawn to men who showered them with gifts or made lofty promises, but to wait for a man who was serious about commitment and marriage.[74] Not surprisingly, heterosexuality was the only acceptable lifestyle for House of Prayer women; what is somewhat surprising is that Grace spoke against lesbianism on several documented occasions. Precisely what this tells us is unclear, but it is quite possible that violations of this policy among church members provoked his comments.[75] Virtue was also linked with attire and adornment. Female church members were supposed to dress modestly because too much exposure could provoke men; on the other hand, they were encouraged to make themselves look pretty. Makeup was permissible, as were nail polish and hair straightening. Grace specifically said that a woman should have at least one different dress for every day of the week, but not a number that would far exceed that, and he encouraged them to buy quality clothing rather than flimsy inexpensive outfits.[76] This posture was not entirely empowering for women, because although they had freedom to express themselves via clothing and adornments, they attended church most days of the week knowing there was an expectation for them to "look pretty" and preferably to wear expensive clothing.

More generally, the role of women in the House of Prayer under Grace's aegis was much like the role of women in mainline churches of the same era: they were the workhorses of the church, the backbone of the organization's social endeavors, and they probably made up the majority of the membership; yet they were largely shut out of the prestigious leadership roles, especially those associated with the development of theology. This is not to say that they were powerless or that they did not have a hand in shaping of the House of Prayer, but in gender equity the church's policies did not distinguish it from mainstream American religious organizations.

There were instances of women's serving in important House of Prayer leadership capacities. For example, Effie Lawrence was one of the founding trustees of the church, as demonstrated by her signature on the incorporation certificate filed in 1927. In the early 1930s, Ann Hodge had the prestige of being the bishop's secretary, a role that was later occupied only by men. Mary Alice Boulware was the secretary of the *Grace Magazine* from its start in the mid-1920s, and by the late 1930s she had become the national secretary of the church's Family Aid Association. Grace's youngest sister, Louise, called Sister Grace, was known as the "spiritual leader" of the Virginia region for many years, and his niece Marie Miller was active in church leadership for several decades, though she was not actually a member. Carolyn Barber was instrumental in organizing youth in the District of Columbia, even getting them to start a publication called the *Grace Youth Gazette* that included several young women on the masthead. And at the time of Grace's death in 1960, the spokesperson at the national headquarters was Annie Bell Jones. Within local congregations, females often served in the office of General Secretary, and outside of the church Grace demonstrated his trust in women's abilities, such as when he hired lawyer Helen Bernard to defend him against a paternity charge.[77]

This sampling of women in important leadership positions shows that there were cases in which women's abilities were recognized and valued by the House of Prayer. However, clear limits were set by the rules. Following Biblical precedent, women were ineligible to become elders in the House of Prayer; they were also forbidden from preaching in any capacity. An example of upholding the Biblical rule was the case of Millie Johnson from Wilmington, North Carolina. At one time, Grace publicly "condemned" Johnson because she had tried to preach in her region. In defiance of Grace, Johnson disappeared with the collection money she was supposed to turn over to him.[78] The fact that she was responsible for a large sum of money was probably typical, since women were at the helm of most House of Prayer auxiliaries. Though they were excluded from guard- and soldier-oriented groups, there were many all-female auxiliaries including the Grace Queens, the Female Ushers, and the Mothers Band. In other church activities there was a tendency to separate by gender, but there was no hard rule about it.[79] Though women were clearly not supposed to engage in any form of preaching, they regularly offered theological interpretation via articles and letters they contributed to the *Grace Magazine* and by testifying in church; this was acceptable because it was not considered serious Biblical interpretation or preaching, nor as attempts to be authoritative.[80]

The House of Prayer also promoted roles for mothers that were based on conservative interpretations of Biblical examples. One year on Mother's Day, the *House of Prayer Quarterly*'s Bible lesson focused on 1 Samuel 1:20–28, in which the grateful and faithful Hannah waits until her child is weaned before bringing him before God. Rather than celebrating Hannah's devotion to God, the House of Prayer teaching about these verses focused on women's responsibility for ensuring their sons were raised within the church. "Now Mothers," the explanation posited, "will you give your sons to one that can teach them and that is Sweet Daddy Grace, the present Prophet in the House of God. . . . Mothers are you raising your sons for God or for the government? You are responsible for the service they render."[81] While Mother's Day was celebrated by reminding mothers of their duties, in contrast, the Father's Day teaching focused on the greatness of spiritual fathers who spend all of their time in devotion to children, and used the examples of Moses and Daddy Grace as great comforters and teachers.[82] In a similar vein, Elder Mitchell, the author of many *Grace Magazine* articles, taught that women were not associated with bringing salvation in the Bible; rather, humans are spiritual children of God the father. Mitchell emphasized paying homage to the perfect, pure fatherhood of God, especially as found in the Lord's Prayer in the eleventh chapter of Luke.[83] Motherhood was a secular, earthly connection of one person to another, whereas fatherhood was a divine link; hence women and men did not share the same spiritual privileges in the world.

For men, women, and children, Grace ultimately wanted nothing less than a serious commitment to the organization and to the faith, and so members were expected to attend services every day of the week unless work or illness prevented it.[84] In a public letter Grace wrote:

> Obey my teaching and do what thus saith the Lord. For the way of the Lord will stand forever, but the way of the unGodly shall perish. I want all of my children to come to the House of Prayer every night. Idleness and slackness is dangerous because just at the time when you turn back, darkness will come into your life and you will be lost forever. If you lose your leg, come limping. If you lost your eye come looking with the other.[85]

He also warned that sinful behavior was not eradicated by being on friendly terms with the bishop himself. As one member paraphrased, Grace said: "Don't think because you come to see me in my dining room and tell people how great I am and give me a dollar that you are going to Heaven."[86]

The breadth of church behavioral policy, the emphasis on church leaders as living examples, and the explicit punishments for broken rules all cut narrow moral paths through the lives of House of Prayer members. It is striking, then, that when questions arose about Daddy Grace's moral conduct, church members and leaders found it inconceivable that he could break either church rules or American laws, and therefore forgiving him for trespasses was completely unnecessary. In his early years of leadership, Grace would not have anticipated the boundlessness of their confidence in him; as a human, he would have expected that followers would lose trust in him if he broke the law.[87] However, Grace's 1934 Mann Act trial was his first serious accusation of deviance from American law. The Mann Act, which forbids transporting someone across state lines for illicit purposes, was originally intended as a measure to control prostitution, though in Grace's case it was invoked somewhat differently. Grace's trial in New York City, attended by many followers and reported in nationwide newspapers, revealed details about his personal practices that appeared to violate numerous House of Prayer standards. The revelations had the potential to disintegrate the House of Prayer membership base, which was still in its formative years. Strikingly, follower reaction was quite the opposite.

Not only did followers unabashedly proclaim his innocence from the start, but what they considered the senseless persecution of their leader caused them to unite more strongly both in his defense and as a religious community.

The Mann Act Trial Testimony

The testimony of Grace's March 1934 trial was lengthy, and, as one might expect, the twenty-one people who testified contradicted each other about what had happened and when.[88] According to Minnie Lee Campbell, a House of Prayer member and the person on whose behalf the case was initiated, Daddy Grace transported her across state lines for illicit purposes that resulted in the illegitimate birth of a son. Her version of the story began in mid-October 1932, when the bishop gave her a ride from Brooklyn, New York, to Philadelphia. She said that as their car passed through New Jersey he attempted to rape her. As Campbell explained in court, Grace "threw me down on the floor of the car and got on top of me, took up my dress, his pants were unbuttoned. I was wiggling, I tried to holler, and he put his hand over my mouth, and I could not say a word. . . . Then he tried to play with me and hug me up until I got to Philadelphia." There was no consummation at that time, however.

In Philadelphia, Campbell sometimes worked cleaning Grace's home, and she claimed that during the weeks following the incident Grace made passes at her several times. At the end of October, Grace told Campbell that a job playing piano for a House of Prayer in Baltimore was available, and so she again accompanied him on a car trip. During this trip she said he told her, "Minnie Lee, I did not bring you here to play the piano. I brought you here to be my sweetheart." He threatened to leave her in Baltimore without money if she would not comply with his wishes. The pair went to Washington, DC, where they stayed overnight at the House of Prayer rooming house on Logan Circle. There, Campbell was assigned to a room with a little girl, but before she went to bed Grace told her, "I want you to come up to my room, and I mean come up. I am going to leave the door unlocked, and come up." Campbell said she had complied and had intercourse with Grace that night but returned to her assigned bed before dawn. The following day she was sent to Baltimore where she remained for several months, playing the piano. She testified that Grace was the only man she had ever been intimate with, and so when her son was born in late July 1933 she named him Charles M. Campbell.[89]

The overall structure of Grace's version of the events did not differ from Campbell's, but on several key details he told a different story. For one, he said the car trips from Brooklyn to Philadelphia and from Philadelphia to Baltimore had occurred on two successive days, not two weeks apart, and that they had taken place in the middle of November. Additionally, he maintained that he had never had any sexual interaction with Miss Campbell, nor had he ever even entertained such thoughts. Grace also provided information about why they had been in Brooklyn in the first place. Grace's lawyer called witnesses who testified about the events that transpired in Brooklyn just prior to the ill-fated automobile journey, as well as about the character of both Minnie Lee and the bishop. And, in the lengthiest part of the testimony, Grace spoke in his own defense.

Grace testified that he had known Miss Lucille Campbell, a dedicated House of Prayer member and his secretary in Brooklyn, for several years. In the middle of November 1932, he received a telegram from Lucille asking him to come to Brooklyn to settle a problem. He did as she asked, bringing with him Lucille's younger sister Minnie Lee, whom he was meeting for the first time. Once there, an ecclesiastical trial commenced because the problem, it turned out, was that Minnie Lee and two church members named Helen and Mary were involved in a sexual relationship.[90] Finding them guilty, Grace ordered all of them to cease their behavior and no longer live together. At the end of the day he returned to Philadelphia with Minnie Lee, whom he described as huddling in a corner of the back seat during the ride, sniffling into a handkerchief and looking ill. Before leaving Brooklyn Lucille had asked him to keep her sister away from the other two women, Grace said, and so at some point it occurred to him that she could be sent to Baltimore, where a piano player was needed for a new House of Prayer mission. Thus, the day after the trial Grace again sent for Minnie Lee, and this time they set out for Baltimore, ultimately spending the night in Washington. Grace described that the bedroom to which Minnie Lee had been assigned in the Washington house was quite far from his, and that to get to his room she would have needed to pass by the dining room. As others also attested, that very same night an elderly woman who lived in the house was sick, and she was being tended around the clock in the dining room. Hence, the possibility that Minnie Lee could have come and gone from an upstairs bedroom unnoticed by anyone was unlikely.

Daddy Grace further explained that after Minnie Lee had been in Baltimore a couple of months, her employer, Mrs. Cunningham, had reported that she was not working out. Mrs. Cunningham herself testified that this was because she had discovered Minnie's Lee's pregnancy. Though Minnie Lee denied the pregnancy when confronted, Mrs. Cunningham witnessed her trying to induce a miscarriage by drinking a concoction involving turpentine and vinegar. When he was next in Baltimore, Grace gave Minnie Lee money and told her to return to New York. After that, he heard nothing of her for several months until Lucille requested money for her sister, explaining the pregnancy and telling him that Minnie Lee earned barely enough to support herself. Grace acknowledged in court that he had sent money, just as he sometimes did for others in need. "I did not see how I could claim to be a minister of the Gospel and the Christian faith and let my own people go too bad and I won't help them," he testified. He also instructed Lucille to give Minnie Lee a portion of the House of Prayer collection on at least one occasion. Eventually it came to Grace's attention that Minnie Lee claimed he was the father of her unborn child; because that point was not relevant to the charges in the case, the trial testimony does not clarify his response.

Numerous witnesses for the defense were called to comment on Campbell's character. Several claimed they had known, in the autumn of 1932, that Campbell was having a sexual relationship with House of Prayer minister Daniel Lewis. Among these witnesses was Bessie Perkins, Lewis's sister-in-law. The testimony of several people suggested that Minnie Lee had been pregnant prior to her trip with Grace, because she had been sick to her stomach and had mentioned missing her menstrual period. A regional bishop for the United Methodist church, who did not personally know Daddy Grace but was acquainted with both Campbell and Lewis, testified that Lewis had confided he was the father of her baby. Others attested to Campbell's general promiscuity. These included Calvin Davis, who said he had given money to Minnie Lee in exchange for sex in October or November 1932. Alice Jones and Irene Brown said that in early 1933 they saw Campbell entering a "sporting house" with a particular gentleman on several occasions. Robert Miller said that in the spring of 1933 Lewis, his wife, and Campbell all slept in the same bed together in a New York apartment

Miller shared with them. House of Prayer member Hattie Frost said that when she lived with Campbell a man named Mr. Austin used to "visit" regularly. And finally, two different women from Savannah testified that when Campbell lived there she ran around with a married man named Ed Felder, and that threats from Felder's wife forced Campbell to move to New York when she was only 16 years old. Though each defense witness—with the exception of one little girl—denied they had been prepped carefully before testifying, the clarity of their memories of routine events from nearly eighteen months earlier shows that they had been. Together, they painted a vivid picture of Campbell as a woman with compromised morality and a sordid past.

The prosecution made an effort to call Grace's character into question likewise. Grace testified that he had never had sex with any member of his church, and though the plaintiff's lawyer called no witnesses who challenged this testimony, he nonetheless managed to ask leading questions to suggest Grace was guilty of immorality. For example, bringing a Caucasian woman into the courtroom, the lawyer asked Grace numerous questions about her. Grace acknowledged that he knew the woman, Miss Ella Wilks, as well as her parents and family, because they had lived near him in Boston.[91] He also knew she had been involved with his church in approximately 1920 or 1921, but he could not remember exactly what her involvement was. The plaintiff's lawyer then asked Grace if he was the father of her 11-year-old son, Jeremiah. Grace denied this, but when pressed he admitted that two or three years earlier Miss Wilks had asked him to take the child away, and so Jeremiah had been staying in Philadelphia with a woman Grace knew named Mrs. Giddens. The plaintiff's lawyer suggested, though Grace denied it at all turns, that Grace had seen Miss Wilks outside in the court hallway the day prior and told her not to testify. He also suggested that Grace had regularly paid child support for Jeremiah. The prosecutor was skilled at introducing new information and casting a shadow on Grace merely by asking questions, even though Grace consistently answered no to these and other questions.

Others testified to Grace's innocence. His chauffeur, John Hero, said he was certain no sexual assault had occurred during any car trip because his mirror provided a full view of the backseat. Several female House of Prayer members testified that they had taken church-related car trips many times with the bishop and that he had always behaved like a perfect gentleman.

Most interestingly, neither Daniel Lewis nor his wife were called to testify in the trial, though the defense suggested Lewis was the most likely candidate for the father of Campbell's baby.[92] According to Grace, Lewis left the House of Prayer in August 1933 after a financial disagreement; this is also hinted at in the letters Grace wrote to Lucille around that time. Grace mentioned during the trial that he thought Lewis had subsequently gotten involved with the Church of the First-born in Philadelphia. Aside from the conflicting snippets of trial testimony, there is no additional information about Lewis's alleged involvement with Campbell. However, Fauset's dissertation notes offer a strikingly similar, perhaps coincidental, story, that may provide a clue. In his research on Prophet Cherry and a Black Jewish group in Philadelphia called the Church of God, Fauset described the case of a man named "D.L.," who, just like Lewis, was originally from Georgia, was married, and had at one time been a minister in the House of Prayer. D.L. told Fauset that he had "severed his connection when it was demanded of him that he 'take the rap' for a serious offense involving the leader." The offense is elsewhere specified as "some trouble over a girl."[93] If Fauset's D.L. was the Daniel Lewis named in Grace's Mann Act trial, and if D.L. is to be believed, then there is reason to doubt the testimony of all of Grace's witnesses because it shows they may have been asked to commit perjury to support the defense. However, even if it were absolutely certain that D.L. was Daniel Lewis, he could have had a motive to lie to Fauset about his past. Hence, we will never know the actual circumstances of Lewis and Campbell's involvement, nor whether Grace asked Lewis to take the blame.

Ultimately, at issue in this case was not whether Grace and Campbell had intercourse nor whether said intercourse was consensual or rape nor whether Grace was the father of her child. Instead, the question was whether he had violated the Mann Act, which forbade him from taking a woman across state lines for sexual purposes. In other words, Did Grace have surreptitious illicit intentions when he first asked Campbell to go with him to Baltimore? The jury believed he had, and so returned a guilty verdict. Grace was remanded until sentencing and spent five nights in Manhattan's West Street Jail, the Federal Detention Headquarters for the area. The following Wednesday, March 21st, he was brought back to court and sentenced to one year and a day in "a penitentiary or prison camp."[94] The lawyer immediately filed an appeal, Grace paid a seventy-five–hundred–dollar bond, and he was released, but within moments he was rearrested on a charge of failing to support his child. He again posted bail and was allowed to go free until a springtime hearing on the child-support issue.[95]

Consequences of the Mann Act Case

Throughout the trial and in the weeks after Grace's conviction, newspapers reported on the most salacious details of the case. As a result, articles emphasized the likelihood that Grace was the father of Campbell's son, the possibility that he had asked people to lie on his behalf, his apparent impropriety with church funds, and the curious relationship between the bishop and Ella Wilks, who was typically described as "a white woman whose child the bishop admitted he was taking care of as his own."[96] Though these stories were not accurate accountings of what had been emphasized at trial, they did become the general record of what had occurred, which was then consumed by the public. Grace supporters packed the courtroom each day, but they represented only a fraction of House of Prayer members. Church members who wanted information about the trial would have been hard pressed to ignore the front-page news stories about it, even if they preferred to get information from church-mediated sources. In other words, even if they were told not to believe what they read, certainly many church members must have been well aware of the sordid accusations against Grace and the point-by-point attempt to dismantle his reputation.

Neither Grace nor his followers were willing to speak to the press about the case. An official statement released by Elder Mitchell expressed, "We will follow our leader to the end. The worthy name of Daddy Grace is all that is needed for our success."[97] Numerous Houses of Prayer sent out similar statements of unwavering support for the bishop. Those members who were willing to speak with reporters made comments such as, "It is all untrue, Daddy Grace is pure."[98] Meanwhile, Minnie Lee's sister Lucille expressed her disgust with the bishop in poetry, in a twelve-stanza condemnatory poem called "Daddy's Sins Have Found Him Out" that was printed in the *Baltimore Afro-American*.[99] A portion of it read:

> Lord, he had a gang of witnesses
> And they came from everywhere;

Really Brooklyn had to stop and wonder
Had he brought the whole House of Prayer.
Everyone was telling lies
On a poor little motherless child;
They may as well hush their mouths
Because Daddy's sins have found him out.

Regardless of his pending appeal, newspapers continued to paint a guilty picture of Grace, even referring to him as a "convicted white slaver."[100] As Grace told followers, he believed the distortions of the trial already printed showed that any efforts to correct them would be futile. Hence, comments from Grace himself about the case were few and far between, such as the lone rhetorical question overheard by a reporter during a Norfolk dinner: "Why should I have to leave New York to attack her if I wanted to, as she said I did?"[101]

In the days after the trial, Grace regrouped in private in Washington, DC. He knew there was much at stake in upholding a good reputation with his church members and he would have been concerned about making a confident and upbeat showing after the arduous trial. The location of his first public appearance, one week after sentencing, was strategically chosen for its devout member base: Hampton Roads. He first stopped in Newport News, which the papers described as "a triumphal entrance into Virginia, very much like the Palm Sunday experience of Christ."[102] Grace spoke at the Ivy Avenue House of Prayer, recounting events from the trial and saying the press had maligned him. He derided his conviction, said that Minnie Lee had been motivated to lie because she sought attention, and proclaimed his innocence. Followers came in droves, eager to hear his side of the story; the newspaper noted that the Newport News church was "packed with people, reminiscent of when the bishop first introduced himself and his type of religious worship to the city."[103]

Two days later Grace preached in Norfolk, sermonizing on the theme of conviction and drawing Biblical parallels. "I'm convicted! Convicted!" Grace exclaimed, according to excerpts printed in the *Journal and Guide*. "Tried in the courts of the United States and convicted! Why then do you follow me? Why not go to some other church? I'll tell you. Every Christian church is led by a convicted man, a man convicted as I was by the courts of the land. Was Jesus Christ not convicted?"[104] Grace used the story of Jesus' crucifixion to emphasize his own disregard for the godless American court, which could not possibly understand his innocence. "Only the court of the Almighty is the one which can pass judgment. . . . Conviction is not guilt. Christ was convicted but was he guilty? . . . Convicted! It means nothing to me. Do I look worried?"[105] Toward the end of the sermon Grace calmed, and asked for followers' continued faithful support regardless of what the future held. He also urged them to stay together even if he was not there to lead. The change of his tone from righteous to conciliatory did not detract from his overall message; Grace had successfully spun his conviction to symbolize anti-Christian persecution, and he planted the inspirational idea that there was nothing more Christian than following a "convicted man."

Grace's comeback in Hampton Roads culminated on Easter Sunday, when House of Prayer members not only celebrated the risen Christ but also feted Daddy Grace with a grand parade in Newport News. Ten thousand people stood along a route that wound through both African American and white neighborhoods to watch several dozen auxiliaries and numerous bands in parade. When Grace left town after the festivities, followers were well aware that he would soon deal with more aftermath from the lingering charges. None could be certain when he would have the freedom to return. Grace's reentry into his bishopric had probably been far more successful than expected, with House of Prayer members in Virginia demonstrating their unwavering loyalty to the church founder, and Grace departed confident that they would remain dedicated no matter what the courts did to him. Even the local paper effused that because of his robust following in Hampton Roads, "the bishop could hardly have picked a better place for his farewell campaign before the 'crucifixion' than eastern Virginia."[106]

While there had clearly been parts of the trial testimony that made both the plaintiff and the defendant appear less than innocent of numerous things, the written record shows that the government's case against Grace regarding a Mann Act violation was weak. In fact, whether he did or did not violate the Mann Act and whether he did or did not behave inappropriately toward Campbell are not what makes the case so interesting. Rather, the Mann Act case created an important moment in House of Prayer history: the moment when followers took a leap of faith. Their faith in Grace transcended worldly accusations on a mass level, and in turn set an institutional precedent for the difference between the rules of Christian behavior for members and the rules of

Christian behavior for the bishop. Rather than losing respect for Grace, follower devotion to him and belief in him strengthened because of the Mann Act ordeal, and he became a living martyr. Rather than Grace's questionable choices, it was evil that caused outsiders to persecute an innocent man, and they believed he would ultimately be acquitted because God was on his side. Followers did not merely forgive him for all of his alleged trespasses—seducing and raping Minnie Lee, having sexual relations with various female church members, fathering children out of wedlock, allowing church donations to be handed over to a particular follower, overlooking the illicit activities in which elders were engaged, asking people to lie on his behalf, and ordering others not to testify against him—they found each accusation utterly inconceivable, incompatible with the Daddy Grace who had been sent to them by God. In effect, the Mann Act trial gave Grace a promotion within his own church.

Two months after his initial conviction, Grace achieved partial redemption when another New York court determined that he was not the father of Minnie Lee Campbell's son. The judges were said to have been particularly swayed by the delivering doctor, who testified that the baby had been born at full term and therefore had been conceived in October.[107] Grace's appeal of his Mann Act conviction went to court in the fall, and in November he was found innocent of the charges. Essentially, the decision was overturned on a technicality: the court found that it did not have jurisdiction in the case. Although the circumstances suggested that Grace may have violated the Mann Act, there was scant evidence that he had done so in the Eastern District of New York. The opinion also made note of the alleged assault on Campbell in Grace's car, calling it a "highly incredible" story, thus suggesting the higher court had not found Campbell's testimony compelling. The charges against Grace were thrown out and the Mann Act debacle was over for good.[108] Because Minnie Lee had made significant alterations to her testimony during the paternity trial, her overall credibility had been weakened; this is likely the reason the Mann Act charge was never refiled in the appropriate district.[109]

The Mann Act case was by no means the only legal battle Grace faced in his early years of ministry, but in many ways it was the most severe as well as the most beneficial. Grace learned that the faithful had not abandoned him even in the face of serious criminal charges; rather, the problems had seemed to bolster member devotion to the church and to him. On a widespread level, House of Prayer members perceived that unjust persecution was at the heart of the Mann Act case and instead of abandoning their faith they committed to it even more deeply. Although the particular case of Daddy Grace precedes the theory, social scientists have observed patterns of members' increasing their commitment to an organization in the face of persecution of either the organization or its leader.[110] House of Prayer members could have reasonably walked away from the church when Grace was accused of committing a federal crime. They also could have walked away when the trial testimony revealed numerous behavioral indiscretions on the part of Daddy Grace. Instead, Grace received their wholehearted praise and support. The celebration of Grace in Hampton Roads was just one piece of evidence that, from city to city up and down the East Coast, the Mann Act case had actually caused an increase in member commitment to the House of Prayer.

In the long term, it was not just the thrill of following a martyr that affected the House of Prayer ethos. The stigma of the Mann Act case also had an impact on the followers as individuals and, in turn, the church as an institution. Newspapers mocked the loyalty of members to Grace because of all that had been exposed during the course of the trial, regardless of his ultimate acquittal. At some moment, each member of the House of Prayer must have examined his or her own faith in order to determine if he or she would stay with the church. As each person decided that Grace was more credible than the courts and his accuser, the story became more than Grace's: the Mann Act trial became a story of the institution because every one of the thousands of members of the House of Prayer had to deal with its consequences.[111] The case caused their faith to become more clearly defined, first for individuals and in turn for the church as a whole. Two important aspects of the renewed faith included a new, higher standard for unadulterated belief in Daddy Grace, and clearer distinctions between the behavior acceptable for members and that permissible for the bishop.

After his success in Hampton Roads, Grace began to use the Mann Act case to exemplify persecution of the innocent. For example, at a Washington, DC, banquet, attended by both church members and a handful of invited city officials, Grace spoke about various aspects of community improvement in which he planned to engage. He specifically mentioned that such projects could be enhanced by better connections with other African American leaders. As a backdrop, he discussed some of the details of the Mann Act case, ultimately labeling it a "frameup."[112] Through the juxtaposition of these things, Grace implied that his success caused less visionary people to conspire against him, and that allowing such false persecution was harmful not just to his church but also to African American communities more broadly. Similarly, the following year during a birthday celebration Grace again discussed his legal troubles, "figuratively . . . ripp[ing] open his mantle to display his wounds."[113] He praised those who had had the wisdom and faith to see him through the ordeal, and he again asked for support from Black leaders and professionals. Later that year he was still pursuing the same theme, publicly describing himself as: "the poor man whose name you see in the papers all the time. I am suffering to prove the gospel true to these, my people. I am the one who has been arrested and put in jail with no one to come to the court to prove their charges, for I am too powerful and they are less than men."[114]

Over the years, as more legal problems came and went for the bishop, they became part of his repertoire of victory stories. Boasting that he won ten court cases between 1934 and 1936, Grace declared, "I'm proud of my troubles. . . . Some say I'm soft because I don't have people arrested for what they try to do to me. But that would not be the spirit of Christ."[115] For Grace, legal troubles became a new kind of capital that he used to garner support. Similarly, followers proudly discussed Grace's track record of arrests and court battles, even years after the fact. More than a decade after the Mann Act trial, for example, one member offered a reinterpretation of it relative to a story in Genesis. "Joseph, too, was arrested for violation of the Mann Act because of a woman's lies," the follower said, referring to the wife of Potiphar.[116] Clearly, for followers these legal predicaments became part of a figurative badge of merit they wore as proud members of the United House of Prayer. The badge demonstrated that Grace was a convicted man who, like Christ, always overcame because the grace of God was upon him.

4

He Ousted God from Heaven

In the late 1930s, a student of religion at Howard University began a chapter of his master's thesis by writing, "Though not a deity on an equal level of popularity as Father Divine, some of the saints have crowned [Bishop Grace] with majesty and honor."[1] With this simple reflection, James Daniel Tyms became the first in a long line of scholars who felt compelled to measure Daddy Grace against Father Divine, the leader of a religious group contemporary with the House of Prayer. But Tyms forged a path that few scholars after him bothered to follow. His thorough and engaging text, never published, correctly distinguished the work and theologies of Daddy Grace and Father Divine, and concluded that the only similarities in their organizations came as consequences of their newness. But Tyms's conclusions did not define the field, and instead most subsequent work determined that Daddy Grace was but a shadow of the more influential Father Divine, called "God" by followers, and the House of Prayer was simply a less interesting version of Divine's group, the Peace Mission.

Because Tyms's work was unpublished, the public academic conversation about the relationship of Daddy Grace and Father Divine truly began in 1944 with Arthur Huff Fauset's *Black Gods of the Metropolis*. Fauset's anthropological project, which continues to be referenced today by a wide variety of scholars, was to understand some of the new forms of religion founded by Black leaders that were thriving in urban environments.[2] Fauset provided individual profiles of five religious groups, compared the groups with each other, and measured them against mainstream Christianity.[3] At the time that Fauset wrote, the preponderance of marginal, Christian-derived groups in African American communities was a phenomenon that researchers were just beginning to examine, therefore his study was pioneering in its scope and original in its attempts at explanation. However, his research demonstrated that these groups did not necessarily have theology in common, and though

Daddy Grace, July 1, 1952. Courtesy of Sargeant Memorial Room, Norfolk Public Library, Norfolk, Virginia.

in several cases they had organizational and developmental similarities, the religious impetus of each group was distinct.

Significantly, Fauset suggested comparisons of Daddy Grace and Father Divine, and the primary similarity he articulated was that each man was worshipped as a God by his followers. Fauset described that in the House of Prayer, "the beliefs boil down to a worship of Daddy Grace. God appears to be all but forgotten."[4] In the Peace Mission, he likewise witnessed that, "Father Divine *is* God."[5] While Fauset noted the slight distinction between Grace as a divine messenger of God and Divine as God himself, their Christian context put both men on equal footing in having a divine status at all. Fauset also overstated the degree to which

Divine's religion corresponded with Holiness belief, thus causing an inaccurate picture of similarity between the two churches' theologies. Important to note is that Fauset's theme of the similar theologies emerges more strongly in his comparative section than it does in his individual chapters on the House of Prayer and the Peace Mission, therefore in many ways his comparison is uneven. Finally, one other major way that Fauset likened Grace and Divine was implied in the parameters of the study: both men were Black leaders of "urban cults." Though this was simply a functional category for Fauset, his highly regarded work set a precedent and the idea of pairing the men remained present in subsequent literature.

It is remarkable that most historians of American Religion who have written on Grace and Divine in the past half century have discussed the two men in the same breath, even as they have become somewhat more aware of the theological differences between them. Scholars place them side by side to discuss things such as urban African American religion or Black religion in the Depression era; yet older categories such as these have not offered fruitful insights for the study of African American religion in decades.[6] Instead, the newer trend in histories has been to consider a group's theological identity as equally important to its social or developmental history. As the academics have selected topics to include in their tomes on religious history, many have chosen not to write about Daddy Grace at all.[7] However, when Grace is mentioned, it is invariably in a context that links him with Father Divine.[8] An examination of the American-religious-history texts reveals no exception to this rule. The two men are implied to be of a similar ilk, and the tendency is to collapse their identity into one portrait; ultimately that portrait looks far more like Divine than Grace. The following brief survey exemplifies this phenomenon.

In 1937, Elmer T. Clark wrote a survey book intended as descriptive and neutral, titled *Small Sects in America*. Clark's five broad categories of sects are of his own design and based on his observations and assessments of the groups included. In the first edition, Grace and Divine are mentioned in separate sect categories. In the expanded, post-Fauset, 1949 edition, the discussion of Father Divine immediately follows that of Daddy Grace in the chapter featuring "Charismatic or Pentecostal" sects. No explicit connection is made between them, but it is clear that Clark has come to think of them as comparable. Most telling is a single sentence found in each edition but changed in one important way. In the 1937 edition, Clark writes: "Multitudes are always ready to follow spectacular leaders like 'King Benjamin' of the House of David and Bishop Grace of the House of Prayer"; by 1949, Clark has edited the sentence and replaced Grace's name with "Father Divine of the Peace Mission."[9] Apparently Clark considered their leadership qualities interchangeable, and it is likely he took his ideological lead from Fauset's work.

The first wave of significant American-religious-history texts were written in the mid-1960s to accompany higher education courses on the academic study of religion, and by that time all accounts of Grace and Divine were posthumous. Three of the major texts are worth noting. First, Winthrop Hudson's 1965 *Religion in America* follows Fauset's work by describing "exotic cults in an urban environment" founded by African Americans; Grace and Divine are both given as examples, though he writes that the Peace Mission "was even more bizarre" than the House of Prayer.[10] Hudson produced a new edition of this text approximately every eight years; by the fifth edition, he had added the detail that these churches were alike not just because they were urban and Black, but also because the leaders were considered divine.[11] All of this comes readily from Fauset, who is footnoted as his source. In Sydney Ahlstrom's highly influential *Religious History of the American People,* rather than including Grace in his section on Black Pentecostalism and Divine in his chapter on "the Communitarian impulse," the two were his only examples of "cults." These were explained as groups with "new doctrines and new grounds for authority, including new scriptures and even new messiahs."[12] The implied similarity was that they were both new savior figures who were successful in the "cult business." Ahlstrom's description is essentially an uncritical acceptance of Fauset's work, and though Ahlstrom's list is relatively accurate in describing the Peace Mission, it is an incorrect description of the House of Prayer on all points. Last, the first edition of Catherine Albanese's well-known *America: Religions and Religion* is a more unusual attempt to describe the two leaders. Placing Grace and Divine in a subsection on Black "cults," Albanese tries to make sense of Fauset and explain why the churches are alike. However, to do so she is forced to discuss obscure points, such as that these faiths link the "ordinary" with the "extraordinary" and that the leaders personify God's tenderness toward Black people.[13] Perhaps recognizing that the comparison was a stretch, Albanese ceased to include Grace after the second edition.

Among the major American religion texts, Albanese offered the most interesting commentary on the men if only because she attempted to deepen the conversation. Others simply reverted to the standard sound bite; Richard Wentz, for example, wrote that the House of Prayer and the Peace Mission were of the same type because of the leader's divine status, his otherworldly abilities, and the overall blending of various faith traditions; Peter Williams noted that Grace and Divine were the same because they were "consummate showmen," but he inexplicably added that they were "prophets of new Black religions that repudiated Christianity."[14] Scholars who specialize in African American religion have scarcely done better, making the same generalizations about Grace and Divine as "flamboyant messiahs" of "exotic groups."[15] The one laudable exception to the trend is Hans Baer and Merrill Singer's sociological analysis of African American churches of the twentieth century.[16] Their book evaluates the place of individual churches in the American struggle for racial equality, and they typologize churches based on a matrix of social, religious, and political attitudes. Using this typology, they clearly distinguish Grace from Divine, and they also discuss the House of Prayer as an institution with a history distinct from the personal history of Daddy Grace. They are the first scholars who truly move beyond the common assumptions grounded in Fauset's work.

In sum, most scholars who have discussed both Grace and Divine have done so in a way that merely echoes Fauset's early 1940s assessments, and they have not bothered to consider whether any value remains in comparing the two men. It is now appropriate to interrogate the theologies and practices of the House of Prayer and the Peace Mission in order to elucidate their distinctions. This will reveal that although they had overlap in time, in place, and in audience, they were in fact very different religions led by men with vastly different ideals and motives. Furthermore, it allows us to see that Grace's response to Divine, and Divine's response to Grace, have been unrecognized dynamics that can explain some of the long-term institutional evolution within both the House of Prayer and the Peace Mission.

Grace and Divine Compared

Although a casual appraisal may make it appear that there are numerous similarities between Grace and Divine, most of these points are superficial rather than substantive. The brief inventory that follows demonstrates that most of their similarities are not particularly relevant to the religious institutions they founded, and therefore amount to little more than coincidences. Divine, originally named George Baker, was born just a year and a half before Grace, and like Marcelino Manuel da Graca was named for his father.[17] Both young men spent their early years in a Black society that was enduring the remnants of a colonial mentality: Grace in Cape Verde, where love of all things Portuguese dominated the culture, and Divine in an African American section of Rockville, Maryland called "Monkey Run," where residents struggled socially and economically to be respected as full citizens in a postslavery society. Each young man left home at about the age of 20 to begin an independent life for himself, and along the way worked in various positions of menial labor. Jumping ahead to their midlife years, both men experienced important developments in their ministries in the year 1919. For Grace, this was the year he opened his first House of Prayer in West Wareham, Massachusetts. For Divine, it was the year he and his wife, Peninniah, bought a home in Sayville, Long Island, and opened their first permanent religious center there.[18] Both men went on major missionary trips in the winter of 1923: Grace abroad to Egypt, Jerusalem, and Portugal; and Divine to the Southeastern United States, accompanied by ten followers.[19] Each man witnessed a membership surge in his religious organization approximately fifteen years into its existence. Over the years, both Grace and Divine received much publicity, which at times bolstered the strength of their organizations and at other times fostered turmoil; much of this publicity related to either the divine nature of the leader or church property. Regarding the former quality, Grace and Divine were both perceived as claiming divinely sanctioned power or divinity itself; in terms of property, each drew attention to church properties and/or what appeared to be church properties as a means of gaining public respect.[20] Both men died within the first half of the 1960s and left their organizations without clear directives for the future. Retrospectively, we can see that each man founded a unique religious institution that particularly flourished among African Americans and acted as a revitalizing power in many members' lives.

Divine Distinguished

The similarities, however, end there. As leaders, the men had distinct approaches; as religious bodies, the two churches were far from one another in most of their beliefs, rituals, and social structures. A more detailed consideration of the Peace Mission's history and development will elucidate this point and further show the faulty nature of the scholarly conflation.[21] Father Divine began itinerant preaching in the first decade of the twentieth century, when he was known as the Messenger.[22] As his travels exposed him to new teachers and ideas, his theology evolved, and so too did the structure of his ministry. By 1917, when he arrived in New York City with a handful of followers, Divine's teachings had become a consistent package with various theological influences including New Thought, Ethiopianism, and Holiness, and rituals that sometimes had the vigor of Pentecostalism but had a structure that was all their own.[23]

In the 1920s, when the Peace Mission was located in Sayville, Divine hosted weekly communion banquets with talks. Persons willing to travel there were welcome to feast, participate in activities, and stay at his home, all free of charge. Some chose to join the small group on a permanent basis, moving to Sayville and finding work through an informal employment service managed by Divine. At that time, those who became full-time live-in members were called Angels, while those who were not ready to make the complete transition but remained seriously interested were called Children.[24] To demonstrate their new lives in the spirit, Peace Mission members generally took new personal names, such as Margaret Faith, Peaceful Serene, Charles Cheerfulness, and Glorious Illumination. Divine attracted increasing numbers of curious people to his Sayville home during that decade, so that by 1930 his vision was turning to expansion and movement.

Following on his New Thought influences, Divine taught that the nature of the universe is divine and thus good. As created beings, people are individualizations of God, and so their lives are reflections of their alignment with the divine spirit. In other words, Divine's followers believed that the physical was an expression of the spiritual. If a person was happy, healthy, and successful in his or her material life, it was because he or she was appropriately abiding by the divine spirit. Despair, illness, and other troubles were manifestations of a life lived out of step with God.[25] Attaining a high quality of life in the present world was emphasized over and above the mainstream Christian concept of preparation for a heavenly afterlife. In addition, Divine's followers believed that the Christ principle was now being expressed in this world as a Black man, their leader, in order to help overcome the tremendous racial strife in America.[26]

As evidence of their religious purity, Peace Mission members followed a moral code akin to that dictated by Holiness traditions but even more stringent. They were prohibited from smoking, drinking, gambling, and any form of obscenity or vulgarity. Modest, formal attire was required at all times. Honesty was emphasized, as was making amends for past debts and other trespasses. Regardless of their marital status prior to joining, full-time followers severed family ties, became celibate, and henceforth socialized only with other members. The genders remained segregated for almost all forms of social activity within the Peace Mission.[27] There were even taboos on the use of certain words, for example "hell" and "damn"; this prohibition was extended to any words considered derivative of these.[28] Those who broke rules demonstrated that their spirits were not right with God, and serious offenses resulted in a request for them to leave the group.[29]

The Peace Mission's primary religious practice was the communion banquet hosted by Divine. The food sharing itself was an important element, but the banquets usually included talks by Divine, spontaneous testimonials by members, and long periods of lively singing; however, any of these latter activities could also occur as independent rituals.[30] Because they did not have "services" similar to those of Protestants and Catholics, in which an agenda of prayers, readings, and ceremonies was performed by rote, Peace Mission rituals were beyond the bounds of mainstream Christianity. This fact, combined with a multiracial following and followers' sincere belief that Divine was God, often caused incredulity, suspicion, and disdain among outsiders.[31]

Despite the conflation of the two churches and leaders in academic work, even the brief sketch above demonstrates that Peace Mission theology and ritual practices were distinct from Grace's United House of Prayer. As discussed in earlier chapters, the House of Prayer is a Christian church that, despite reluctance to affiliate with any denomination, is theologically aligned with Pentecostalism. The Peace Mission, on the other hand, has never been easily categorized, though historians and sociologists have placed it all across the map of American religion in attempts to do so. Certainly its New Thought ideology and its members' unabashed pride in their leader's divinity distinguish it theologically from Grace's more mainstream Protestantism. Though both churches demanded commitment, full-time membership in the Peace Mission was a comprehensive lifestyle that included drastic changes to one's financial, social, and family life; the House of Prayer merely expected that members would attend services several times a week and join a church auxiliary. Although both churches' codes of moral behavior were similar, in the Peace Mission a transgression was grounds for potential expulsion, whereas occasional backsliding was normative in the House of Prayer. In the simplest of terms, the difference between the Peace Mission and the House of Prayer is the difference between a Utopian community and a Protestant church.

By the mid-1930s, both religious groups had experienced several years of consistent growth. Grace and Divine had transformed from being leaders personally known by most followers to being idolized and idealized figureheads; they were admired from afar because most new members had few opportunities to meet their founding father. The limits of both men's leadership became increasingly similar: though each was the unquestionable head decision-maker for his religious body, each faced the problem that he was unable to monitor carefully what happened in his geographically widespread churches. Grace and Divine were continuously figuring out how to guide their flocks and experimenting with aspects of their leadership as they encountered the changing circumstances of their own churches. Despite their substantive differences, over time the men's leadership roles had developed similarly. Though they might have had valuable insights to teach each other about how to be the strong and consistent leader of a burgeoning religion, they never did so in any kind of friendly sit-down meeting. Instead, Grace and Divine's actions demonstrate competitiveness and territorialism, and it is from this spirit that they learned lessons from one another despite themselves.

The Emergence of Harlem

Late 1930s Harlem was the stage where the drama of Grace versus Divine was performed. At that time, Harlem was still a young place with a growing identity. Though it is technically a neighborhood on the island of Manhattan in New York, by the 1920s Harlem was considered the most vital African American "city" in the United States.[32] Its new recognition was a by-product of what is now called the Great Migration: a migratory trend of African Americans moving from the rural South to the urban North, which began in approximately 1915 and lasted several decades. This movement of peoples brought tremendous change to the cultural and material landscape of cities in which the migrants settled.[33] The Manhattan neighborhoods where Black people were relegated, such as the Tenderloin and San Juan Hill, were already overcrowded when the Great Migration began, and furthermore many long-time residents were being displaced as construction progressed on Pennsylvania Station and the new business district around it.[34] Every day Manhattan had more African American residents with fewer places to go. The desperate need for more residential space led to the first trickle of Black people into Harlem.

Harlem had been built up by investors in the last decades of the 1800s as a kind of experiment in neighborhood creation. The investors built the new neighborhood on spec, trusting that the populace would come. By 1900, when they expected to be seeing huge profits, they instead discovered that the new neighborhood was not luring enough residents.[35] Although they had succeeded in creating a posh suburb of white residents, the buildings had only partial occupancy and new businesses were reluctant to establish themselves there without enough demand. Economically, Harlem the neighborhood was not a success.[36] It was thus as a fight against profit loss and with an eye toward growth that a few white investors allowed African Americans to move into their empty Harlem properties.[37]

The change began in the vicinity of 135th Street and Seventh Avenue, where the first Black residents moved in in the early years of the twentieth century.[38] From that epicenter, each year the African American community in Harlem expanded a little further, though not with geographic uniformity. The neighborhood transformation was aided by the flight of whites.[39] The boundaries of "the Black neighborhood" at any moment in time are difficult to pinpoint, both because of definitional problems (is a Black neighborhood defined by number of residents, culture, or something else?) and because of the rapid movement of people. However, census records indicate that by 1920 African American residents were concentrated in an area roughly bordered by Park and Eighth Avenues on the east and west, and 126th to 146th Streets south and north; and by 1930 this area had stretched northward, southward, and as far west as Amsterdam Avenue.[40] The new residents infused Harlem with a vibrant cultural life reflecting the fabric of Black peoples who made it their home. Harlemites now included native New Yorkers; migrants from southern parts of the United States, especially from the Carolinas, Georgia, and Virginia; and immigrants of African descent from places such as the West Indies.[41] Additionally, Harlem still had non-Black ethnic pockets, such as Italians in the southeastern section and Latinos on the southern tip.[42] But the African American presence seemed to override all else, and by the mid-1920s the name "Harlem" was nearly synonymous in popular parlance with the phrases "Black Cultural Mecca" and "Black Ghetto" alike.

Living in the "Three Harlems"

In literature, in the news, in the history books, and in peoples' memories and impressions, there were and there are at least three versions of Harlem that existed concurrently in the 1920s and 1930s. One Harlem was the colorful arena of Manhattan night life, where African Americans sang, danced, and played jazz, and where white people went to socialize in the high-fashion clubs. The all-Black floor shows at places like Connie's Inn and the Cotton Club included singers and dancers of various genres, scantily clad house chorus girls, and orchestras conducted by people such as Louis Armstrong and Duke Ellington. Some clubs, like the Lenox, allowed entry to both Black and white customers with the rule that there could be no mixed social parties; others such as the Cotton Club allowed entry to African Americans only if they were light skinned or famous.[43] There were also predominantly Black venues for socializing and dancing, such as the Savoy Ballroom and Rockland Palace; these were far bigger in scale than the white clubs and attracted consistently large crowds by featuring the most popular musicians available.[44] For those who preferred theater over the nightclub atmosphere, the all-Black cast of the Lafayette Theater on Seventh Avenue entertained with plays such as *Very Good Eddie* and *Macbeth*.[45] In the mid-1930s the Lafayette's former managerial team opened the Apollo Theater on West 125th Street, which drew crowds to its more ostentatious shows and quickly rose to prominence on the Harlem entertainment circuit.[46]

A second Harlem was far from the nightlife playground; it was the dangerous slum, a place of loneliness, disillusionment, and despair. Segregation and overpopulation were two significant causes of the slum conditions. Between 1910 and 1920, the migration of southerners caused New York's Black population to increase by sixty thousand people; between 1920 and 1930, one hundred seventy-five thousand more came.[47] Since most migrated as single people it was difficult for them to find appropriate and affordable apartments in the Harlem buildings, which had predominantly been designed for very large families; at the same time, segregation prevented them from living in other parts of Manhattan. New experiments in living arrangements provided solutions to the housing problem, such as roommates, apartment lodgers, and beds rented by the half day.[48] The overpopulation led to more rapid wear and tear, and many property owners chose to ignore the situation rather than maintain the buildings. As the years passed, the grand apartments of Harlem transformed into dilapidated, tenement-quality dwellings.[49] Garbage, filth, rodent infestation, and fire hazards increasingly became part of the neighborhood, as did skyrocketing rates of death and disease. Without comfortable homes, backyards in which to play, or enough community space, many young people spent their leisure hours on the streets where prostitution, drug use, and juvenile delinquency were all prevalent.[50]

The third Harlem was in between the playground and the slum; it was the basic, everyday Harlem. This was the Harlem that was simply home to average African American families and individuals living relatively nondescript lives. They went to work, ate meals together, attended church, perhaps joined a social club, and weren't necessarily engaged in either of the other Harlems that existed around them, although they knew they were there. Some people worked just to maintain their standard of living; others hoped to move to Sugar Hill, the more upscale section of Harlem around Edgecombe Avenue. Those who already counted themselves among Harlem's upper-middle class strove to maintain a respectable and peaceful community. By the late 1920s, the average Harlemite rarely had to venture outside of his or her neighborhood, because everything a person needed—from social agencies to social clubs—had opened a branch there, effectively making Harlem a convenient city unto itself.[51] Unfortunately for the average family, it was also a very expensive city; prices for everything from food to rent were exceptionally high in Harlem despite the low salaries that most African Americans were able to earn.[52]

After the stock market crashed in 1929, financial troubles reverberated throughout New York's African American community. The Great Depression ultimately caused downgrades in all of Harlem's subcultures: it shrank and dimmed the nightlife, it exacerbated and expanded the grim ghetto situation, and it caused most average families to become poverty stricken. Many who were employed as unskilled and semi-skilled laborers, such as domestics working for white families, lost their jobs quickly. Those who held professional positions maintained them longer, that is, until skilled white people willing to work for "Black wages" displaced them. Even those at the top of the social ladder encountered hardship; for example, Black doctors who continued to provide care often could not collect payment for services, thus they sank to the poverty level even though they remained highly respected in the community.[53] Because the various forms of public assistance could not make a significant dent in Harlem's poverty, local organizations forged new alliances to aid the community creatively. The National Urban League offered a job placement service and vocational training; the Harlem Cooperating Committee on Relief and Unemployment assisted residents with applications for public and private aid; various individual churches provided meals, clothing, and shelter without requiring the needy to fill out forms and answer personal questions; and the "Don't Buy Where You Can't Work" campaign urged boycotts of white stores that refused to hire African Americans.[54]

Father Divine's Kingdom in Harlem

Yet of all the solutions to unemployment, homelessness, and poverty that emerged in Harlem during the Great Depression, the cooperative strategies developed by Father Divine's Peace Mission Movement were of singular genius. In the late 1920s, when increasingly large groups began traveling from Harlem to Long Island to visit Father Divine's community, his Sayville neighbors stopped seeing Divine as the polite leader of a small religious group and began seeing him as the commander of a vast number of Black people. Residents cloaked their fear and repugnance in disturbance-of-the-peace citations against the group. After an escalating series of clashes with Sayville residents and law enforcement over alleged violations, Divine decided the fight was not worth his trouble. In 1932 he took the opportunity to move his Peace Mission to

Harlem, where he already had a large following. There, his local popularity grew, and many people who had been sporadic visitors to Sayville became full-time members.[55]

Divine's national following also multiplied in the early and mid-1930s. A handful of speakers, including John the Revelator, Walter Lanyon, John Lamb, and Faithful Mary, traveled extensively, delivering Father Divine's message and acting, in a sense, as missionaries. His ideas attracted considerable attention among those interested in New Thought. In mid-Atlantic cities, in parts of the Midwest, in towns along the coast of California, and in countries including Canada, Switzerland, and Australia, new Peace Mission "extensions" opened.[56] Divine himself traveled infrequently and rarely went further than a short distance from New York City, but the Peace Mission expanded exponentially without his direct control.[57]

The Peace Mission swiftly became the object of public fascination. Father Divine made regular splashes in the New York newspapers, and gained both attention and notoriety as two books were published about him and articles appeared in *Christian Century, American Magazine, Time,* and the *New Yorker.* The American public was awestruck by the fact that Divine appeared to provide for his many followers from an endless wallet, yet he also publicly refused donations. People were curious and often skeptical about the origins of his money, and many articles raised this question. Meanwhile, the Peace Mission's expansion made Divine look like a man of great means. He seemed to mastermind and finance endless new businesses in New York, including Peace Mission restaurants, dry cleaners, rooming houses, markets, garages, and beauty shops. It was believed that he owned many properties, that he personally housed and employed those in his community, and that among the rewards for followers were lavish banquets, day cruises on steamships, retreats in the country, and picnics at large estates.[58] It is difficult to know how much Divine tried to dispel these distorted notions; there is certainly evidence that he told interviewers he owned nothing, yet when stories were published about him the "wealth" and "possessions" of an uneducated Black man with a large following were inevitably highlighted. However they were constructed, the myth and mystique of Father Divine the benefactor were publicized and believed.[59] The truth was probably less interesting to most writers in need of captivating material. The truth was that Divine owned no property; that all Peace Mission members classed as Children paid either in money or labor for their living space; that Divine himself employed very few people, though he did provide ideas and assistance to those in need of work; that few of the entertainment rewards for followers were organized under Divine's aegis; and that followers themselves were the proprietors of the businesses associated with the Peace Mission.[60]

At the heart of the myths were impressions that Father Divine owned many buildings. In fact, contrary to appearances, he had not purchased a single piece of property since his acquisition of the Sayville home in 1919. Since he later signed that home over to a Peace Mission member, he had not personally owned anything since 1930.[61] All of the residences, businesses, and meeting halls, whether owned or leased, were held in the names of members who accepted the financial responsibilities for those properties. In many cases, such as with the Ulster County "Promised Land," property was owned collectively by groups of members who had pooled their money. In other instances, new converts allowed their homes to be freely used by the Peace Mission. And in some cases, one or two followers took the responsibility for holding a lease on a space that was used by many.[62] Divine's personal policy of nonownership extended to things such as the limousines in which he rode, the airplane in which he flew, and the Peace Mission tour buses.[63] He owned nothing, yet everything having to do with the Peace Mission was popularly believed to be his.

The reason followers were at the economic helm, rather than their leader, stemmed from Divine's philosophy on finance. He stipulated that one should not engage with monetary institutions nor use any kind of credit system, and that one should never be a passive recipient of charity. He taught that everyone should live a debt-free life. This meant that not only should one pay off outstanding debts, no matter how old, but one should also not take on new debt. Every form of credit was considered immoral, including business loans and mortgages, and because Divine also frowned upon the idea of paying interest or fees, organizations utilizing such things were condemned. Divine had no admiration for relief-oriented programs including those that grew out of the New Deal, and he did not believe in charity. Self-help, cooperation, and God's reward were the only acceptable methods for socio-economic advancement according to his teachings. In essence, this meant that Peace Mission Angels did not use banks, did not have insurance, did not belong to unions, and never bought anything until they could pay for it in full. Although unusually stringent, Father Divine's unique combination of ideas about money and monetary institutions were the impetus for material salvation for many of his followers during the Great Depression. Peace Mission enterprises flourished in New York, New Jersey, and other places where large clusters of members abided by Divine's economic teachings. They put his ideas into action, pooling their resources and labor to create projects from small barbershops to large rooming houses to vast farming collectives. Because they organized themselves into single financial units, they could afford to open new businesses; because members also lived cooperatively, their living expenses were not high; because Divine taught them to provide goods for fair prices, they passed their savings onto the public (a policy known as "selling the best for the least"); and as a result of all of these things, in poverty-stricken Harlem in the middle of the Great Depression, Peace Mission businesses were extremely successful.[64] As Watts astutely points out, although Father Divine devised the economic plan, he never forced anyone into it; therefore, it was Peace Mission members who put his strategy into action and made it successful praxis.[65] Furthermore, Divine's "strategy" had not been a response to the Depression; it was simply the consistent message about economics that he had preached since his Sayville days. He did provide guidance on purchases and leases, and he accepted donations from profitable Peace Mission businesses, but because followers themselves bought property when they decided the circumstances were right he saw no need to own anything himself.[66]

The Peace Mission's Downward Turn

After several years of good fortune and growth, the Peace Mission's luck changed. Over the course of 1937 the reputation of Father Divine and his organization was stained, perhaps irreparably, by a run of negative incidents that included legal problems, violence, and accusations of impropriety. The onslaught of legal troubles began in April 1937, when three men visited the Peace Mission headquarters in Harlem during a crowded speaking engagement to serve legal papers on Father Divine. As the men were being urged to leave, a skirmish broke out; in the end, two of the men were beaten and the third was stabbed with an ice pick. Charges were filed against Divine and several members, but Divine had fled the scene and could not be found. Days later, police discovered the esteemed leader hiding behind a furnace in a Connecticut extension.

Though he was subsequently cleared of charges, the publicity around this episode was vast, negative, and embarrassing.[67] Just after the initial incident, prominent Peace Mission leader Faithful Mary took the opportunity to defect. She and Divine had been at odds over some money and a property in High Falls, New York. When Divine went missing, Faithful Mary denounced his leadership, appropriated the building in question, and took several of his followers with her. In addition to filing a suit against him, in short order she published an exposé that alleged sexual impropriety and racketeering in the Peace Mission.[68] Meanwhile, former member Verinda Brown also took Father Divine to court. Divine refused to return several thousand dollars that Brown and her husband had donated to the Peace Mission while members of the organization. In a May 1937 hearing the court ruled in Brown's favor, finding mismanagement of funds. Divine filed an appeal and the case ultimately dragged on for years, but in the meantime scores of former members followed Brown's example and attempted to sue for return of donations.[69] In another incident that same month, two followers were charged with medical neglect by the Children's Society when one of their children died of tuberculosis; as was typical, the accusation received more press coverage than did the fact that the charges were later dismissed.[70] All throughout this period, the Peace Mission also endured bad publicity about leader John the Revelator. During the previous winter he had seduced Delight Jewett, the 17-year-old daughter of a Denver couple who attended Peace Mission gatherings, and he brought her to New York with him. The story went public after the FBI filed charges against John the Revelator for violation of the Mann Act, and in the summer of 1937 he was tried and found guilty.[71]

It was not long before these controversies rippled outward to the streets and affected average Peace Mission members. In June, two fights occurred near the Harlem Heaven and contributed to the growing idea that Peace Mission members were not truly peaceful. In the first, a female follower of Faithful Mary was beaten by two men who remained loyal to Divine. In the second, which occurred only a few hours later, two dozen Peace Mission members were attacked when people threw glass and rocks at them as they left the headquarters. This caused a small riot among all those around, and a number of people were injured.[72] Additionally, several fires destroyed properties used or owned by the Peace Mission around this time, and the fires appeared to be caused by arson.[73] The organization was certainly experiencing stress.

Under normal circumstances, Divine's somewhat impersonal leadership style was balanced by two nurturing female figures in the movement: Faithful Mary and Divine's wife, Peninniah. But at about the same time that Faithful Mary defected, Peninniah became quite ill, and she was sent to a hospital in Kingston for the remainder of the year. Her husband was an infrequent visitor during her long stay. Although her absence from Peace Mission functions was noticeable, Divine did not see fit to explain her whereabouts to followers. Reporters, however, seized the opportunity to highlight Divine's negligence in caretaking, and made certain that followers knew full details of Peninniah's situation.[74]

The medical community also weighed in on the Peace Mission. Following on the heels of these internal problems, lengthy, negative assessments of Peace Mission members were published in the *Journal of Abnormal and Social Psychology* and the *Journal of Nervous and Mental Disease*. In them, Divine was described as mildly manic-depressive, and Peace Mission members were characterized as "suggestible," wanting "to escape the world of reality," and fearful of many things.[75] Though these articles came to differing conclusions about what could be said of the relative mental health of members, neither offered flattering portraits of the Peace Mission.

External suspicion of the group by both average citizens and official institutions was dramatically increased by all of these incidents, and animosity toward them became palpable in Harlem.[76] Though Divine himself had spent years withstanding the challenges of those who opposed him, his troubles now regularly spilled over and tangibly affected large numbers of followers. The group became internally weakened. As Watts writes, "Despite a history of conflict and rejection, members of the movement had never encountered the concentrated hostility they experienced in 1937."[77] The incidents continued to trickle over into the next year, and by the day in February 1938 when Daddy Grace came to town, what had once been Divine's kingdom was now a compromised entity ready to be overthrown.

Daddy Grace Overthrows the Kingdom

Father Divine's headquarters, called the "Number One Heaven," was far from Harlem's central business district at 135th Street and Seventh Avenue, but it did not want for activity.[78] The bustle of a popular shopping strip along 116th Street attracted drifters and other sketchy characters to the area, and they often trickled over to West 115th Street where they loitered in search of a way to keep busy.[79] Peace Mission shops and living spaces occupied several buildings on West 115th between Fifth and Lenox, and for several years the Number One Heaven had been located at 20 West 115th in a space leased from the Union Square Savings Bank for a small monthly sum.[80] On one side of the Heaven was a garage, and on the other, an abandoned Polish Synagogue.[81] This section of Harlem contained a very high proportion of what E. Franklin Frazier termed "fourth-class dwellings"; such a designation was not an attempt at objective measurement, but rather a measure of these buildings relative to other properties in Harlem.[82] Often characterized in the newspapers as ramshackle, 20 West 115th Street was not a drastic improvement from the depressed neighborhood surrounding it.[83]

According to the story recounted many times to newspapers by Grace's friend and real estate advisor, Edward Rogall, Grace's triumph on West 115th Street began in February 1938 when he first heard that Father Divine claimed to be God. Grace, offended, felt called to intervene, and directed Rogall to inquire about the status of Divine's Number One Heaven. It is nearly implausible that Grace had not heard that Father Divine claimed the title of God prior to 1938. Certainly he was familiar with Divine, as evidenced by a 1935 story in the *Afro-American* in which Grace declared he was more powerful than both Father Divine and Elder Michaux. It is believable, however, that Grace refrained from publicly reacting to the Divine-as-God idea until he was in a position to use the situation to his advantage. Rogall's inquiry revealed that, true to form, Divine's space was rented by one of his followers, Blessed Purin Heart, and furthermore the bank was interested in selling the property. Grace took immediate steps to purchase it and came north from Washington to pay the two-thousand-dollar deposit in cash. Despite Grace's zeal, Rogall insisted they visit the building and examine the interior before signing the papers.[84]

The essentially three-story building, faced in tapestry brick, was originally the home of a fraternal organization.[85] Passing through the arched front doorway, Grace and Rogall would have entered a foyer lit with a series of electric chandeliers that one author described as "gaudy."[86] The first floor had an assembly space, and the finished basement contained a large kitchen and a room the Peace Mission used as a banquet hall; together these could hold about five hundred people. The second and third floors contained rooms suitable for offices or living quarters, and a small penthouse-like structure crowned the building.[87] At forty feet wide and one hundred feet long, the space was easily large enough for Grace's plans. He returned to the Union Square Bank offices in lower Manhattan and signed the purchase agreement that same afternoon.[88]

Grace subsequently went public with the news that he would evict Divine and establish the northern headquarters of the United House of Prayer in the Harlem building. He made it clear that any Peace Mission members who wished to stay behind to truly experience the Lord's presence in the building would be allowed to remain; as for the future of Father Divine, Grace deigned to say, "I will not drive him out of Harlem. . . . I will just let him stay. Poor fellow. . . . I will give him peace and pity."[89] In an official statement, Divine told the press that the building had been purchased "according to My own Instruction and according to My own Endorsement," adding that, "the Kingdom of God is not bound to . . . material places."[90] Careful never to use Grace's name, he specifically stated that he and his followers bore no ill will toward the purchaser.[91] Grace, on the other hand, was quite willing to make disparaging public comments about Divine, such as his rhetorical toss to Divine via the press: "Go explain to your flock how come God Almighty can be evicted!"[92]

In the sensationalized clash between Grace and Divine that began to unfold, local newspapers were active participants if not leaders. The *New York Times,* for example, immediately labeled the situation a rivalry of religious leadership stemming from Grace's disapproval of Divine. The *Times* encouraged rancor among Divinites by printing statements such as the one from Rogall that described their tour of the property: "Father Divine's people apparently thought [Daddy Grace] was some new angel or messiah because they kept bowing and curtsying to him all the time we were there."[93] Similarly the *New York Age,* the newspaper targeting the city's Black elite, was nearly celebratory about the potential conquest of Father Divine. Its coverage was undergirded by the idea that Divine had monetary problems, describing his kingdom as "tottering" and suggesting that financial woes were the reason Divine did not buy the building himself.[94] In time, the *Age* wondered if Divine might disappear from New York rather than face mounting troubles such as lawsuits instigated by former Peace Mission members.[95] Furthermore, the *Age's* initial coverage of Daddy Grace had an air of optimism: "Unlike Divine," one reporter wrote by way of introduction, Grace was a respectable evangelist of devout Christians.[96]

In the weekly *Amsterdam News,* the coverage of the two men was far more frequent; most issues of the paper from late February through June carried one or more stories about the purchase and eviction. Because the *Amsterdam News* was prone to tabloidism, each article was peppered with colorful and incendiary phrases to emphasize the theme of competition. Forthwith, they named Grace the instigator in the unfolding "holy war" while calling Divine his "cocky little rival," and Grace's purchase of the building was considered merely the first victory in a series of competitions.[97] By mid-March, the paper speculated that Grace's takeover of the building might lead to a violent response from Peace Mission members. In this "modern battle of David and Goliath," Grace was generally portrayed as the underdog because Father Divine was known for turning seemingly bleak situations to his favor.[98] However, by late April the paper's tone had changed and Grace became the conqueror, despite the fact that he had not yet moved to Harlem. Reporters praised his impending arrival, and dismissed Divine by claiming he was "easing out of the cult business for keeps."[99]

Likewise, many news sources outside of New York City carried the story of Grace's purchase of the Number One Heaven, including *Time* magazine, the *Washington Post,* the *Norfolk Journal and Guide,* and the *Baltimore Afro-American.* In one fell swoop, Daddy Grace catapulted to national renown simply by strategizing, spending, and placing himself in the center of the action. The change in Grace's larger institutional strategies from that point on shows that the experience of buying Divine's "Heaven" was a lesson in church leadership he would never forget.

Grace returned to New York fourteen days after signing the original agreement and completed the sale with a check for the balance of eighteen thousand dollars. He did not answer reporters' questions about when he planned to move into the building, but before climbing into his Packard he purportedly said that Divine could stay in the property just so long as he paid his rent.[100] Two weeks later Grace went to his estate in Cuba for relaxation, with no apparent Harlem relocation date on his calendar.[101] The publicity in New York continued nonetheless. At the end of May, Grace returned to the city with an entourage of followers to start a new chapter of his faithful.

Wednesday, June 1st, was the day the Peace Mission was officially evicted from its kingdom. The morning dawned clear and warm. Father Divine was noticeably absent from the group of laboring Mission members, who spent the better part of the day hauling furniture and bags out of the building. Daddy Grace, accompanied by uniformed assistants, was on hand to watch with several reporters.[102] The *Amsterdam News* claimed that, "Even Father Divine's angels who were busily moving 'God's' junk out of the kingdom put down their burdens and took a good, long look at the man who, though not God, has ousted 'God' from his now erstwhile heaven."[103] Playing to the audience that seemed to be his for the taking, Grace courted newspapers that were widely read in Harlem, but he had little interest in those targeting white Manhattanites. For example, his exclusive eviction day interview went to the *Amsterdam News*; two weeks later, at the public dedication of the building, Grace dismissed *New York Times* reporters to, "Go and see the elders for the write-up."[104]

Divine's approach to the eviction remained steady from February through June: he evinced nonreaction, and when directly asked he assured questioners that life at the Peace Mission was business as usual. Both he and secretary John Lamb asserted that the Number One Heaven had become too small for the organization and therefore was not something they wished to own; contrary to this, the *Times* reported that a Peace Mission member had made an insufficient counteroffer on the building.[105] In the days leading up to the eviction, Divine told his followers: "A place several times as large as this one has been partially secured, but as there was a lease on the building and it is occupied by others" the Peace Mission could not move in immediately.[106] He announced that his office would relocate to 123rd Street, but that he was considering eventually moving his entire headquarters to Kingston or possibly Stone Ridge. He advised them that banquets would be held at a variety of smaller locations in the future.[107] On eviction day Divine busied himself by giving talks at two other Peace Mission locations, yet he did not mention a single word of the commotion taking place on West 115th Street.[108]

It is clear that in the short term Divine was adversely affected by the eviction. The Peace Mission had experienced high amounts of turmoil over the course of the previous year, and the physical decentralization of his organization exacerbated the stress on Divine and his followers. Despite his assurances of order, a careful study of the paper trail demonstrates that when 20 West 115th Street was lost, the Peace Mission Movement no longer had a New York hub. Prior to eviction 115th Street served as many things: the primary offices of the Peace Mission, the location for most of its New York City banquets, the auditorium for talks by Divine and other leaders, a residence for members, and Divine's personal home. And, although Divine did not have tangible control over Peace Missions, the Number One Heaven was at least symbolically the international headquarters. After eviction, the organization lost its focal point. Divine's new office on 123rd was several blocks from the main banquet hall on West 126th. Speaking engagements had to be held at various locations, including rented auditoriums and smaller Peace Missions in the greater New York area. Though Divine's followers were able to find homes in other local extensions, Divine himself no longer seemed to live anywhere in particular, and in a modified strategy he increased his travel schedule so that he was on the road several days every week. In the autumn, he appeared to settle into a new building on Madison Avenue, after which the pace of his travel slowed. A newly renovated banquet hall in that same building was dedicated in January 1939; from then on, banquets were held about half the time on 126th Street and the other half on Madison.[109] Although the Madison Avenue building was able to serve multiple purposes, never again did Divine have a headquarters in New York akin to what the Number One Heaven had been, and members used to visiting the Number One Heaven would have been well aware of the differences created by the decentralization. Divine knew that it was of the utmost importance for everything to appear to be running smoothly despite the internal and external disruptions facing the organization. Furthermore, Divine realized that it was imperative that he never allow such a tremendous upheaval of his space to happen again.

Grace, meanwhile, joyfully settled in at 20 West 115th Street. After a work crew redecorated the interior in red, white, and blue, followers came from other cities with their uniforms and musical instruments to celebrate the grand opening of the newest House of Prayer.[110] To further mark his territory, Grace called in James Van DerZee, Harlem's renowned portrait photographer. Van DerZee had been the official photographer for Marcus Garvey, and among his many well-known, regular clients was Father Divine.[111] Van DerZee shot Grace's portrait in the redesigned assembly room of West 115th Street, and Grace sent copies to Houses of Prayer around the country for framing and hanging. A few weeks later, he packed his bags and headed off on his usual convocation tour.

Long-Term Effects

In the long term, Grace succeeded in gaining a Harlem following and establishing a viable House of Prayer. More importantly, his tangle with Divine led him to revelations about methods for church growth; specifically, he learned about the effects of owning high-profile real estate and of receiving intense publicity. He learned that although the relationship was tortuous rather than direct, one could effectively buy social status by purchasing something newsworthy. Despite its ramshackle nature, the purchase of the Number One Heaven was a public coup for Grace because the building itself had already received a great deal of attention for several years. For example, a survey of *New York Times* coverage of Father Divine in 1937 shows that of the more than ninety articles about him that year, a vast majority specified the address of his headquarters as 20 West 115th Street. Thus its reputation, rather than the location or quality of the structure, made the Harlem building a trophy. But additionally, the fact that he had displaced Divine was of major importance internally. The House of Prayer members took pride in the conquest of Divine's territory. For instance, a full nine years after the eviction a reporter in Charlotte saw a sign posted at the local House of Prayer that touted Grace as the "only man" with the power to take over Father Divine's Heaven.[112] Clearly, some members felt a certain rivalry with the Peace Mission, and the fact that Grace had one-upped him gave them collective pride.

Divine too learned a lesson about the impact of property ownership based on his ouster from Heaven. After the dust settled, he made a major shift in leadership strategy and in the structure of the Peace Mission, and these changes were directly affected by, though not solely the result of, Daddy Grace's manipulations. For the first time in twenty years Father Divine began to buy property himself. He started slowly and quietly, with a building in Philadelphia. In his messages to followers, Divine put a new emphasis on the importance of property ownership rather than rental. He followed this with a second important change:

the Peace Mission officially incorporated as a religious institution, with bylaws, a board of trustees, specific parameters for church assets, and a clear role for himself as the head of the organization with ultimate veto power.[113] By the end of the 1940s, stories about the Peace Mission's wealth had returned to the papers, though its real-estate holdings still did not match the growing House of Prayer empire. Comparisons notwithstanding, by the early 1960s Divine and his churches had acquired properties in five states and six foreign countries that were valued at close to ten million dollars.[114]

Also worth noting are other interactions between Grace and Divine involving property, if they can be called interactions. It appears that for a few years following the Harlem incident neither man's decisions occurred in a vacuum; rather, the two were silently responding to one another, with Grace doing much of the instigating. Divine's very first purchase, the year after his eviction, was a former hotel in Philadelphia located just around the corner from Grace's local headquarters on Fitzwater Street.[115] Three years later when Divine permanently left New York City for Philadelphia, he chose this hotel as his new international headquarters. Not to be outdone, Grace opened two more Houses of Prayer as close as possible to Peace Mission strongholds in Philadelphia; this despite the fact that the city was geographically vast and had a substantial African American population, thus rendering such maneuvers unnecessary. In 1941, Grace opened a church on 12th Street in North Philadelphia, a mere four blocks from a Peace Mission on Poplar Street, and after Peace Mission members collectively bought a large property in West Philadelphia in 1943, Grace purchased a former Baptist church nearby.[116]

Perhaps Grace simply kept himself amused with his attempts to provoke Divine, or maybe he was sincerely offended by the religious assertions of the Peace Mission leader. His motivations are unknown. But property was not the only device he used; beyond being quietly territorial, Grace was also willing to challenge Divine in a less subtle fashion. In 1956, when asked by the young reporter Charles Kuralt for his thoughts on Divine, he replied: "Father Divine is an imposter. He says he's God. Do you know what he really is? A lying old fool. I dismiss him."[117] The following year, Grace commented to North Carolina reporters that he thought Divine had been dead for at least two years, and to fool people the Peace Mission was "using someone else for his voice and the person stays in a room away from the audience."[118] Grace's speculation was picked up by the Associated Press and published nationally. Though it was true that Divine's appearances had become infrequent, he was still alive. When attempts by his followers to dispel the rumor failed, Divine responded indirectly to Grace's claims by holding a public reception.[119] Just as they had years earlier, the newspaper columns again described the two men side by side, calling Grace the "rival evangelist" of the man who had once been "the most famous Negro cultist of his day."[120]

More important than these shenanigans, however, was what Grace had learned about the power of high-profile property. A change in Grace's financial strategy began the moment of his Harlem takeover. He had always believed in buying property for the church, whether land or buildings, but up until 1938 the specific things he purchased were not noteworthy. They were most often empty lots or small buildings to be used as Houses of Prayer. From 1938 forward, his focus in real estate became showy purchases. While a few were used for the church, many were simply occupied apartment buildings that brought in a modest income for Grace; followers neither lived nor worked in these buildings. Others were lavish homes for the bishop. All received press coverage and brought increased attention to the church, and trophy purchases seemed to become both a hobby and a church management method for Grace. He often took time out to discuss his buildings with reporters, occasionally bragging about their monetary value, and pictures of the buildings themselves regularly turned up in the press.[121]

Grace's collection of high-profile purchases added up over the years. In April 1941, he bought the historic Ahavath Achim Synagogue in New Bedford, claiming it would be used as a new House of Prayer.[122] Two years later he purchased a well-known New Bedford mansion called the Nye House, complete with its antique furnishings and artwork, as a home for himself when he was in town.[123] In 1947 Grace focused on adding New York properties to his collection, acquiring four in one year. Two were apartment buildings on Edgecombe Avenue in the Sugar Hill section of Harlem; one was a picturesque apartment building at 800 Riverside Drive that later graced the cover of the *Grace Magazine*; and the fourth was a swath of land at the corner of 125th Street and 8th Avenue in Harlem. The latter property remains one of the highest income-producing properties for the House of Prayer today.[124] In 1953 Grace bought two New Jersey properties: the Savoy Theater in Newark, and a twenty-room mansion for himself in Montclair, and he also acquired the El Dorado apartment building in Manhattan.[125] In 1956 he set his sights on Detroit, selecting two more items for his collection. The first was the former Oriole Theater, which he planned to use as a new House of Prayer, and the other was a fifty-four-room mansion styled on a French chateau that had previously been the home of Prophet Jones of the Church of Universal Triumph of the Dominion of God.[126] In 1958, he bought a large property in Bridgeport, Connecticut, commonly called "the Castle" due to its having been modeled on a castle along the Rhine River.[127] That same year, Grace acquired the building that would be the last addition to his trophy real estate collection: a furnished eighty-five–room mansion in the Berkeley Square section of Los Angeles. After the purchase, Grace regaled reporters with a long list of his properties, bellowing: "[This] makes forty-one houses!"[128]

The most iconic property of Grace's collection was the El Dorado, located on the Upper West Side of New York City between 90th and 91st Streets. One of several twin-towered apartment buildings along Central Park, it was modeled on the luxurious San Remo fifteen blocks south. Faced with brick, tile, and terra cotta, the El Dorado has always been considered an excellent example of Art Deco detailing. When it opened in 1930 it contained 186 apartments, each with between three and twelve rooms and a private terrace; it was later subdivided into smaller spaces.[129] After Grace's purchase of the building in 1953 the El Dorado became a symbol of power and achievement not only for the bishop but for his followers as well. As noted by numerous researchers, in many Houses of Prayer around the country, hanging on the church wall at the altar beside a portrait of Daddy Grace was a framed photograph of the El Dorado.[130] Thus, Grace's high-profile real estate served many purposes: it was an investment; it was a means to publicity; it was a bit of a hobby for Grace; and most interestingly, it was a point of pride for House of Prayer members nationwide to know that they were part of the church that owned glamorous buildings.

Though it was often said that Grace paid cash, in full, for these extravagant properties, this was not necessarily the case. He may have paid outright for small buildings, but he took mortgages on properties such as 800 Riverside Drive, the apartments on Edgecombe Avenue, and the El Dorado. He also regularly overstated what he had paid for buildings; for example, though he claimed to have paid eighteen million dollars for the El Dorado, after his death paperwork revealed the price had been less than a quarter of that figure.[131] In addition to the popularized buildings and mansions, Grace continued to acquire other properties throughout the years, such as small businesses, apartment buildings, and plots of land. The records of his transactions indicate that especially in the 1940s and early 1950s, he was nearly as busy speculating as he was ministering and preaching.

Were it not for Daddy Grace's whimsical idea to oust God from heaven, the United House of Prayer might never have grown to become a multimillion dollar empire. Grace's competitive nature was stimulated by the Harlem incident and as a result he was inspired with new ideas for how to increase his church, his wealth, and his reputation as a powerful religious leader. Divine, too, was not unaffected, though he took the high road and demonstrated that he would not be goaded into negative interactions with Grace. The attack on his Number One Heaven was a factor influencing Divine's change in church policy on property, and it led to his overall tightening of the organizational reins on the Peace Mission. It is for these reasons that the Grace-Divine composite figure of written history is worth deconstructing; taking apart their complex relationship reveals more about each man as a person and as a religious leader—distinct in both message and motivations—than does the composite stock character portrayed in much religion literature.

5

My Joy Is Completed in Charlotte

During the 1940s and 1950s, Daddy Grace's last two decades of leadership, the United House of Prayer was in its heyday. The congregations in Charlotte, North Carolina, had grown to become the numeric stronghold of the church, and the city was subsequently described as the "pulsating heart of Daddy Grace's religious and financial empire."[1] Charlotte churches held some of the biggest and most exuberant convocation events, and the members and leaders, in an effort to prove their own worth, always tried to raise the most money for the church. Due to the heightened activity level in Charlotte during these years Grace visited the city more frequently than other places, staying in his large home in the Brooklyn neighborhood. Ironically, while Grace basked in the success of his Charlotte churches, Brooklyn was literally being dismantled all around him, piece by piece. The city had determined that the land Brooklyn occupied would be put to better use as the government district of the downtown area, and so between 1940 and 1970 the cozy neighborhood was gradually replaced with imposing courthouses and municipal office buildings. The United House of Prayer on South McDowell Street, Brooklyn's newest and most expensive structure, was among the last buildings demolished.[2]

In the postbellum years when Brooklyn first began to grow, Charlotte was just an average-sized town of about five thousand. Between 1880 and 1930, the convergence of railroad lines and the growth of cotton mills and other trades caused Charlotte to expand rapidly and become a small city, and during this time its population increased nearly elevenfold. The town square, at Trade and Tryon Streets, officially divided the Charlotte map into quadrants called wards. Prior to Charlotte's growth, the neighborhoods within the wards had never been classifiable as being home to any particular type of people; instead, each contained intertwining pockets of peoples of all races and class levels. However, as the decades of the late nineteenth and early twentieth centuries passed, neighborhoods became more distinct and ultimately more segregated. Specifically African American neighborhoods were found within each ward as well as in the surrounding suburbs. For example, in the southeast neighborhood called Cherry, many Black families owned newly built homes with yards. To the northwest, a Black community gradually formed around the campus of Biddle Institute, which became Johnson C. Smith College in 1923. Just beyond Biddleville lay Washington Heights, a streetcar suburb for African Americans who could afford both homes and daily transportation to the city. Brooklyn, the most vibrant of Charlotte's many Black neighborhoods, was located just beyond the center of town in Second Ward.[3]

Brooklyn's initial draw began when the first school in the county for African American children opened in Second Ward in the 1880s. On the heels of the Black families who were drawn there came churches, meeting halls, clubs, a library, and eventually a high school. Brooklyn's commercial district flourished after the turn of the century, when an increasing number of racist policies threatened Center City businesses owned by African Americans, and they began moving en masse to Brooklyn. Though not the only Black neighborhood, by 1925 Brooklyn was unquestionably the heart of Black life in Charlotte.[4]

Like other urban African American enclaves, Brooklyn contained people whose jobs and incomes varied widely. The neighborhood's housing ranged from grand two-story homes with wrap-around porches and manicured lawns to tiny shotgun-style wooden enclosures, and as often as not these houses were located on the same blocks. Brick apartment buildings and other small but sturdy homes peppered the neighborhood. There were few sidewalks in Brooklyn and most streets were not paved until the late 1940s, so in bad weather the muddy roads were difficult to traverse for both vehicles and pedestrians.[5] The worst residential part of Brooklyn was much like slum areas in other cities. Poorly maintained wooden homes, built close together, were available for the inflated price of a dollar or two a week. Those built on the edge of Sugar Creek were tiny one-story homes with small porches, barely more than shacks. The backs of these homes faced the creek, which was used as an all-purpose water supply, and their most modern conveniences were a single fireplace and a toilet that worked only in warmer months, if at all.[6] Just a few blocks from Sugar Creek, in a crime-ridden section called Hell's

Half Acre, was Daddy Grace's red, white, and blue two-story home, identifiable by the big neon sign on the lawn that read: "Welcome, Daddy Grace."[7]

Grace purchased his McDowell Street home in 1931 in order to have a residence near the Brooklyn House of Prayer. After his initial tent meetings in 1926, a group of followers helped clear land to build a church on South Long Street, which was a simple structure with sawdust on the floor, often likened to a barn or a warehouse.[8] At that time South Long Street was mostly residential, so the church was surrounded by small wood-frame houses without yards. On Sunday mornings, the sound of the tolling bell from a nearby Congregational church was the community signal for everyone to hurry up and get to their places of worship. On the weekdays, Brooklyn was likewise a picture of quaint life: women socialized and gossiped as they did the washing or congregated at a passing produce truck, children spent carefree summer afternoons playing in the pristine hills or swimming in the creek, and men often worked six days a week, laboring long hours to support their families.[9] The House of Prayer thrived in this environment for over twenty years before Grace considered moving services to a larger building on a more commercial avenue. In 1949, he purchased several plots of land on busy McDowell Street, catty-corner from his home, and in the early 1950s reportedly spent nearly three hundred thousand dollars erecting the most extravagant of his new churches, a gigantic House of Prayer that included a cafeteria, a beauty parlor, and two auditoriums and that had a capacity of several thousand.[10]

Despite Grace's zeal for building, the power brokers of Charlotte would not allow the Brooklyn community to flourish indefinitely and had already begun to tear it down.[11] In 1930, Brooklyn was comfortably situated between two Second Ward white neighborhoods: Belmont, primarily blue collar, and Elizabeth, primarily white collar. By the end of that decade, however, Second Ward was changing overall in the direction of becoming more white, more moneyed, and the location of much new construction, and city leaders were helping that process along. The first clear steps in Brooklyn's demise began in the 1940s in part due to pull factors in the northwest region of the city. The creation of a new Black high school in the northwest, as well as homes designated as available for Black purchase, drew many upwardly mobile residents away from Brooklyn. A housing project built in the northwest also attracted segments of the Brooklyn population. Much of this was strategic planning from outside of the African American community: federal money and programs of various types infused the city, and government planners had to choose what they would do with it. With a vision of a new area for industries and government buildings, Brooklyn became their target, and so its population had to be removed. Between 1940 and 1970, Brooklyn experienced many phases of redevelopment as it was disassembled section by section and became decreasingly attractive as a residence; by 1970 it was completely gone. Despite the gradual nature of the process, many African American businesses were permanently closed, and in the final stages many families found that the need for housing exceeded the supply. While the new government district that replaced Brooklyn was streamlined and efficient, the neighborhood became just a memory.[12]

Grace's Calendar Year

In the midst of these phases of destruction, Charlotte was developing into a House of Prayer stronghold, and as a result Grace visited it more frequently than other places. Though he was constantly on the move, his annual travel calendar was fairly consistent. In the summer months he went from one House of Prayer convocation ceremony to another, typically in a pattern that allowed him to move southward from New York to Florida. His stops along the way usually included but were not limited to Buffalo, New Haven, New York City, Philadelphia, Wilmington, Baltimore, Washington, DC, Newport News, Norfolk, Winston-Salem, Charlotte, Columbia, Augusta, Savannah, and Miami. Sometime between the end of convocation season and the beginning of his winter travels, Grace usually made another visit to Charlotte. Afterward he would disappear for a while, spending part of the winter in warmer climates, sometimes for relaxation and other times for proselytizing. His warm-weather destinations included Los Angeles and Cuba, but most likely he also spent time in places where he had no Houses of Prayer and could therefore be somewhat anonymous.[13]

When the weather in the Northeast began to warm, Grace started his travels anew. In the spring he made the rounds of various House of Prayer hub cities, such as Newark and Philadelphia, making a point to attend when invited for special celebrations. For example, in March 1948 he attended the Grace American Flag March, an event organized by a young woman in the Charlotte congregation. Part of the celebration included waving of flags during a service while the band played a song called "Three Cheers for Daddy Grace." Later, a woman who had recently traveled to Cuba with Grace spoke to the congregation about her experiences.[14] Grace enjoyed himself at the event, staying a night longer than originally planned. Adorned in his purple suit with gold trim, he stood before the congregation and lavished praise on them, saying: "The sky is holding me in Charlotte. The four winds of the earth [are] holding me in Charlotte. Tonight my joy is completed in Charlotte; I am so high until you can't go over me, so low you can't go under me, so wide until you can't go around me, you must come straight in by me."[15] Because Charlotte churches planned many special events to which the bishop was specially invited, Grace often passed through in March or April, and then again in late June for Emmanuel day, the anniversary of his first tent meeting in Charlotte.[16]

His busy travel schedule makes it difficult to pinpoint exactly where Grace "lived" at any given time. Although he specifically said that he preferred his homes in Philadelphia and Washington, DC, it does not appear that he spent large amounts of time in either place. In fact, in the 1940s it appears that Grace spent much of his down time residing in New Bedford. In the 1950s, however, he spent decreasing amounts of time at the New Bedford mansion, preferring instead warmer climates, such as Los Angeles. In his absence Grace's many homes were cared for by church members. In Charlotte, for example, the McDowell Street residence was maintained by Elder Sloan Harvell and his wife, who acted as live-in caretaker and housekeeper, respectively.[17]

Grace's busy travel calendar was not merely a personal preference; it was both a church regulation and a culturally ingrained habit. According to the House of Prayer's General Council Laws, "All states must have a calendar of yearly events" for church members. Every church had to observe standard House of Prayer celebrations and plan unique events each year. Any pastor who did not follow the calendar was to be reviewed and potentially fined.[18] As a result of these regulations, up and down the East Coast there were always church events happening that Grace could attend.

But beyond mere rules, in many ways Grace's schedule mimicked the pace of life he had known growing up in Cape Verde. On his home island of Brava, each month of the year had been easily identifiable by the ceremonial events taking place. The long-evolving blend of Catholic feasts, African ceremonies, and various pragmatic interests had created a festival tradition on Brava that amounted to frequent punctuation of the moments of the year. Harvest, the New Year, the Wedding Season, the return of ships from America, and saints such as Saint Helen and Saint Anthony were just a few of things celebrated annually.[19] Each event was preceded by many days of decorating and food preparation, and the celebrations themselves included drumming and singing, processions with ceremonial banners, men performing on horseback, a mass, and the raising of a ceremonial mast. In addition to the large community gatherings were smaller, localized feasts that were considered more closely African in origin. Some of these were distinguished by intense pageantry, such as the inclusion of a ritual "king" and "queen" of the festivities.[20] On top of these gatherings were various extended family events such as baptisms, weddings, and funerals, all of which might last two or three days apiece. The combination of these events could keep the average Bravan busy with ceremony nearly year-round. Those who were abroad sometimes returned to visit for certain feasts, and if they could not, they sent money to assist with the work. Most of the religious feasts were financially sponsored by a person or family who had made a vow to the saint being celebrated, and sponsorship was considered a privilege and honor.[21]

Convocation

Within the House of Prayer structure, Grace effectively recreated an annual calendar like the one he had grown up with on Brava, where time could be identified by the festive events taking place. The most important ceremony in the House of Prayer was convocation, which occurred every summer. In East Coast towns where Houses of Prayer were located, the official end and start of each church year was signaled by convocation. Its Biblical basis is found in the Hebrew Scriptures. In Exodus 12:16, which is part of a larger set of instructions given to Moses and the Israelites upon their release from Egypt, God tells them: "And in the first day there shall be an holy convocation, and in the seventh day there shall be an holy convocation to you; no manner of work shall be done in them, save that which every man must eat, that only may be done of you." Further details are provided in the twenty-third book of Leviticus.[22] House of Prayer General Council Laws stipulated that con-

Daddy Grace baptizes in a pool, Augusta, Georgia, circa 1940.
Courtesy of Milledge Murray, private collection.

vocation was to be the major event of the year. Each minister was required to be a "booster" of the occasion, encouraging not only his members but the other ministers in the area to participate and to contribute funds to make the occasion successful.[23] Funding also came from individual members of the sponsoring church, as every person was required to pay an annual convocation fee.[24]

Convocation was not a single event. Typically, it involved various musical performances, several days of church services with guest speakers, a mass baptism, a night on which Daddy Grace spoke from the Holy Mountain, and opportunities for auxiliaries to present themselves publicly, often in one or more parades. Grace did not usually participate in the entire sequence of convocation festivities in any town, which might last as long as a week; instead he allowed the ceremony to build and he arrived toward the end as its crescendo. In Charlotte, however, where the House of Prayer convocation was affectionately called "one of the gaudiest, noisiest events of the year in North Carolina," Grace was more typically present for several days.[25] As the national church expanded, attendance at convocation events took up an increasing amount of Grace's time. From the early 1940s on he spent a quarter of every year traveling from convocation to convocation, with the season lasting from July through September and occasionally spilling over into the months on either side.

For many of the faithful, baptism was the most significant part of convocation. Because only the bishop had the power to baptize, and because he did so only on the last full day of each convocation, the annual ceremony was the single opportunity for members to take part in the Christian rite. In the House of Prayer baptism was not limited to new members; many followers were baptized every year, and some would travel to different convocations so that they could be baptized multiple times in a given season. Members understood water baptism as a ritual of purification from sin, rather than a one-time rite signaling a permanent change of one's moral nature or spirit.[26] This is made explicit in the creed, which stipulates: "We believe in water baptism for the redemption of sin."[27] Exemplifying this belief, one member told a reporter that yes, she had been baptized the year before, and she would do it again this year, and if possible she will do it next year too. "Why? . . . Because it [feels] good. You get clean on the inside and on the outside."[28] Said another, "It takes all the evil away."[29]

House of Prayer baptisms were public events that attracted as many spectators as faithful. Photographs often show people crowding around to watch the event, with those to be baptized distinguished by their all-white attire. In his earliest years, Grace baptized followers in local rivers and lakes; in Charlotte, he first baptized in nearby Sugar Creek, and when larger groups were amassed he arranged trips to the Catawba River. In time, many Houses of Prayer built outdoor baptismal pools. Grace would bless the pool at the start of the ceremony, then bestow temporary power on the elders to baptize the faithful. Sometimes, he stood at the front of the line and touched each person's shoulder just before he or she descended into the pool. Then the bishop looked on as elders standing in the water dunked each individual and helped them

Participants in fire hose baptism in Harlem, 2004. Author's collection.

move through the water.[30] The annual baptism was thus a lengthy process that required several hours and numerous assistants to complete. Additionally, many people spent time filling jugs with baptismal water to take to others in need or to use later themselves. To make it more comfortable, refreshments were sold nearby so the event was combined with leisurely picnicking. A refrigerated truck decorated with House of Prayer slogans sold refreshments, Grace Royal Vitamins, and other church merchandise from its window. In the late 1940s this truck traveled with Daddy Grace and was present at every convocation event.[31]

In several cities, including Philadelphia, New York, Detroit, and Washington, DC, Grace made it his custom to baptize followers in one fell swoop beneath the gushing stream of a fire hose rather than one by

Daddy Grace at convocation in Charlotte, North Carolina,
1959. Courtesy of the *Charlotte Observer*/File Photo.

"Daddy Grace let his benevolent glance sweep the throng as he rode along."[45]

For over two decades, a highlight in Charlotte's convocation parade was captain Shedrick Ford. Ford, dressed in a red and blue uniform with gold braid, marched through the streets leading the crowd with his head held high and chin in the air. In later years he explained that his style of marching, with knees rising to midtorso level, was based on what his brother learned to do when serving in the First World War. Occasionally Ford would throw in "a sharp kick or twist" for entertainment's sake, but he always approached his role as leader of the parade with focus and sincerity.[46] Behind Ford came groups of House of Prayer members, often from several different cities, both on floats and on foot. Each person wore the uniform of his or her auxiliary, such as blue robes for the Grace Jubilee Choir, green and orange outfits for the Grace Soul Hunters, brown cowgirl costumes for the Grace Mexican Girls, turquoise evening gowns and tiaras for the Grace Queens, and white uniforms with gold and red braid for the Grace Ushers. Some auxiliaries carried banners or flags bearing slogans such as "The Grace of God Is the Only True Way to Bear this World in Peace," "Daddy Is My Friend," and "Dad Is My Rock." The parade always included bands—string bands, shout bands, concert bands—either marching in formation or playing their instruments from the bed of a truck. Sometimes the parade included things more fantastic than usual, such as a man performing acrobatic tricks while riding a horse, or more inexplicable than usual, such as a man proudly carrying a Confederate flag. As group after group processed through the streets of Brooklyn, House of Prayer men served as parade security and traffic controllers, and they often rode on horseback and carried visible guns. The local police made it known that they welcomed church support in the job of crowd control.[47]

One of the final ceremonies during convocation was the presentation of funds to Daddy Grace. Each pastor had to turn in a "convocation report" that was written in both narrative and tabular format, accounting for all activities and transactions since the previous year's convocation.[48] Then, during a service, each of the local auxiliaries was called before the crowd to present the bishop with the fruits of its year-long fund-raising. Grace rarely gave praise to any group, instead typically saying that its amount was fine but that he knew the group could have raised more. The tally was publicly announced and added to the score for that House of Prayer. Essentially, each church competed with all other Houses of Prayer nationwide to be the highest fund-raiser of the year, and tremendous accolades and prestige were bestowed on the victorious church. Similar to what had occurred in Cape Verde, the most successful fund-raisers were rewarded with special titles, such as "Convocation King" for the pastor of the church, and for the remainder of the year the area where the winning House of Prayer was located was referred to as "Victory Land." After all of the regular convocations had taken place, the season culminated with more services and a celebratory banquet in Victory Land, described by Fauset as a "monster-master convocation." The festivities were paid for by the losing churches and attended by Daddy Grace.[49]

Money, Hierarchy, and Structure in the House of Prayer

The vast quantities of money collected by Grace during convocation season were the endpoint of a long process. Devoted followers, through their auxiliaries, worked all year to raise these funds and it was an honor to give them to Grace for "the upbuilding of the Kingdom of Heaven."[50] Outsiders were suspicious of the "focus" on money in the House of Prayer; journalists, for example, often asserted that Grace used his followers to raise money and then he squandered it on whimsical purchases for himself, like mansions and fancy clothing. Likewise, the ostentatious display of money during House of Prayer events was disturbing to those Christians who normally relegated monetary issues to the private sphere. The House of Prayer tradition in which a three-dimensional cardboard object was covered over with followers' dollar bills, such as a "money tree," a "money house," and the "money barbecue," was considered offensive by some.[51] Neither Grace nor House of Prayer members understood money in the same way these outsiders did. From their perspective, money was necessary for the work of the church, and it was an honor to donate it publicly. Furthermore, raising money did not make them feel "used," because auxiliary membership brought them joy. By participating, they found a group of like-minded Christians to meet with for a common purpose; they developed pride in working for their religious community; and they gained a sense of belonging. Fund-raising was only part of what any given group did, and they understood that the money their efforts yielded automatically belonged to the church. Grace, as the benevolent leader and business manager, was the natural recipient of the funds because he knew best how to redistribute the wealth to further the work of the House of Prayer.

Though participation in an auxiliary was truly appealing for many followers, it is also true that during Grace's reign it was a requisite for full church membership. Additionally, requirements for some of the more prestigious auxiliaries could be strict. In order to participate in a band, for example, members had to attend several hours of rehearsal each week, purchase their own uniforms, pay monthly dues, and follow extra behavioral rules, especially when they were acting as representatives of the church.[52] Such rules were necessary because auxiliary membership was a form of lay service in the House of Prayer, and so it was a privilege as much as a duty. In fact, these rules were quite basic compared with those for leaders in higher levels of service; auxiliaries were merely the simplest form of hierarchical structure within the multilevel House of Prayer.

At the top of the hierarchy was Bishop Grace, whose role included the power to select, ordain, and supervise ministers. On behalf of the church's members he was the owner of all church property, including donations. Though he employed several lawyers and business advisors in different cities, none of them was fully apprised of the monetary details of the church, and therefore Grace had sole knowledge of church financial affairs. He referred to Biblical precedent for his role, pointing out that in various time periods God repeatedly chose a single man for special missions, such as Noah and Moses, who bore the responsibility of being the primary decision-maker on behalf of many. Grace was that man for the true Christian congregation of the twentieth century.[53] Grace's mandate read, in part: "The general assembly and congregations of this organization shall have no power whatsoever to interfere with his visions, rights or powers in building and making growth in the said congregation, neither shall they have power to judge or condemn him. . . . According to the words of the Apostle Paul, he is only to be judged by the Almighty God."[54] However, it was also true that the church constitution stipulated that the bishop could be removed for reasons such as violations of church rules and incompetence.[55]

Grace wanted his full-time pastors to be beyond reproach. He handselected each one, and his criterion was that they did not need to be the most accomplished people as long as they were ethical, honest men. Although Grace believed that, "No preacher should go to school to learn to preach," potential pastors were required to train for the ministry under a more senior elder (or, in the early years, under Grace himself), to study the Bible, and to learn basic business strategies.[56] As elders, they had to abide by strict rules, keeping in mind that there was little distinction between a pastor's personal behavior, his behavior as a leader, and his role as the top representative of his particular House of Prayer. For example, one rule stipulated that: "Any minister riding sisters in their cars shall be arrested and tried."[57] In addition to serving as good examples, ministers of individual Houses of Prayer were the de facto managers of all local House of Prayer businesses, from stores to apartment buildings. Despite their many responsibilities, few elders worked solely for the church, and their pay consisted of the offering collected on one designated night of the week. However, the General Council Laws asserted that each minister in good standing was to be cared for if disability or old age rendered him unable to work, and the church insured each one for funeral expenses.[58]

Below the elders, numerous officers served as church leaders including secretaries, deacons, auxiliary presidents, a treasurer, and those on administrative committees. Many of their responsibilities, outlined in the General Council Laws, were designed to prevent financial abuse within the church. For example, elders were never allowed to handle money themselves, but they were held accountable for all money raised and spent. Special committees were responsible for banking and bill paying, but several people, called "checkers," were designated to review the committees' transactions periodically.[59] Like pastors, officers were also held to behavioral expectations. The Laws stipulated that any officer who behaved in a disrespectful manner toward another had to pay a fine; officers could also incur fines for unexcused absences from business meetings.[60] The myriad opportunities in the church for service and leadership coupled with responsibility allowed nearly every member of the House of Prayer to contribute a part of him- or herself. Even a child wearing the uniform of his auxiliary could feel that he or she was a valued member of the church community, and could take pride in the part he or she played.

On a broader organizational level, each House of Prayer belonged to a regional district, and on occasion district representatives met for planning purposes. Districts were chaired by the pastor of what was called the Mother House, which was usually the largest church in the region. District chairmen were in turn accountable to Daddy Grace, who had a headquarters building in Washington, DC. The headquarters housed the two national business units of the House of Prayer: the Grace Publishing Company, and the Family Aid Association, both of which were managed by the Washington Mother House. Until 1955 Elder Ernest Mitchell was the pastor of the Mother House in Washington and served as one of Grace's most trusted assistants. He was the secretary of the *Grace Magazine* and wrote many of its more substantive articles, particularly those on theological themes.[61] The publishing company appears to have been primarily occupied with the *Grace Magazine*, which came out three times a year and was intended for the national audience of church members.

The Family Aid Association (FAA) was a larger entity than the publishing arm. Grace's friend, real-estate developer Samuel Keets, had the idea to start an insurance program for House of Prayer members' funeral expenses. He thought it would be an attractive program because many poor members of the church were unable to afford decent funerals and burials, though it was also clearly intended as an income-producing venture for the two men. Grace and Keets incorporated the FAA in Washington, DC, in 1930. Those who were insured paid a membership fee to join and two years of high monthly premiums; in the third year and beyond, they paid only twenty-five cents a month to an officer in their local congregation in order to maintain the policy. When an insured person died, his or her family received up to two hundred fifty dollars for funeral expenses. Grace served as president of the FAA and earned 25 percent of its gross; essentially, he was paid this fee because without his involvement few people would have joined. In time, Keets determined that he was not able to earn enough to make the FAA a worthwhile endeavor. He suggested to Grace that they expand the types of insurance the FAA offered, but Grace declined because he felt it was already an unwieldy business. Keets resigned, and Grace arranged for the work to be divided among district chairmen and managed by the Washington headquarters.[62]

Because of the House of Prayer's clear emphasis on members' raising money and ceremoniously handing it over to the bishop, Grace never earned a reputation for being munificent. This was further promoted by writers who openly suspected Grace of being motivated by greed rather than concern for the well-being of his members. Fully one-third of Fauset's precedent-setting study, for example, focuses on the role of money in the House of Prayer, including interpretations such as that church contests were primarily "for the purpose of increasing the totals which are to make up the collections for the leader," and determining that Grace had much in common with "the numerous entrepreneurs who exploit the possibilities of various media in order to turn a financial profit."[63] In contrast to suggestions of avarice, Grace often gave his financial assistance to those who asked, and he did so without needing public fanfare. For example, the Dwiggins Nursing Home in Charlotte, owned by two House of Prayer members, was financed in large part by a donation from Grace.[64] When individual Houses of Prayer needed funds to erect new buildings, Grace loaned them the money with a low interest rate.[65] At one time he even acted as a lender when a small church in Charlotte unrelated to the House of Prayer needed a building, though as part of the arrangement the church sometimes had to allow his elders to preach there. There are also numerous instances of Grace's giving money to struggling single mothers during his early years of ministry.[66] Beyond the business realm, he was also considerate of his family. He bought homes for relatives, such as his daughter, Irene, and despite his estrangement from former wife Angelina he covertly paid for the long-term hospitalization of their teenage son, Marcelino. Upon his death, various IOUs and informal loan notes were found among Grace's personal items, some written many years earlier but never collected on. His will stipulated that any outstanding debts owed to him for real estate were to be erased.[67] In sum, although the bishop could not necessarily be described as charitable, neither was he greedy or insensitive to those in need; he was a businessman who sometimes demonstrated generosity.

Grace's Family Troubles

The bylaws, the designated leadership roles, the annual cycle of events, and all of the other established church structures made the House of Prayer a well-oiled machine by the 1940s. For Grace, this must have been helpful, because during the last two decades of his life several family struggles competed for his attention. The bishop preferred to keep his most personal troubles out of the public eye, and so with few records to follow, it is difficult to determine how he may have been affected by the various challenges that faced him. What is clear is that despite what he experienced on a personal level, Grace maintained his glamour, his frenetic travel schedule, and his frequent appearances. Perhaps when family issues were most stressful, submerging himself in work brought him fulfillment and joy.

According to Grace's daughter, Irene, in the late 1940s the bishop offered to adopt Irene's son Norman, who had just started school. Grace wanted to bring Norman to live with him in Washington and possibly to groom the boy for the ministry. Irene agreed to the arrangement, and Grace directed his sisters to buy clothes and toys for Norman in preparation. Seeing all of the new things, Irene began to worry that her father's inclination was only to make her son materially comfortable, rather than to care for him truly. When the day came for Norman to move, Irene refused. She never regretted her decision, but she acknowledged that the situation created the first serious strains of tension in the family.[68]

Not long after this incident Grace's elder son, also named Norman, was killed. Norman had served overseas as an Air Force corporal from 1942 to 1945, and after his return he was active in the church, sometimes traveling to Cuba to manage his father's estate. In July 1947 as Norman was driving to Charlotte to join his father, his jeep flipped over near Richmond, Virginia, and he was killed.[69] The House of Prayer community shared in the grief. As one church member memorialized him, Norman "was always struggling to bring Sweet Daddy Grace's words to its [*sic*] highest level. Brother Norman Grace died as a warrior on the battlefield for Sweet Daddy Grace."[70] But rather than attend his son's New Bedford funeral, Grace continued working, and arrived three days later to incur the wrath of his daughter and first wife. Following Norman's death there was confusion about who was responsible for various funeral-related expenses. Norman's mother, Jennie, subsequently filed suit against Grace and his sister Louise for reimbursement of a portion of the costs; Louise countersued. The paperwork and ill feelings dragged on into the early 1950s, and only exacerbated the rift between Grace and his sisters and nieces on one side and Jennie and Irene on the other. Irene, who sided with her mother, permanently lost touch with her father because of the disagreement.[71]

In 1948, a year after Norman's death, Grace's son Marcelino, from his second marriage, was placed in a mental facility for long-term treatment of schizophrenia. Marcelino ran away from the hospital in the spring of 1951, and for most of that decade his parents had no idea what had become of him.[72] Though they were not close, this could not have been easy for Grace, as Marcelino had been the only child with whom he still had any contact. A few years later, Grace's own mortality may have come more clearly into focus, as his sister Eugenia died in the summer of 1955.[73]

With his children and grandchildren no longer present in his life, and with his remaining siblings now elderly, it is no wonder that Grace's work consumed his life. His joy, it seems, really was completed by the members of his congregation, his "children," who always looked to him as their "Sweet Daddy." His happiness came from witnessing the perpetuation of his most precious offspring, the House of Prayer. And whenever he went to Charlotte to visit his largest, most vigorous following, his joy was most complete.

A *"Better Class" Gentleman in Charlotte*

When the first waves of slum clearance were taking place in Brooklyn during the 1940s and 1950s, Daddy Grace's friend Joseph Samuel Nathaniel Tross lived comfortably across town. Tross was one of Charlotte's Black elite. Born in British Guiana (now Guyana), he had been raised within the Black professional class and sent abroad to Oxford for his education. In his late teens he moved to the United States and, two decades prior to arriving in Charlotte, earned his bachelor's degree at Howard University. Later, in Pittsburgh, he earned a doctorate in religious education. In the early 1920s Tross taught philosophy and religion at Livingstone College in North Carolina, and in 1932 he made his permanent home in Charlotte with his wife, Geneva, and daughter, Florence. In Charlotte, Tross got involved in many projects. He began editing church school literature for the African Methodist Episcopal Zion Press, and he also published several books under its aegis including *This Thing Called Religion* and *The Meaning of Education*. He became secretary for his division of the American Bible Society, and for a short while he pastored the China Grove AME Zion Church. Tross also had his own weekly radio program that broadcast on local station WBT, and, in 1949, he became the publisher of the *Charlotte Post,* the city's secular Black newspaper.[74] As an accomplished citizen, Tross was known to keep company with respected Black leaders in Charlotte, such as Thad Tate, Arthur Grier, Fred Alexander, and Clinton Blake; less well known was his friendship with Daddy Grace.[75]

Beyond his elite credentials, Tross's personal beliefs also made him easily fit in with the "better class" of Black residents, who "promulgat[ed] a philosophy of race progress based on education, property ownership, and moral propriety."[76] The "better class" perspective grew out of the enslavement period, when Black people in Charlotte had been taught to look to white people for help rather than helping each other. In the twentieth century this ideology remained manifest in the goals of local leaders, who tended toward accommodationism. They strove for assimilation and white acceptance rather than agitating for real equality, despite the fact that these goals did not encompass the broad range of

Charlotte's Black citizens' viewpoints. These leaders advocated a single strict path as the one to racial uplift: Christian living, education, and ownership.[77] Though there was nothing inherently wrong with these goals, the fact that social distinctions were measured by them generally meant that poor Black people of Charlotte remained at the bottom of the social structure because they rarely achieved more than "Christian living" on this scale. At the same time, the leaders had accomplished few changes to Jim Crow customs that deemed all of the Black residents of Charlotte second-class citizens.

Tross's beliefs and actions readily fit in with the ideals of Charlotte's "better class." Although he was active in working to improve race relations, his methods were conservative. He eschewed demonstrations, preferring instead calm meetings of community members willing to think across race and class lines in attempts to solve problems.[78] Rather than pointing out racial inequality at every turn, Tross insisted he was "color blind . . . and thank God for it."[79] He was a member of the local association of Christian ministers, an organization that, three years prior to the official desegregation of Charlotte in 1963, chastised college students for their protests against segregation and commended the Charlotte mayor for his efforts toward racial "friendly relations."[80] Though he worked on many issues, including school desegregation and getting Black officers on the local police force, Tross was among the leaders whom some residents considered "too cautious" about race relations.[81] Activist Reginald Hawkins, for example, criticized Black leaders who merely affirmed the strategies put forth by white elected officials, and insisted these changes were mere tokens.[82]

Tross's conservatism also managed to alienate people when he served as a minister. When he became the pastor of Weeping Willow AME Zion Church in the late 1940s, he earned a reputation for being strict about rules and order. For example, he distributed a copy of the *Methodist Book of Discipline* to each lay leader and insisted they meet with him monthly to discuss various points. Any leader who felt he was above the rules was promptly dismissed from his post. Members described Tross as "businesslike" and as a maker of "strong decisions," and some left the church, dissatisfied with his style of leadership.[83] Tross was certainly a man of integrity and determination; a religiously motivated humanitarian who directed his efforts toward improvement of the quality of life. But because he was a stalwart of "better class" ideals and strategies, he was not admired unequivocally in Charlotte.

Grace's Visits to Brooklyn

It was in Charlotte that Daddy Grace and Tross met and became friends, though how this connection first occurred is not known. Because of his local status and connections, Tross would have been an attractive associate for Grace, so it is possible that the bishop pursued a relationship with him. When Grace was in town he often invited his friend for a meal at his home, where volunteer church members obsequiously waited on them. As a frequent guest, Tross confirmed witnessing Daddy Grace's occasionally tossing crumbs to the servers. "I have to admit that I didn't care for that," he said.[84] But though it made him uncomfortable, he did not feel it was his place to intervene. In Tross's opinion, despite any shortcomings, Grace was a "religious genius," and he enjoyed their intellectual exchange.[85] On one occasion, he asked Grace why he spent his money on churches and fancy real estate rather than founding institutions that could be more directly beneficial to followers. Grace explained that he felt there were limits to what he could do as well as limits to what people were ready to receive. "I represent all my people," Grace told him, "and all people can be lifted only a little at a time."[86] Improving self-esteem and self-respect, then, were ground-level objectives for Grace, but he was not unaware of the need for aid and other forms of social uplifting. He simply believed that achieving a feeling of worth and dignity within American society was of foremost importance for a majority of his followers. Years later, Tross reflected that his friend had taken "a rock no other builder would use and made it the cornerstone of his church. But he gave those people there a new self-identity. They had somebody who wanted them. He gave them hope and something to be happy about."[87] Grace's unusual methods, Tross felt, were thus deliberately and successfully designed to appeal to his target audience of religious consumers.

Grace and Tross Exchange Ideas

It is notable that in his latter decades Grace began to show signs of looking beyond the scope of his own church and toward wider involvement in the community. This ideological thread was taken up and developed much more fully by his successor, Daddy McCollough, but the seeds for it were planted by Grace. The consistency and independence of Houses of Prayer such as those in Charlotte probably allowed Daddy Grace to feel secure enough to turn his attention away from regional management and toward a broader picture. Interestingly, when one considers some of his actions during the 1940s and 1950s alongside those of his friend Dr. Tross, it appears that the two men thought through ideas about leadership together. The numerous parallels between them suggest that their occasional dinners were paired with fruitful conversation about how to run a successful church. Though it is possible, even likely, that Grace initially befriended Tross because of his status in the community, the longevity of their friendship demonstrates that each man found in the other a true friend whose intellect he admired.

One way in which Tross may have influenced Grace was to encourage him to work more overtly on issues of racial concern. In the 1940s, Tross put much energy into the push to get Black officers on the Charlotte police force, which was ultimately a successful campaign. Grace had never been one to speak out on race issues, instead insisting they did not affect him. The first and only evidence of Grace's working on an issue of racial civil rights came right on the heels of Tross's feat, when, following in his friend's style of the dignified meeting, Grace sat down with the mayor and police chief in Charlotte to discuss getting taxis to carry Black riders. Tross's charitable efforts may also have rubbed off on Grace, if only briefly. When Tross directed the North Carolina Bible House in Brooklyn, he ran a drive for donations for the needy each year at Christmastime. Beginning with the Christmas of 1947, Tross increased his attention to this work and expanded the charity to a year-round endeavor. The only known charity drive led by Grace occurred that very same year. He encouraged his churches to spend the year collecting clothing for people in Cape Verde, and in December 1948 Grace paid for the shipment of what he called "Christmas Cargo" to the islands.[88]

Tross may also have been the one to encourage Grace to put more attention on church writings. As a firm believer in publications that would allow members to read and study theology and religion on their own, Tross had long been involved in writing for the AME Zion Church. As he implored in the introduction to a denominational anthology, "We must . . . write to be heard and to influence. Without literature the Church must inevitably lose its hold on the masses, and the masses look to the press for their education and guidance."[89] Grace may have seen the wisdom in Tross's words, because in 1941 the Long Street House of Prayer in Charlotte begat a new publication, the *House of Prayer Quarterly*. As stated in the preface to each issue, "the purpose of printing this literature is to set forth and make known the truth of the Scripture concerning Sweet Daddy Grace, and the House of Prayer for All People." The *Quarterly* contained three months' worth of Sunday School lessons that would be taught in church that quarter but that could also be studied at home. Each single-page lesson included a Bible excerpt, a "Main Thought," and a list of daily Bible readings for that week. The Main Thought usually contained two kinds of information: commentary on the theological and historical significance of a passage, and an explanation of how the passage related to the present day, often with emphasis on how the House of Prayer's work or Daddy Grace himself could be understood as exemplifying Biblical instruction.[90]

Changes also developed at the Grace Publishing Company during this era. Though the company did not add new religious literature to its repertoire until much later, its publication, the *Grace Magazine,* transformed from a mere record of church events into a vehicle for religious guidance. Around 1950, the magazine was redesigned to look more like a professional publication. Elements of its typesetting were altered, and the page size became slightly smaller, and both of these changes enhanced its appearance. And it was no longer a free publication; it now cost fifteen cents an issue. Most importantly, its focus changed. Until the 1940s the magazine's contents were inwardly focused, intended to appeal primarily to House of Prayer members. Articles recounted events, praised and affirmed the power of Daddy Grace, provided localized news such as travels, weddings, and obituaries, and reminded people of things such as FAA meetings and Bible studies. But around 1950 the magazine became more outwardly focused, and the types of information printed were more clearly intended for a broader audience that did not consist solely of loyal members. Now the magazine contained articles with more context about the House of Prayer organization and its beliefs, it praised the power of Grace in a way that promoted him rather than merely affirming him, and it included more lengthy listings of House of Prayer addresses along with each minister's name. The changes that came to the *Grace Magazine* may well have been another way that Grace incorporated Tross's suggestions about educating, guiding, and influencing the masses via the written word.

Tross, too, seems to have tried out some of Grace's management techniques. During his short tenure as pastor of Charlotte's Weeping Willow AME Zion Church in the late 1940s, Tross made numerous changes that bear striking resemblance to the House of Prayer. As with House of Prayer auxiliaries, where membership in the organizations helped to increase people's commitment to the church, at Weeping Willow, Tross created numerous new lay organizations such as choirs, missionary societies, class leaders, and stewards and stewardesses. As with the House of Prayer's strength that was on display each year during convocation, Tross emphasized the church's appearance. When people walked through the door on Sunday mornings he wanted ushers ready and attentive, he wanted the service always to begin on time, he wanted the choir to get crisp-looking new robes, and he wanted the music directed by someone who had the time and skill to devote to it. In another move much like Grace's style, he reorganized church finances so that funds were put into one pot managed by the board of trustees instead of allowing each group to control its own money. He conducted a review of all of the parachurch organizations, added more people to the board of trustees, and designed a long-term plan for expansion of church facilities. Last, though Tross increased the number of laypeople involved in leadership of the church, he sometimes made decisions without consulting anyone below him, just as Daddy Grace did.[91]

Grace's noteworthy activities during his last two decades of religious leadership were essentially limited to his experimentation with small aspects of the institution he had created; aside from this, his activities remained stable. His dabbling with community issues and charity, his creation of a new publication for religious education, and his adjustments to the church's house organ suggest that he was beginning to consider issues of outreach in a way not seen in earlier decades. This was partly due to his church's being a streamlined organization that no longer required constant management, and partly due to the influence of his friend Dr. Tross. When combined, the seemingly disparate elements of what we know about Grace in Charlotte—the nature of the neighborhood where he lived and worked, the convocation ceremonies he held, the design of his calendar year, his personal troubles, and his friendship with Dr. Tross—show a portrait of the church in its glory years under Grace, when the institution essentially ran itself and Grace merely needed to make appearances. This freedom allowed Grace to surrender some aspects of leadership as he simultaneously began to lead on new, more subtle levels. His experiments with church structure and focus during these later years, especially those experiments influenced by Dr. Tross, set the stage for developments within the church after his death. Charlotte, then, is the ideal place to view both the House of Prayer in its heyday and Bishop Grace beyond the crest of his directive leadership, as he adjusted and perfected his joyous creation.

6

Chaotic Confusion

Daddy Grace tried to prevent the unhinging of the House of Prayer. Five days before his death on January 12, 1960, Grace recorded a live sermon in Los Angeles titled "You Must Be Born Again." When members listened to this recording during funeral services for the bishop, newspapers erroneously reported that Grace "preached his own funeral."[1] Most of his sermon's message focused on the third chapter of the Gospel of John, and Grace reminded listeners that to be a full believer in Christ one had to experience baptism both by immersion in water and suffusion in the Holy Spirit. Grace also repeatedly stressed that the United House of Prayer for All People was the only true path to salvation. But then, in the final few seconds of his recording, Grace suddenly broke form. He put down his Bible, stopped preaching, and slowed his words. Perhaps he sensed the trouble that would disrupt the church for years to come and wanted to warn members against it. Perhaps it was random chance. But in nearly prophetic tones he cautioned: "My little bit, your little bit, talking against each other because we jealous, oh, [that's] bad business children! Remember what I say: if we together, we'll stay together. Because together we will stand. But divided we will fall."[2] The very next day, Grace had a heart attack, and four days later he died. The church did not heed his warning. It became not only divided, but also embroiled in costly lawsuits that lasted for more than a decade; despite this, the church did not fall.

The Funeral Cortege

Grace's sisters Sylvia and Louise flew to Los Angeles and arranged for their brother's body to be taken on a cross-country train ride aboard the *Sunset Limited*; meanwhile the church announced that public viewings would be held in six cities on the East Coast. The family reached

Charlotte, North Carolina, on the evening of January 17th, and a crowd awaiting Daddy's arrival milled inside the station. His body was promptly taken to the House of Prayer on McDowell Street, where hundreds more stood outside in the rain.[3] Reporters badgered congregants for stories about the departed leader but they were hesitant to talk, and attempts were made to chase photographers away, such as when one elder scolded, "We have respect for Daddy Grace and his departure is not for commercial practices."[4] Inside the church, in a brass coffin with a glass lid, Grace was dressed in a dark suit with gold trim and a fresh rosebud on the lapel. As at every subsequent funeral stop, Grace's coffin was carefully placed on a dais and surrounded with elaborate flower displays; a large brass band played both mournful and upbeat tunes; and uniformed guards and contribution baskets flanked the coffin. The mourners patiently waited in a long line for their chance to see Daddy one last time.[5] Grace remained in Charlotte for one day before being placed in a hearse and taken north to Newport News, Virginia, where the scene was repeated at the Ivy Avenue House of Prayer; then it was on to Washington, DC. In Washington, despite a long wait outside in the windy cold, several thousand people passed through the Mother House of Prayer to view Grace's body. Inside, a reporter wrote, "women shrieked and fainted, [and] men burst into tears and had to be escorted bodily from the bier."[6] Despite the grief of some, the crowds were mostly orderly and the extra police the district put on duty for the funeral were not needed.[7]

After twelve hours in Washington, Grace's body was taken to Pennsylvania, where on the morning of the 21st an estimated four thousand mourners assembled near the Fitzwater Street House of Prayer in Philadelphia for a procession. Five girls in white uniforms, carrying flags and rifles, walked in front of a car laden with flowers. Behind it came Grace's hearse, and behind Grace, the crowd. Inside, Daddy's throne stood empty; other signs of his absence included his desolate coatrack with a single empty hanger, and his silver pitcher and goblet turned upside down on a table. "Sweet Daddy is not dead," an elder reminded the mourners during the sermon, "He is in every one of us."[8] The viewing in Philadelphia lasted until dawn of the 22nd, when the motorcade again amassed. Now fifteen cars strong, Grace's cortege traveled to the next House of Prayer stop in Newark, New Jersey. There, Elder Stephen welcomed a crowd of hundreds to the elaborately decorated space and the rituals of last respect continued.[9]

While Daddy Grace passed through all of these cities on the incremental journey to his final resting place, his nephew Manuel was arranging the most elaborate of the funeral ceremonies in New Bedford. The reds, whites, and blues of the Kempton Street House of Prayer were repainted, banners were hung, life-size cutouts of Daddy Grace were positioned, and lighted floral displays shaped as Bibles, crosses, and hearts were arranged on the podium. As soon as the convoy crossed into Massachusetts, state police joined in to escort it to the city line of New Bedford, where local police took a spot in the procession. Three cars of church officials preceded the Cadillac hearse, and when it arrived, uniformed Grace Soldiers solemnly carried the body up the steps into the church. Over one thousand mourners waited outside while a private ceremony for Grace's family and close associates took place. Once the viewing was opened to the public, Grace lay in state from Saturday until Tuesday morning. Visitors of all races came steadily, including church members who had traveled from many regions, as well as local curiosity seekers.[10]

The transcontinental journey finally ended with a formal procession from Kempton Street to the cemetery on Grace's fourth day in New Bedford. Leading the procession were the Grace Soldiers of the Cross, followed by a group of church elders. Three cars contained, respectively, Grace; his two sisters and niece; and his daughter, grandchildren, and ex-wife; and behind them walked the crowd.[11] At Oak Grove Cemetery Grace's body was put in a rented holding vault, intended as temporary. Plans were being drawn up for a mausoleum to be built on the da Graca family plot at Pine Grove Cemetery. Little did anyone realize that with the onslaught of litigation the church was about to endure, there would be no money readily available for such a memorial. As a result, Grace's body remained in the five-dollar-a-month vault until October 1964, when his marble tomb was completed and his body could finally be laid to rest.[12]

Grace's Messy Estate

Within days of Grace's death, bureaucratic chaos ensued in the church nationwide. Since he had not appointed a successor, it was unclear to most members how a new bishop would be chosen. Additionally, Grace's financial affairs had never been an open book. He had always employed numerous lawyers and advisors for his money matters but none were knowledgeable about the entire picture, and his own record keeping was scant. Church leaders did not know the answers to basic questions such as precisely what property the church owned, how many bank accounts existed and who would be able to access them, and what items belonged to Grace's personal estate. This confusion made the environment ripe for lawsuits about money and power.

Grace's will, written in November 1948, left small amounts of money to twelve specific people: his four siblings (one of whom, Jennie, was by then deceased); his two remaining children, Irene and Marcelino; Irene's three children; and nieces Marie, Mildred, and Olive. The total of all these payments was only in the tens of thousands of dollars. Both children felt snubbed due to the small sums they were willed, as did Grace's first wife, Jennie, who received nothing, and all three filed lawsuits contesting the will. While Irene and Jennie reached an out-of-court settlement that was reported to be in the neighborhood of two hundred thousand dollars, Marcelino's case was ultimately dismissed.[13] After the specific payments, the remainder of Grace's personal estate was left to the church. There had been great potential for litigation here too, because many properties commonly thought to be owned by the church corporation turned out to have been owned by Grace personally; the fact that he left all of his remaining assets to the church solved these problems. Nonetheless, numerous conflicts over church property arose, and these ultimately became far more volatile than the family disagreements about the will.

It is hard to know whether Grace's poor record keeping made lawsuits truly inevitable, or if it was just that people viewed his death as an opportunity to skim wealth from the estate. Either way, attacks came from every direction. For example, beyond the basic troubles with the will, Grace's niece Marie Miller sued the church for back pay of nearly forty-six thousand dollars for services she had performed.[14] Another niece, Mildred Lopes, sued the church because property she claimed to have temporarily transferred into Grace's name for safekeeping during her divorce had been inadvertently left to the church.[15] In New York City, Grace was one of two people named in a nurse's hundred-thousand-dollar lawsuit that alleged negligence in building maintenance had caused her on-the-job injury at the El Dorado.[16] Even the school board in New Bedford saw Grace's death as an opportunity: they wanted his County Street property in order to build a new elementary school, and discussed using eminent domain to usurp it.[17] But the most daunting of all the suits came from the government. Claiming that Grace had failed to pay enough income tax for several years, the IRS froze all of Grace's personal and corporate assets until it could determine what was owed. The initial estimate of taxes owed was $5.9 million; the IRS eventually settled for $1.9 million in June 1961.[18]

It was not unusual that the IRS expected such a large amount, because the House of Prayer's wealth was commonly believed to be much greater than it was. After his death, it was widely reported that Grace's estate was worth between sixteen and twenty-five million dollars, and some estimates were even higher. To straighten out issues of taxes and inheritance, both his personal property and the church assets needed to be surveyed and assessed, and a variety of people were assigned by the courts to help with this task. The two executors named in Grace's will declined to serve, and so a Boston judge appointed lawyers Roy F. Texeira and Rosalind Poll Brooker to administrate. Texeira also represented Jennie Lomba in her claim against the will, and he was therefore both an administrator of and a challenger to Grace's will.[19] By mid-1961 the new executors determined that Grace's personal estate was worth approximately seven hundred thousand dollars, primarily held in real estate in North Carolina and New Bedford. The most valuable individual properties were the County Street mansion and an apartment building in New Bedford, his Cuban estate, and the half-million dollar converted hotel in Los Angeles.[20] But beyond the few payments willed to his family, the legal fees, and the inheritance taxes, the rest of this personal estate went to the church.

The Church in Receivership

Assessment of the church property was a more complicated process than assessment of the personal estate, in part because of lawsuits against the church's new and controversial leadership. Upon Grace's death the Council of State Chairmen, made up of elders of the eight church districts, convened swiftly and chose Walter McCollough of Washington, DC, as their temporary leader. A formal election was to be held a few weeks later. When asked if he hoped to be elected permanently, McCollough told inquisitors, "I hope not. I've got my hands full"; and so speculation began about possible candidates for the bishopric.[21] In New

York, a front page *Amsterdam News* headline announced: "Elder Henry Price to Succeed 'Daddy' "; one week later, the paper reported that Price was "in a deadlock with elder McCollough."[22] Price, the pastor of the Harlem church, was considered a contender because he had frequently been crowned Convocation King as reward for raising the most money of all the churches nationwide.[23] Meanwhile, the *Philadelphia Tribune* wrote that there was a "Bitter Fight for Top Post," and tossed two other names into the ring: John Williams of Norfolk, Virginia, whom Grace purportedly called to his deathbed, and Arthur Price of Newport News.[24] Arthur Price, readers were reminded, had long been a highly praised elder and had once been referred to as "next in rank to the bishop."[25] In their own efforts at a scoop, the *Baltimore Afro-American* predicted Melvin Adams from Charlotte, who was reported to be "one of the elders closest to Daddy Grace"; meanwhile the *Pittsburgh Courier* predicted it would be William Revis of Los Angeles, whose physical resemblance to Grace would make him the most effective man to "perpetuate the image of Sweet Daddy."[26] Despite the newspaper hype about competition among potential successors, the actual choice was controversial among only a small minority. In early February, a general election was held and McCollough was officially chosen as bishop.

McCollough immediately took on the visual mantle of Daddy Grace, the first step in his transformation from a soft-spoken and conservative pastor into a colorful leader. He grew his hair and nails long and started to adorn himself in jewelry and bold fabrics, and he asserted that everything in the church would proceed as usual.[27] Most members were pleased with the new leader. But in June 1960 one group of dissidents filed suit against McCollough in federal district court, claiming his election had been fraudulent because it had not followed House of Prayer bylaws, and that therefore he had no right to control church funds and affairs.[28] Upon examination of the record, Judge George L. Hart agreed that McCollough had not been elected according to regulation. Furthermore, it was clear that a much larger array of problems had accompanied the death of Bishop Grace—for example, the church was still trying to figure out how much money and property it had, and where these assets were located. Deeming their plight "chaotic confusion," Hart temporarily removed financial management power from all church leaders, put the church assets into receivership, and ordered McCollough to step down.[29]

The receiver appointed, William B. Bryant, was a man whose experience up to that point was mostly in the area of criminal law. Upon the start of his service for the church in August 1961 he became the first African American attorney ever to manage such a major estate case in the district, and years later he said that the prestige of the case permanently opened a new door for other Black lawyers.[30] Bryant's job was to figure out what steps were necessary to convene a proper election; to assess the church property, including determining what business transactions had occurred since Grace's death; and to manage the church assets during the interim phase without a bishop. Under detailed instructions from Judge Hart, Bryant got to work sorting through the chaos.

McCollough, though he no longer had access to church money, completely ignored the legal ruling and continued to preside as bishop. The judge specifically forbade McCollough from "referring to or calling himself as 'Sweet Daddy' or 'Daddy' . . . [or putting] himself in the position of leader, quasi-leader, bishop or chief official" as well as from wearing anything that might suggest he was the bishop. The dissident group reported to the courts that despite this order, McCollough was "making appearances in a gold tuxedo, followed by attendants trailing a white satin runner, and fanned by girls in cocktail dresses."[31] Hart found McCollough in contempt of court.[32] Bryant, the receiver, eventually finished examining the House of Prayer bylaws and convened a new election in April 1962. Walter McCollough was again elected, 410 votes to 52, and was legally recognized as the House of Prayer's "spiritual adviser and chief executive officer."[33] One of his first acts as bishop was to dismiss several pastors who had been a part of the suit against him.[34]

In short order the discharged pastors reestablished themselves as ministers in an organization called the True Grace Memorial House of Prayer. With a small but significant following, Elders Noble Harris, Randall Roberts, James Long, Paul Lawson, and Thomas Odell Johnson were among those who led the break. In their first two years, churches started in Savannah, Miami, the District of Columbia, and Philadelphia; later locations included California, Maryland, North Carolina, and New York. Originally True Grace operated much as the United House of Prayer had, except that the ministers worked collaboratively rather than having a bishop in charge; they later agreed to elect a bishop although they remained somewhat decentralized.[35]

Internal conflicts, such as the break-off group and McCollough's treatment of pastors, had no effect on the job of the receiver, Bryant, whose duties regarding financial affairs continued for about a year following the election of McCollough. Bryant made regular reports to the courts about his accounting processes. As Grace's personal finances were gradually resolved, large chunks of money were paid out in taxes and legal fees, and many assets passed from Grace's personal estate into the church holdings. By early 1963, Bryant concluded that the total worth of the church was approximately $4.5 million: $1.3 million was located in twenty-four church bank accounts held in eleven states; and $3.2 million was the market value of all the church property, scattered among thirteen states. These properties ranged from vacant lots to modern buildings, and most were located in Georgia, North Carolina, and Virginia, but the single most valuable piece of church real estate was the block of property located in Harlem on the corner of Eighth Avenue and 125th Street.[36] The more famous of Grace's New York City buildings had all been sold in a transaction begun covertly by Grace in November 1959 and completed by McCollough amidst public controversy in March 1960. Thus the apartments on Riverside Drive and Edgecombe Avenue, as well as the beloved El Dorado, were no longer part of the House of Prayer's kingdom.[37] With Bryant's duties completed, the remaining treasure was officially handed over to McCollough as church trustee.

The Phantom Church Lawsuit

Though McCollough was the new leader free and clear, the chaos and confusion were far from over. All of the legal transactions thus far were nothing compared to the byzantine lawsuit that began in Philadelphia as a result of the ingenuity of one man named James Walton. Seemingly innocuous and unlikely to work, Walton's idea and the perseverance with which he pursued it generated an enormous amount of paperwork and legal expense; it also caused litigation to drag on into the 1970s despite many judgments in the church's favor.

James Walton, a Philadelphia resident who had never been a member of Grace's church, was part of two different phantom organizations that had incorporated in the state of New Jersey. The first, Mankind Homebuilders, Inc., was a company that claimed to be involved in all aspects of building care, from design to construction to management. Mankind incorporated in New Jersey in December 1959, at which time Walton served as its treasurer.[38] The second organization, the United House of Prayer for All People, Inc., was a new church that incorporated in Essex County, New Jersey, in April 1960.[39] The church had several trustees, of which Walton was one, and he also served as its president or "moving spirit." These organizations were "phantoms" in that they existed almost solely on paper. There is no evidence that either organization ever did much of anything beyond the mere act of incorporating—that is, the builders did not build anything, and the church held no services—nor is there evidence that the organizations even existed outside of a single room in West Philadelphia where they shared office space for a brief period in 1960. Despite this, on paper Mankind claimed to employ eight people, and the church had lawsuits filed against it at least three times.

In April 1960, Mankind entered into a contract with the phantom church. What Mankind was enlisted to provide was both vague and nonsensical; one lawyer called its duties "at best bizarre." For example, Mankind was supposed to,

> Obtain and complete many of the objects of the House of Prayer for All People. . . . Some of the objects are to erect, construct, maintain and improve houses, buildings, sewers, drains or work of other kinds on any lands of the House of Prayer for All People or upon any other lands, and to rebuild and improve existing houses and buildings thereon.

The president of Mankind later summed it up by saying the company's job was "to take care of all non-religious affairs." In exchange, the church agreed to pay Mankind $38.6 million by May 4, 1960, and to make ongoing payments of $500,300 to them every fifty-three days.[40] The church failed to pay Mankind though the company claimed to have completed the first portion of the agreement as specified in the contract. On May 24th Mankind went to the Prothonotary of Philadelphia and filed a claim against the church; based on the terms of the signed, notarized contract made between them, the judge ruled in Mankind's favor. Almost instantaneously, the news got out that the United House of Prayer for All People owed a building company $38.6 million plus interest and legal fees.

As Mankind attempted to get the payment fulfilled, it sent legal notices to more than two dozen banks holding accounts in the name of the United House of Prayer for All People. Several banks, confused by the paperwork, refused to allow funds to be withdrawn by anyone until the problem was resolved by the courts. In reaction, McCollough's United House of Prayer for All People petitioned to be allowed to intervene in the case. McCollough's people insisted that the accounts in question did not belong to the phantom New Jersey church, but to them. In addition, they told the judge, publicity surrounding the case was affecting them negatively because of a perception that their church was in serious debt. They argued that public confusion had the potential to harm their business ventures. The judge agreed that McCollough's church had a vested interest in the case, and allowed it to become an additional defendant or "intervenor."

Just as McCollough had once ignored orders to not act as bishop, both phantom organizations ignored injunctions to halt their activities while the courts sorted out the facts. Mankind continued attempting to garnish bank accounts. The phantom church's trustees posted "No Trespassing" signs written in legalese on Houses of Prayer in the Philadelphia region, and when McCollough came onto the property they got a warrant for his arrest.[41] Mankind had trouble keeping lawyers on its side—probably each attorney dropped out when he realized the extent of the legal circus in which he had become involved—and by 1963 the company had changed counsel seven times.

Concurrent with all of this, in a separate civil action brought against the phantom church, a New Jersey judge ruled that this new church's name was problematic. Since Daddy Grace had incorporated his organization in that state in 1954, the second church should never have been allowed to incorporate with such a similar name. The group was ordered to file a certificate of name change; in apparent compliance, the phantom church filed papers to dissolve its corporate status altogether, and the group created a board of liquidating trustees to oversee this process.[42] At no time, however, did any judge decide that the ruling on the contract would be changed; in other words, according to legal decision, the phantom church that was in dissolution still owed Mankind $38.6 million.

Walton was proving himself to be a slick litigant and strategist, and Grace's four decades of haphazard record keeping made it all the more difficult for McCollough's side to defend itself. Walton masterminded a wide variety of legal proceedings that were all an effort to get money and property that did not belong to him, and depending on what he was trying to achieve he would intermittently stress that McCollough had no business in the case because his church was not involved in the Mankind contract, or that his own church, and not McCollough's, was the actual organization founded by Daddy Grace. Walton's personal shenanigans began early on; for instance, once when the parties convened in court and the intervenor's lawyers had not yet met James Walton, he masqueraded as a friend who had been sent to inform the court that "Mr. Walton was out of town," and so the case had to be continued. Walton kept the paperwork coming, even subpoenaing McCollough to depose in Philadelphia as part of the phantom church liquidation procedures; this caused McCollough to file charges of harassment. Walton filed liens on church property and refused to release them despite being tossed in jail, and he passed bad checks under the church's name.[43] At one point, Mankind demanded that the receiver, William Bryant, give the company one million dollars to continue operations. Bryant replied in writing: "This is ridiculous, Mr. Walton." Calling the claim "fictitious and fraudulent," Bryant advised Walton that if he continued the charade he "might find [him]self looking on the inside of one of the penitentiaries." Walton remained undaunted, and pulled more people into the fray. He sued the phantom church on behalf of his late wife, Alta Parker.[44] Walton claimed that Parker, who had died in late 1963, had worked for the new church for slightly more than two years. In July 1962 the liquidating trustees voted to pay her eight hundred thousand dollars for her services and they issued a judgment note. Since the phantom church never completed the payment, Walton filed suit against it on behalf of her estate.[45]

It may have been Walton's ability to flip-flop from a legally savvy person to a bumbling idiot that helped earn judgments in his favor. The courts could not believe that this simple-seeming man was anything but sincere about his contract and the payment. An example of his slickness is found in a cross-examination by the intervenor's lawyer, Mr. Harper. Walton, being questioned at length about the various roles he played in the phantom church, its liquidating board, and the building company, smartly avoided answering in any way that would reveal an intentional conflict of interest. But when cornered, he would suddenly play dumb, as in the snippet below. The lawyer had just pinned Walton into admitting that Parker had never submitted a bill for services to the liquidating trustees.

Harper: Upon what basis then did the figure of eight hundred thousand dollars—who suggested the figure of eight hundred thousand dollars at that meeting?

Walton: I don't know exactly how it came about, but the figure was rendered somehow.

Harper: Who was present at the meeting?

Walton: The figure was entered and agreed upon. It wasn't exactly what you might call "who was present" or whatnot.

Harper: Who was present at the meeting?

Walton: We don't have presidents now.

Harper: Who was present at the meeting? Who was physically present at the meeting? Who attended the meeting?

Walton: The people who entered their signatures on the notes.

Walton's dense and forgetful persona clearly frustrated the lawyer who was trying to get straight answers, and the line of questioning was successfully derailed.

Ultimately, the problem for McCollough's side was that if the phantom church legally dissolved but the judgment note was not stricken from the record, a church named the United House of Prayer for All People would still owe the Mankind company millions of dollars. This could harm McCollough's potential business ventures simply because of confusion with his church, and so he continued trying to get the judgment expunged. In 1965, his lawyers were tiring of the extensive paperwork and the ridiculous claims being put forward by Walton. The suit on behalf of Walton's wife was nearly the last straw. They appealed to the judge in a cogent brief:

The plaintiff [Mankind] appears before this Court allegedly clothed with corporate legality, but under the hard glare of the piercing light of honesty, what is it? . . . In another devious attempt, the plaintiff is commencing suit against the so-called dissolved corporation, hoping doubtless, by arrangement that its complaint will not be answered and a default judgment obtained thereby. It will then be in the same place as it was, with a note of stupid and astronomical amounts with which it can then, again, harass the legitimate defendant Intervenor Corporation.

As at other times, the courts did not completely agree with the intervenor's perspective, and the case kept going. By late 1966, McCollough's church had had enough. Its lawyers realized it was unlikely that the contract ruling would ever be stricken. They also came to see that at least legally, all judgments to date had supported the fact that every bank account in question belonged to the real United House of Prayer, and that the United House of Prayer was in no way related to the phantom New Jersey church nor the contract made with Mankind. The intervenors decided they had gotten what they had come for, and asked to be excused from the case. The judge consented.

This, however, didn't change the fact that the $38.6 million note from the phantom church to Mankind Home Builders remained outstanding. It remains outstanding to this day. That allowed Walton to continue grifting the church periodically; at various points, he found people and institutions who did not know about the fake church with the similar name, and he was able to use the ruling to skim money from church bank accounts. For example, in the early 1970s a New Bedford Bank paid Mankind $2,100. McCollough's church again had to file a lawsuit to get the money returned, even though legal fees likely cost more than the amount taken.[46]

McCollough Institutionalizes the Church

Despite all of the lawsuits and periods of monetary instability, the House of Prayer not only maintained its institutional dignity under Mc-Collough, but it also improved its reputation amongst the general public. Rather than allowing newspapers to bait him with suggestions of turmoil in the church ranks, McCollough kept a calm demeanor. Of his new position, he demurely quoted a verse from the New Testament book of Hebrews: "Let us therefore come boldly unto the throne of grace, that we may obtain mercy, and find grace to help in time of need."[47] This bishop's strategy with the media was different from Grace's, and instead of striving for the House of Prayer to be the center of attention he severely tightened the reigns on publicity. McCollough and his elders kept comments about church troubles to a minimum, refusing to air their dirty laundry in the newspapers. Without gossipy angles and flamboyant episodes, reporters lost interest; one bittersweetly noted that McCollough was, "No show biz character by any means."[48] The church fell out of the headlines and off of the front pages, seemingly slipping into obscurity.

McCollough was originally from Great Falls, South Carolina, and had become a member of the church in the early 1930s when he was about 15 years old. He served for a time as Grace's chauffeur, and by the late 1930s was training for the pastorate at a Washington, DC, mission where he served as assistant minister. By the late 1950s McCollough was the proprietor of a dry-cleaning shop and also served as the full-time elder of the M Street House of Prayer in Washington, a post he took over after the death of Elder Mitchell. In his personal life, he and his wife, Clara, had four children, and he was a long-time Prince Hall Mason. Originally described as "conservative, both in speech and appearance," after the election McCollough began changing his personal style to fit Grace's mold better and ease the transition for church members.[49] Though he kept a low profile with the media, he became a vibrant presence within the church, maintaining the bishop's typical schedule of travel appearances. He gradually transformed himself from humble Elder McCollough of Washington, DC, into Sweet Daddy McCollough, a flashy leader who constantly toured the country to lead convocations and conduct baptisms as had his predecessor. He encouraged those who were able to travel with him aboard new vehicles called McCollough Luxury Liners.[50] As he grew into the role, many products were renamed with his prefix such as McCollough Shampoo, *McCollough Magazine,* and Daddy Grace McCollough Pine Soap, which bore a picture of the new leader on the wrapper. Auxiliaries took on his name as well, such as the McCollough State Band, the McCollough Notes of Charlotte, McCollough's Specials, and the McCollough Sons of Thunder.[51]

But McCollough was not a Daddy Grace flunky: as it turned out, he had a deliberate agenda that would eventually move the church in new directions. Once his power had been established and accepted, the new bishop began to steer the church away from some of the more ostentatious activities members were used to. Grand parades, for instance, were limited to only three cities, and fire-hose baptisms, though not completely eliminated, were mostly replaced with pool baptisms.[52] Like Daddy Grace, McCollough always welcomed anyone and everyone into the fold, saying, "We take rejects from other churches"; and perhaps as evidence of this he allowed some membership requirements and behavioral rules to be eased.[53] Though the importance of auxiliary participation was still emphasized, daily church attendance became less typical of even the most devoted members. McCollough never claimed the ability to heal, but he introduced a new type of gathering called the Spiritual Hurricane—basically an intense late night prayer service—in which healing could be the focus. More important than these surface-level changes, though, McCollough had substantive messages to communicate to people, particularly about modes of self-help. Unlike Grace, McCollough made a point of providing leadership on social justice issues, and he consistently promoted clean living. He preached to church youth about the evils of drugs, and he preached to adults about the importance of eliminating debt. And in case anyone missed out on what he wanted them to hear, McCollough frequently wrote pamphlets and public letters to keep church members informed of new initiatives.[54] These were significant changes in focus for the House of Prayer, bringing it more in line with ideals and practices found in mainline African American churches of that era and reducing its overall tension with broader society.

Like the financially savvy Grace, McCollough made wise investments for the good of his institution, but rather than acquiring trophy properties he turned his attention to projects that directly served church members and had the potential to increase their personal dignity. It was often repeated that McCollough had a dream of Black self-sufficiency, and his efforts demonstrated that he intended to move toward this goal by improving the quality of his church members' lives first and foremost. In 1971, the bishop used his own money to begin the McCollough Scholarship Fund, which offered members grants for college study. Preparing the House of Prayer for the long term, in the late 1960s he started the McCollough Seminary in Richmond, Virginia: a one-year program that offered training in scriptural interpretation, ceremonial rituals, and House of Prayer regulations.[55] In time, the church opened day care centers, cafeterias, and elderly homes in the church's stronger regions, and the organization bought houses for its ministers. A new church auxiliary called the Coalition of Concerned Citizens was founded in several cities, and it offered services such as tutoring, food banks, youth employment programs, voter registration drives, and informational speakers. Another auxiliary McCollough helped develop was the Back the Attack Club, whose members focused attention on combating church legal troubles and any type of outsider provocation. And, not forgetting about church growth, McCollough continued to open new Houses of Prayer and renovate older ones.[56]

Meanwhile, the bishop also paid attention to the larger communities where his congregations were situated. In 1974 the House of Prayer purchased a plot of land near the Mother House in Shaw, which was at that time a poor District of Columbia neighborhood. With great ceremony, including a press event with public speakers and gold-plated shovels, McCollough kicked off the construction of a ninety-unit apartment building. The House of Prayer announced with pride that the church would pay for the building in full as it went; in other words, it was not taking out a mortgage or requesting any other kind of federal assistance. This went along with McCollough's oft-quoted maxim that, "You can't dedicate something to the Lord that you don't own."[57] Partly because of the project's success, in the late 1970s Washington's mayor, Marion Barry, gave the church a valuable plot of land so that it could build another apartment building—this one for people with low and middle incomes—with an adjacent shopping center; a decade later, the church built a third.[58] In addition to facilitating community improvement, McCollough made himself an asset to the political forces in the District of Columbia, often creating a stir around his endorsements of candidates and thereby creating a voice for himself on local issues. By the mid-1970s he had become a well-known community leader in Washington. McCollough received a variety of public honors including two Presidential Commendations in 1976 and 1980, and a Distinguished Community Service Award from the National Urban Coalition in 1985.[59]

Beyond his résumé of accomplishments, McCollough's leadership is also significant because he was smart enough to learn from Daddy Grace's mistakes and to fix the problems. After suffering through the years of instability following Grace's death, McCollough was able to pick up the pieces and put them back together, and then he implemented institutional changes intended to prevent such catastrophes in the future. He revised the original General Council By-Laws to provide more detail about election procedures, monetary accounting, and the institutional power structure.[60] From the troubles created by James Walton's phantom church, McCollough learned the importance of having the House of Prayer legally incorporated in every state where a congregation was located. He also learned the hard way that all bank accounts and property needed to be clearly titled in the church's name. He saw firsthand that taxes needed to be carefully paid because the government had the power to freeze assets. And he ultimately seemed to conclude that the church would continue growing without all of the frenzied publicity and hoopla of which Daddy Grace had been so fond. Because of his changes, most of the bewildering financial and leadership troubles that had beset the church upon Grace's death did not affect the institution when McCollough's reign came to an end in 1991.

The House of Prayer under Daddy Madison

Samuel Madison was already a septuagenarian when McCollough died in March 1991, and he too had personally known Daddy Grace.[61] Originally from Greenville, South Carolina, he had become a pastor in Washington, DC, in the 1970s. Madison took over the bishopric in much the same way that McCollough had: he became temporary leader upon the bishop's death, and was officially elected two months later, in May 1991. Madison received 360 of 570 votes cast, with most of the rest going to the late bishop's son Charles Leon McCollough. And, similar to what happened in McCollough's succession, but on a much smaller scale, a lawsuit was filed by unhappy congregants challenging Madison's election. Though the case was quickly dismissed by the judge, more lawsuits followed, including several bitter fights between McCollough's family and the church. For example, his widow, Clara, sued the church over small-scale valuables that each side claimed to own; almost all of this property was awarded to the church.[62] When Clara discovered that the memorial crypt for her husband would not have room for her, she sued to have his body exhumed and reburied on a private family plot in another cemetery.[63] In 1993, McCollough's son Charles had his preaching credentials rescinded after allegedly failing to demonstrate the appropriate respect for Madison as the new bishop; this did not result in a lawsuit, but it did cause waves of strife among House of Prayer factions. But these were all minor personal issues when compared with what had occurred after Grace's death, and they caused relatively little trouble. And, despite the fights with the family, Bishop Madison maintained that McCollough had been "a great spiritual adviser" and that the church's esteem for him was not diminished by such troubles.[64]

Assuming the title Precious Daddy, Madison followed the organizational footprint left by McCollough, and most church practices have not undergone change. He continued building new Houses of Prayer, undertook a multimillion dollar renovation of the Harlem worship space, and oversaw the completion of other building initiatives. He kept

late 1970s it had moved to a place much closer to the religious mainline, to a category once known as "established sect," and that is essentially where it remains today.

Two definitional structures used by New Religious Movement (NRM) scholars show why the House of Prayer could reasonably be called a cult or a sect. Under one system of definition, used especially by social scientists, a religious group's origins are the main factor for measurement. Thus, if a group began as a break from an established church it is considered a sect; if it began independently, such as by being based on a new teacher, new revelation, or new God, it is considered a cult. By this definition, Grace's church is always going to be classified as a cult whether one is focusing on the past, the present, or the future.[68] A second system of definition uses ideological social location as the main factor of measurement. A group whose ideas and beliefs are vastly and irrevocably distant from its society's belief structure should be considered a cult, whereas one whose ideas are still within range of the dominant ideological structure would be considered a sect. By this definition, Grace's church has never been anything less than a sect, because it is a Christian religion in a predominantly Christian society.[69]

Another way to think about this issue comes from the American religion field, and particularly African American religious history, where slightly different categories have been used. Here, the words "mainstream" and "mainline" are interchangeable terms used by scholars to describe religious bodies of legitimacy. Usually employed to discuss Protestant religious groups of the twentieth century, these terms explain the extent to which a church fits in with the dominant social and religious ethos of its time, and so they essentially serve the same function as the sociological category "church." Though there has been some debate, in general the Black churches consistently considered mainline in the past several decades are Presbyterian, Methodist, Baptist, Congregational, and Episcopal. As anthropologists Hans Baer and Merrill Singer explain it, "These bodies constitute the 'mainline' or 'mainstream' churches in the African-American community in that their orientation is toward the Black middle class and they have achieved both social legitimacy and stability."[70] Much like "church," mainline religion is then contrasted with groups labeled "sects," "cults," and "storefronts."[71]

Even if scholars could agree on one schema for measurement and precise definitions of the terms in use, distinct categorical boxes such as any of those suggested above fail to explain groups as they change; they merely pinpoint where a group is at a given moment in time, and then freeze it there.[72] Not only do religious societies change internally, but the larger society around them—the city, the country, the political system, the popular culture, the religious climate—also changes. Hence our perception of every religious group is both dialectical and fluid, rather than based on a set of fixed objective standards.[73] Scholars continue to note this among the challenges of categorization, and they debate possible solutions.[74] Sociologist Eileen Barker has repeatedly pointed out an aspect of this problem which she phrases as the question, "When does a new religion stop being new?" To Barker's question we might add the follow-up question, What does a group become when it is no longer "new"?[75] "Cults" do not automatically upgrade to "sects," but there is no name for the transitional status. Numerous religious groups do not fit neatly into any particular category that could be suggested: some are neither cult nor sect, but somewhere between the two, and others linger in the vicinity of the mainline but by virtue of their growing body of beliefs and practices are either moving toward or away from it. It would be especially helpful to have a label for groups that are in between sect and the mainline/church end of the spectrum, as a great number of religious groups pass through this space at one time or another.[76]

The United House of Prayer exemplifies this problem. The church ceased being a "cult" when Daddy Grace died. It was not primarily the beliefs or practices of the church members that had pushed the House of Prayer to the cult end of the spectrum all along; it was caused by society's unwillingness to take the church leader seriously, and its inability to see the church institution as distinct from the leader. In essence, the bishop's flamboyance kept the church locked out of public acceptability. By the time Walter McCollough was elected bishop, the church had already moved toward a sectarian middle ground. Within a few short years McCollough enacted his largest institutional changes, particularly forming programs of social outreach and eliminating some of the less conventional public events. Not only did this move the church into the "sect" realm, but also the more the church became politically and socially involved in the wider communities, the more its socio-religious legitimacy increased. By the late 1970s, when politicians regularly called upon McCollough for endorsement and he received a Presidential Commendation for his leadership, the House of Prayer was categorically located in the interstice between sect and church. Furthermore, because of its developmental stasis since that time, the church remains in that interstice to this day. In other words, the House of Prayer has spent much of its existence in a liminal state on the sociological continuum of church/sect/cult. If we measure it instead on a scale that uses storefront, sect, and mainline church, the result is much the same. The question, then, is what to do with groups that are in these interstices. Does one merely acknowledge the imperfection of the scale? Should new names for additional designations be invented, or perhaps a new scale altogether? Any of these could be legitimate solutions.

I suggest that we begin by incorporating a decades-old term used by sociologist Milton Yinger, the "established sect."[77] Though Yinger wrote about this category at length, including many intricate subdivisions, the category does not appear to have gained any momentum in the academic world.[78] He theorized the category as a step up from sect, indicative of a group in which the organization as a whole is becoming increasingly legitimate relative to the dominant religions. He explained the meaning of the category this way: "The established sect is somewhat more inclusive, less alienated, and more structured than the sect," and Yinger's term readily describes groups in transition.[79] If we evaluate the House of Prayer in terms of both internal beliefs and behavior and external perceptions, under Daddy Grace the church was undeniably far from mainline religion. However, in the absence of a flamboyant leader, and with the modest changes effected by Grace's successor Walter McCollough, the church moved clear through the sect stage and toward the church end of the spectrum. However, the House of Prayer is not there yet, and may never be; instead, the House of Prayer is an established sect.

In addition to its categorical shifts, another reason the post-Grace House of Prayer is compelling is because of how it compares with other religions whose "charismatic leader" has died. Max Weber's work analyzing the institutionalization of charisma offers a prelude to considering these circumstances. Weber suggested that charismatic authority inevitably transforms into either "rational" or "traditional" forms of authority via a process called "routinization."[80] In a broad sense, the House of Prayer does follow this pattern, and so one could place it on Weber's trajectory. Yet this theory has limited use in this case, in part because the process of routinization in the House of Prayer began long before Grace's death, and in part because numerous social dimensions of the church and its members are at issue here, rather than merely the authority vested in the office of the bishopric.[81] Nonetheless, Weber's identification of a multifaceted process that guides groups as they undergo leadership transitions is helpful for considering the overall developmental curve of the House of Prayer.

More recently, specialists in NRM studies have analyzed the courses followed by socially marginal religious groups in the years following the death of their founding leaders. In the preface to his edited volume on the subject, scholar Tim Miller writes, "The conventional wisdom has long been that most new religious movements are so heavily dependent on a single dominant personality that they cannot long survive that leader's passing."[82] He adds that the longevity of new religions has often been written about utilizing a variety of presumptions that appear logical on the surface, but that are shown to be without merit when the actual results are investigated. The essays in Miller's volume demonstrate that the "conventional wisdom" about the demise of groups is not borne out with many examples. Instead, in case after case, new religious groups have emerged from a powerful leader's death with renewed strength after experiencing a tumultuous, but relatively short, interim period. Many times they enter a new phase of institutional development and public acceptance, although this does not necessarily insure their longevity. The worst they tend to experience is a small group's breaking away in opposition to new leadership. Examples of this evolutionary pattern include the Shakers, the Mormons, Christian Science, the Theosophical Society, and the International Society for Krishna Consciousness. These groups not only stayed together, but flourished far beyond original levels of success in the years after the death of the founding leader.[83]

As we have seen, the United House of Prayer clearly follows this blueprint of "postcharismatic fate." There was indeed a time of crisis, upon Daddy Grace's death in 1960. Conflicts over the assessment of his estate and the vacancy of the bishopric dominated the troubles, and many of these battles had to be resolved through the courts. A handful of leaders and members broke away to form a new church. However, within a few short years the institution pulled itself together, and under the leadership of successor Sweet Daddy McCollough the church became a pillar of strength and pride in many communities. Although no longer dominating headlines, when the church did find itself in the news it was for things like scholarships, affordable-housing programs, and awards bestowed upon its bishop, rather than an accidental drowning during baptism, a Mann Act violation, or a fancy new mansion for the bishop. By focusing his changes on the church's public image, rather than on himself, McCollough was able to move it toward respectability among a wider audience. He could not have done this if Grace had not laid solid foundations in the realms of membership and finance; and he might not have seen the need for it without all of the very public problems that arose after Grace's death. Ultimately, McCollough succeeded in taking the chaotic confusion of the "cult" called the United House of Prayer for all People and transforming it into a respectable, nearly indistinguishable, African American religious body within the Pentecostal tradition.

Conclusion

The leadership of Daddy Grace deserves more than the cursory scholarly dismissal it has received for so many decades. As a daring institutional leader and a savvy businessman, Grace was the inspiration and motivational figurehead for a church that affected the lives of hundreds of thousands of Americans over several decades. The House of Prayer gave members a place to invest their creative energies, rewarding them with a community of believers and, often, a unique role within that community. Furthermore, Grace's success would be almost unfathomable were it not for the fact that he achieved the conventional "American dream." Despite being an immigrant from a tiny Afro-Lusophone country and not having an extensive formal education, Grace built a vast organization with less than a decade of effort. He began by connecting small groups of people in both northern and southern locales up and down the East Coast, and he made them feel they were part of a big, important religious community; they, in turn, believed in that vision and helped make it a reality. Using strategies including open letters to his congregations, church publications distributed nationally, regularly scheduled regional events, and an annual touring cycle, Daddy Grace united religious seekers and provided them with social and religious fulfillment. The degree to which he made something out of nothing means he must be counted among not only the significant creative religious strategists of his era, but also with other dramatically self-made men in the North American context, such as John Jacob Astor, Andrew Carnegie, or even the American-born Franklin W. Woolworth. Though his success was in a vastly different kind of endeavor than these entrepreneurs', their paths were the same: all were born into families of modest means, each young man had a vision of a larger enterprise he wanted to create, and each persisted with his goals through every incremental step toward "success."

In fact, one can draw reasonable lines of comparison not only between Grace and other self-made immigrant men, but also between

Grace and numerous categories of success stories. The most obvious comparison is that which has been made for decades: grouping Daddy Grace with other religious leaders of urban African Americans during the same era, such as Elijah Muhammad and Ida Robinson. One might reasonably compare him to other immigrants who became social leaders or to Pentecostal ministers or to preachers whose appeal straddled the Mason-Dixon line or to any number of other possible groups. However, the most beneficial comparison grows out of those factors that are particularly unique to Grace: his uncanny conglomeration of religion, pageantry, money, fame, and scandal. If Grace were alive to embody these characteristics in the present day, surely he would be discussed in the popular tabloids as a celebrity.

In many ways, Daddy Grace was a celebrity preacher: a religious leader who became famous as much for who he was, or was perceived to be, as for what he actually did. After Grace reached a certain level of fame, people would have been hard-pressed to explain whether they went to House of Prayer events because of the particular religious content offered in services or just because they had heard of the bishop. He regularly went on tour to keep his public happy, and in each town admirers flocked around him, longing to see and to touch and to be touched by Grace. Along with them came the curious, who wanted to see what the fuss was about. Like a modern celebrity, Grace traveled in style with an entourage, he dressed in what seemed like costumes, and he had keen sense about publicity and interacting with the media. Though he was merely continuing in the distinctly American Protestant tradition of celebrity ministry, he was among the first to create a path for nonwhite preachers, and his personal style of fame was in many ways ahead of its time. Grace's counterparts in that tradition included men who came long before him, like George Whitefield, Charles Finney, and Dwight Moody; overlapping with him were Billy Sunday and, though less of a character, Billy Graham; and not long after him came men such as Oral Roberts and Pat Robertson. Today, African American celebrity preachers who stylistically echo Daddy Grace include men such as Reverend Ike, Creflo Dollar, and T. D. Jakes, as well as the occasional preacher who straddles religion and politics, such as Al Sharpton. But among Black men of the past, almost none became celebrity preachers based on religion alone; instead most who rose to prominence combined religion and politics, becoming either celebrity preachers who had a foot in politics, or celebrity politicians who had a foot in religion. Such men included Father Divine, Adam Clayton Powell Jr., and Martin Luther King Jr., and by further stretches of the boundaries, Marcus Garvey and Malcolm X. But during the first half of the twentieth century, Daddy Grace stands alone as a Black male celebrity preacher whose message was almost entirely religious, and whose appeal was more along the lines of indulgence and guilty pleasure than education or a plan for social empowerment.[1] This fact does not discredit the legacy of the House of Prayer, nor does it suggest that Grace created his organization haphazardly. Rather, as this text has demonstrated, Grace clearly and deliberately used his cachet as a figure of public fascination to build a religious institution that attracted a unique audience. Grace himself was most certainly an original.

Despite his contributions to American religion, the public is often more interested in hearing lurid gossip about the rich and famous. Questions about Grace's romantic life repeatedly resurface, such as about Minnie Lee Campbell and Louvenia Royster, regardless of their place in the House of Prayer story.[2] For instance, during the course of my research I have frequently been asked whether Daddy Grace was gay. Cultural stereotypes of homosexual men, particularly those related to appearance, presumably drive such questions. Clearly, Grace's sense of fashion was unusual, but I believe it is largely anachronistic to interpret his particular style of dress as a sign of homosexuality. And, though it is true he spent much time with close male companions, during his era nothing about that behavior would have been particularly indicative of homosexual relationships. Furthermore, since he was unmarried for most of his years, it would have been unwise for him to travel and work closely with female companions; we need look no further for proof than the Minnie Lee Campbell scandal, which in fact occurred during his second marriage. So to those who ask this question, I reply that only the ghosts of history know the answer; but I have never found any evidence to suggest that Grace engaged in homosexual relationships.[3]

Beyond the grandeur of Grace's personality, and in addition to the parts of his leadership that contribute to a comprehensive picture of American religion, many aspects of the history of the House of Prayer as an institution add new contours to the growing body of scholarship on Pentecostalism. Today, debate continues about exactly who Pentecostals are and precisely what defines Pentecostalism as a religious tradition.

Historians approach the answers by considering the schools of thought that influenced various religious leaders, the established religious traditions they grew out of, and the organizations they built as a result of these influences. Other scholars who are more theologically oriented will answer the questions by considering the characteristics of belief and practice that unite certain Christians into something uniquely Pentecostal. Believers are likely to define themselves even more narrowly, based on particular beliefs and/or associations. Thus the boundaries demarcating what is or is not Pentecostalism can and do vary widely, including different approaches to the inclusion of Nazarene and Holiness history.[4] Consistently, certain groups have been omitted from the historical record; in fact, for many decades, it seemed the only "correct" history of Pentecostalism was white history of white Pentecostalism. Now the academic accounts of the past have begun to shift, more commonly including African American and Latino Pentecostalism as requisite for a full picture, but still the more marginal forms are pushed to the sidelines. Vinson Synan, historian of the Holiness-Pentecostal tradition, has written that although the House of Prayer has "demonstrated charismatic or emotional phenomena resembling Pentecostal worship, [it has] never been recognized as part of the Pentecostal movement as a whole."[5] In this sense, it does not stand alone: Synan names a handful of African American churches that appear, by way of charismatic practice, to fall within the boundaries of the tradition but that are not typically included in the annals of Pentecostal history.[6] Many would argue that these churches fall too far outside of the mainstream in belief and/or practice to be included; yet this kind of delineation seems to be the precise opposite of what the nature of Pentecostalism has always been. Since the first moment of Azusa Street, and with many precursors to that event, the Pentecostal tradition has been characterized by the fluidity of experiential forms of worship rooted in the direction of the spirit and very much connected to the significance of spiritual gifts.[7] Hence, those churches that spring from that sentiment must be considered part of the tradition, most especially when other aspects such as structure or practices also align with the larger body.

The omission of so many churches from the historical record has the consequence of altering our understanding of the tradition's breadth. Can we fully understand Pentecostal leadership, for example, if we ignore all of the churches whose leaders have been considered crude, unsophisticated, or boorish? Likewise, are we able to understand the range of leadership if we ignore all of the pastors whom Synan refers to as "dominating men who built entire denominations around their personalities"?[8] If such men and their followers are disregarded, our understanding of Pentecostal thought and development is also seriously altered. Similarly, we cannot fully comprehend the extent of spiritual healing if we exclude religious groups that utilize it in ways beyond our comfort level. And certainly there is no way we can understand patterns of numeric growth and expansion, especially as predictive indicators for the future, if random Pentecostal bodies such as those typically dismissed as "storefronts" are excluded from the record.

Other less obvious areas of religious history are also bereft when less acceptable religious institutions are tossed by the wayside. I am reminded of a time, years ago, when I was enlisted to research grassroots Christian organizing. In particular, the inquirer thought I should examine Billy Graham. How did Billy Graham transform from an unknown itinerant evangelist to a man who attracted thousands to every speaking engagement? What strategies did he use when he came to town, I was asked to learn, in order to get people in the door? Today, I know that my colleague's questions about grassroots organizing and religious leadership could just as easily have been answered through the example of Daddy Grace, who did exactly the same thing decades before Graham. Furthermore, there are probably many others whose skills with management and expansion have much to teach us. Instead of merely making the usual assumptions that a figure like Grace would have attracted the most economically and socially deprived individuals to his ramshackle worship spaces, real inquiry shows that he succeeded in neighborhoods of all socio-economic strata, that he attracted people of varying backgrounds, and that he created a structure to unite them as a single worshipping body. Reconsideration of his tactics, therefore, reveals a multitude of data that might be useful to researchers all across the spectrum of religious and sociological study.

Spiritual healing is an important aspect of the House of Prayer that also contributes to our understanding of the ebbs and flows of the phenomenon both within Pentecostalism and within broader Christianity. Many of the healing-oriented preachers in the early Pentecostal tradition operated much as Grace did in his first days, holding extended revival-type meetings with an emphasis on repentance and general spiritual gifts, offering daytime prayer groups in addition to the nightly services, and toward the end of each week, introducing healing as a focal point of the nightly meetings.[9] One thing that differentiates Grace from other healers contemporary with him is that, in the early period, Pentecostal healers primarily remained itinerant evangelists. Though the label "healer" was given to particular individuals, they themselves were more likely to consider healing a minor aspect of their ministerial repertoire. Few of these healers were focused on starting churches. Therefore Grace, like healing evangelist Aimee Semple McPherson, was among a small number who were committed to establishing an institution out of those who, one by one, responded to an altar call.[10] As scholar Nancy Hardesty astutely points out, "Focusing more directly on one person as a dispenser of healing, despite all of their [sic] efforts to give God the credit, changed perceptions of divine healing."[11] Thus, for those who gained reputations as healers and decided they wanted to establish churches, it was a challenge within reach due to the psychological investment believers had already made. In these ways, the House of Prayer is very much in line with common trends of early twentieth-century Protestant healing, but it was unique in its extensive use of proxy devices. Healing by proxy was not only accomplished through letters to the bishop, but also via spiritual remedies made possible by the curative potential of Grace products. In this aspect of practice, the House of Prayer must be counted among only a select few religious groups whose unusual avenues to healing defy both precedent and easy categorization.

Certainly, early Pentecostalism was tumultuous as it sought to organize and define itself, and it was marked by its rapid and repeated schisms. The splits stemmed as much from perceptions of racial and socio-economic barriers as they did from differences in theological interpretation. As the teens turned into the twenties, divided factions aligned more clearly. Many individual African American Holiness churches became affiliated with one of the newly established denominations, such as the Church of God in Christ, the Fire-Baptized Church of God of the Americas, or the Church of God (Cleveland, Tennessee); many people who sought a specifically white version of Pentecostalism moved into the Assemblies of God, and many who sought to reinforce their Holiness roots affiliated with the Church of the Nazarene. By 1925, the major branches of Pentecostalism that remain today had been established.[12] The House of Prayer, as a church that experienced its "official" start and its real growth after this basic stage of Pentecostal development, represented another spiritual-gift-focused alternative for those whose needs were never quite met by the larger choices. It is not surprising that Grace never aligned with any of the larger denominations, because many of his original members had specifically chosen to join the House of Prayer rather than those other denominations to begin with. The unique features of the early church set it apart within the tradition, and with both positive and negative consequences, apart is where it remained. The House of Prayer remained independent as it grew, as it developed a highly respected form of religious music, and as it became a wealthy property holder; but it also remained alone as mainstream ministers worked ecumenically on political issues, as charismatic denominations moved into public respectability, and as the history books were written. It is this work, I hope, that now demonstrates the benefit of bringing the House of Prayer into other conversations in which it could and should have been included all along.

The goal of this text was to start afresh with what seemed to be a tainted subject and to tell the story of the founding and development of the United House of Prayer for All People in a respectful manner. As the work unfolded, I realized that part of my own fascination with Grace as a leader is that for me he represents the opposite of *gestalt*. That is, I find the individual pieces of Grace's leadership style and his church's development at least as compelling, if not more so, than the sum of the parts. The sum is a quirky and cartoonish leader, but that impression belies the depth of each piece of the institution he actualized. In seeing how Grace built his church step by step, we can recognize his ability to assess the state of American religious life and fill a void by combining theology and social experiences. Furthermore, both by tracing its early history and by introducing the changes in the post-Grace years of the church, I have demonstrated that the House of Prayer has evolved without losing its individuality. Although today it is a different kind of institution than what one would have experienced in the early 1930s when Daddy Grace first came to town, its original spirit and unique roots are still visible if one knows what to look for.

In the summer of 2004 when I attended the House of Prayer's firehose baptism in Harlem, I experienced for myself the inimitable spirit of the church, which is not merely historical but is alive and well. When I emerged from the subway that Sunday morning, the convocation event was already in action. Various elders spoke from a stage set up in the middle of 115th Street, while hundreds of people milled about, laughing and mingling and buying food from women at makeshift tables. The sound system did not allow for clarity, so the words of the speakers

Daddy Grace's tomb, Pine Grove Cemetery, New Bedford, Massachusetts, 1999. Author's collection.

were difficult to understand over the carefree noise of the crowd. Buses arrived and more people, dressed all in white, poured into the street. I looked up and around, trying to figure out where the famous building of Father Divine and Daddy Grace had once stood, but the high-rise housing complex that replaced it was disorienting. All at once, a shiny black car eased through the throng and stopped just at the edge of the stage, where a brass band was perched on the curb. Daddy Madison emerged and was helped to the platform, and as he said a few words an assistant held an umbrella over his head to shade him from the hot August sun. The crowd quieted and two men readied the hose. Daddy Madison prayed over the hose, consecrating the water, and as the shout band suddenly broke into joyful song the water surged up and out over the crowd. In the street, people of all ages allowed themselves to be soaked, some dancing and swaying and others merely standing still, with heads bowed and clothes dripping. Some looked to the heavens, some talked with their friends, and others seemed to be adrift in a very personal place. I felt embarrassed to be a tourist, but I also felt deeply connected to this event and its long history. For half an hour, while the rush of water and lively music continued, I circumnavigated the crowd, taking photographs and absorbing the scene. Sooner or later I got too close to the action, and in an instant I took a hit from the baptismal water. Does it "count" if it was an accidental baptism? Although at the time I jumped back and frantically tried to dry my camera with my soggy shirt, I like to think that the surprise splash of water was a sign that I was absolved for committing the acts of research and writing.

Watching the House of Prayer baptism crystallized the spirit of the church for me in a way that articles and artifacts never had, and it made more complicated the question of how much the church has grown away from its roots. The House of Prayer is a different institution today from what it was, but many figurative foundation walls built by Bishop Grace still support it. This text has sought to bring the entirety of that history together in one picture. In addition to offering new insights about the development of the church, the results of this exploration show that Daddy Grace's grandiose persona does not need to be overblown as it has been in the past, as though his behavior were the only thing worth noting about the church, nor does it need to be denied, as if his legacy cheapened or embarrassed the institution. In today's society

BORN JANUARY 25, 1881
CAPE VERDE ISLANDS,
PORTUGAL

DEPARTED JANUARY 12, 1960
LOS ANGELES,
CALIFORNIA

ON JANUARY 23, 1960
RETURNED TO NEW BEDFORD
WHERE HE HAD FOUNDED
THE HOUSE OF PRAYER
FOR ALL PEOPLE

Inscription on Daddy Grace's tomb, Pine Grove Cemetery, New Bedford, Massachusetts, 1999. Author's collection.

we can accept that Daddy Grace was a bit of a character, and way ahead of his time, and appreciate that he was unafraid to plow forward with his own style of conducting business no matter how people reacted to him. For his independence, he must be admired, and for the religious community he envisioned and created, he must be respected. Together, the elements of his church help explain the larger story of Grace's unique contribution to the history of American religious leadership and within that, the broad spectrum of charismatic worship in twentieth-century America.

An Essay on Sources

Sources for this project have been many and varied, and most of them were buried under piles of dust up and down the East Coast. I trust there are many more to be uncovered by the next researcher, and I wish him or her the best of luck in unearthing things that will help us better understand the rich complexity of Daddy Grace and the United House of Prayer. In an effort to orient those interested both in this specific research and in researching African American religious history more broadly, I offer here an explanation of some of the sources used.

Several particular collections were helpful in my work, and will certainly be useful for anyone else studying Grace and the House of Prayer. The Daddy Grace collection at Emory University contains an interesting assortment of items, about half of which relate to more recent history of the church. The folder on Daddy Grace from the MALP Collection at the Schomburg Center contains a bevy of valuable documents, primarily unusual House of Prayer publications. In addition to the House of Prayer publications found at George Washington University, the university's library also owns several unique pieces of Daddy Grace ephemera, such as stamps and jewelry. Photographs of Grace and/or church activities can be found in each of these libraries, as well as in the photograph files of newspapers.

The *Grace Magazine,* the house organ of the United House of Prayer, is one of the single most valuable resources on the church, and so it is regrettable that very few issues are available for study. From what I have been able to ascertain, the *Grace Magazine* began publication in the mid-1920s and was printed three times a year. Probably beginning in the late 1930s and lasting into the mid-1950s, Elder Ernest Mitchell was its editor. In addition to theologically oriented articles written by Mitchell, the magazine contained news reports of church events and letters in which members testified about their faith and spiritual experiences. I have been able to see only four and a half issues of the *Grace*

Magazine; two of these are held by the University of Pennsylvania, two are held by George Washington University, and half of one issue is located in the MALP Collection at the Schomburg Center.

Another internal document, a booklet of Bible study lessons, is the *House of Prayer Quarterly,* seven issues of which are held by Gelman Library Special Collections. Each page contains a short Biblical passage followed by the "Main Thought," which was essentially an explanation of the passage that related it in some way to present-day beliefs and practices. Each lesson concludes with a list of Bible readings for the following week. It is not at all clear who selected these passages nor what criteria were used for selection and arrangement; however, the correlation of certain passages with particular House of Prayer events demonstrates that the arrangement was at least partially deliberate. The overall consistency of the Main Thought may mean that it was written by as few as two people, or that it was carefully edited by one or two people. There seem to be at least two distinct voices in the Main Thought, one that sticks closely to textual interpretation, and another that uses the verse as a springboard for much broader analysis of the human condition. The one early issue available contains a much heavier emphasis on the special role of Daddy Grace than do the later issues.

Many, but not all, articles from the *Charlotte News* and the *Charlotte Observer* were found in the clippings files held by the newsroom library of the *Charlotte Observer.* Although dates stamped on the clippings are supposed to be the dates of publication, in several instances I found this was not the case. Therefore, all references to articles that I found in that collection are designated with the suffix [cc], for "clippings collection"; references to articles from either the *News* or *Observer* that do not include the suffix mean that I located the article in the newspaper itself and therefore can assure the accuracy of the date. The same dating issue applies to articles found in the *New Bedford Standard-Times* clippings collection, cited throughout as "NBST cc" and including items from the *New Bedford Times,* the *New Bedford Evening Standard,* and the *New Bedford Standard-Times.*

This newspaper-dating issue helps to clarify Lenwood Davis's bibliography on Daddy Grace. While Davis provides an important key for starting research on Grace, in fact many of the citations in his book contain errors, making it frustrating to use. While I cannot account for all of the errors, it is clear that Davis used the *Charlotte Observer* library for his references to items in Charlotte papers and that the incorrect stamped dates were reproduced in his bibliography. Perhaps similar issues were the cause of other errors in his volume.

Several newspaper reporters who wrote about Grace in an ongoing way, either in a specific series or more generally, distinguished themselves with their work. Though I cannot be certain about the validity of every point he made, articles by James L. Hicks, executive director of the *New York Amsterdam News,* were accurate in both broad assertions and particular details. I used his work with less trepidation than, for instance, articles by Paul Benzaquin of the *Boston Globe,* who made gross errors of fact in his 1960 article series on Grace. After the bishop's death, Phil Casey of the *Washington Post* put together a decent and compact series that is mostly a pastiche of earlier articles; as a primer on Grace, I recommend his series foremost to any researcher. A 1960 series in the *Baltimore Afro-American* and written by Rufus Wells is particularly interesting because it contains numerous assertions of fact that I have never seen anywhere else. This makes me both curious and skeptical. For example, Wells claims that Grace came to the States in 1900 as a seaman, that he was first ordained in San Francisco, and that his first wife used to call him "Charlie." I could make a long list of such unusual items. Either Wells had a unique source for his information, such as a person or persons who had been close to Grace, or he made these things up. Finally, prior to his illustrious career, Charles Kuralt interviewed Grace in 1956 and wrote a detailed and praiseworthy three-part series for the *Charlotte News.*

Information about *Mankind Homebuilders, Inc., v. The United House of Prayer for All People, Inc.,* and other related cases was found on microfilm at the City of Philadelphia Prothonotary's Office Older Records Division. The film contains over 550 microfilmed pages, not especially in order, of documents related to the case, including partial records from several different cases in other jurisdictions. Testimony from *United States v. Charles M. Grace,* also known as the Mann Act case, was found in a printed case file at the New York City division of the National Archives of the United States.

This project also involved numerous unsuccessful attempts at research. For example, I tried to obtain files from both the Federal Bureau of Investigation and the Tax Division of the United States Department of Justice. Those that came from the FBI were surprisingly disappointing, containing very little of interest. Furthermore, the file for the United House of Prayer for All People contains exactly the same information as the file for Marcelino Manuel da Graca, except that the two files were redacted differently. The most interesting file the FBI sent was, unfortunately, for an entirely different man by the name of C. N. De Grace of Portland, Oregon. The Tax Division of the Justice Department was unable to locate any public records on Daddy Grace. In another corner of the world, despite their best efforts, my assistants, Alexis Adorno and Raque Kunz, were unable to track down any birth or baptismal records for the da Graca family in Cape Verde, though I appreciate their work. And finally, though Marilyn Schuster of Atkins Library Special Collections, University of North Carolina, Charlotte, enthusiastically assisted me, I found nothing about the House of Prayer or Daddy Grace in either the Harry Golden papers or the microfilm collection of Charlotte newspaper clippings.

Portions of the research were undertaken in each of the following places: Paley Library at Temple University, including the Urban Archives; the Charles L. Blockson Collection, Temple University; Lamont Library, Andover-Harvard Theological Library, and the Loeb Design Library, all at Harvard University; the Charles D. Cahoon Local History and Genealogy Room of the Brooks Free Library, Harwich, Massachusetts; the library of the *New Bedford Standard-Times*; the New Bedford Free Public Library; the library at the *Charlotte Observer*; Gelman Library Special Collections, George Washington University; the Robinson-Spangler Carolina Room of the Public Library of Charlotte and Mecklenburg County, North Carolina; the United States Library of Congress; the Prothonotary's Office of Older Records and the Department of Records at Philadelphia City Hall; Howard University Divinity Library and the Moorland Spingarn Research Center of Howard University; Annenberg Rare Book and Manuscript Library at the University of Pennsylvania; the Manuscripts, Archives, and Rare Books Division of Woodruff Library, Emory University; the Schomburg Center for Research in Black Culture, New York Public Library; the Free Library of Philadelphia; the National Archives of the United States, College Park and New York City divisions; Atkins Library Special Collections, University of North Carolina at Charlotte; and the library of the American University in Washington, DC.

Notes

NOTES TO THE INTRODUCTION

1. News release, 16 Aug. 1948, *Claude A. Barnett Papers* (Frederick, MD: University Publications of America, 1986), microfilm part 3, series J, reel 1.

2. Based on Biblical interpretation, Daddy Grace was very strict about not believing in "churches," and so members never refer to the United House of Prayer as a church. However, solely for practical reasons, I do use this word to refer to their religious organization, but I do so recognizing that it would be a distasteful choice for House of Prayer members.

3. Arthur Huff Fauset Papers, 1855–1983, box 4, folder 99, Rare Book and Manuscript Library, University of Pennsylvania, Philadelphia. (Hereafter cited as Fauset Papers.)

4. Alex Poinsett, "Farewell to Daddy Grace," *Ebony*, April 1960, 25.

5. Wilson Jeremiah Jones, *Black Messiahs and Uncle Toms: Social and Literary Manipulations of a Religious Myth*, rev. ed. (University Park: Pennsylvania State Univ. Press, 1993), 12.

6. Paul Hunter, *Prophets and Profits: What's to Be Learned from Daddy Grace and Others Like Him* (New York: Revelation Books, 1996), 72.

7. For examples of such analyses and predictions, see: Albert N. Whiting, "The United House of Prayer for All People: A Case Study of a Charismatic Sect" (PhD dissertation, American University, Washington, DC, 1952), 185–86; John LaFarge, "The Incredible Daddy Grace," *America*, 2 April 1960, 5; *Baltimore Afro-American*, 27 Feb. 1960; *Charlotte Observer* cc, 5 Feb. 1960. As noted in the essay on sources, articles found in the morgue at the *Charlotte Observer*, which includes both the *Observer* and the *Charlotte News*, are designated with the suffix "cc" for "clippings collection," and their dates do not always match the dates of actual publication. Articles taken directly from these newspapers not include the suffix.

8. *Baltimore Afro-American*, 23 Jan. 1960.

9. *Washington Post*, 9 March 1960.

10. Grace's year of birth has been reported inconsistently, ranging from 1880 to 1883; 1881 is the year most consistently given. Because of this range of

birth dates, it is unclear whether he was slightly older or slightly younger than his sister Eugenia.

11. *Washington Post,* 7 March 1960.

12. *United States v. Charles M. Grace,* 2nd Cir. Ct. App. (1934), case file 13440, National Archives of the United States, New York City.

13. Edward Peeks, *The Long Struggle for Black Power* (New York: Scribner's, 1971), 253.

14. *Charlotte News,* 10 Sept. 1949; New Bedford Death Records; *United States v. Grace,* Government's Exhibit 5. Original spellings preserved.

15. Passenger and Crew Lists of Vessels Arriving at New York, 1897–1957, vol. 8011 (roll 3500); New Bedford Immigration and Ship Passenger Lists, 19 April 1902—24 Nov. 1903 (T944, roll 1).

16. He did so, though it was with a bit of difficulty and he pointed out that he did not have his reading glasses with him. *United States v. Grace.*

17. New Bedford Death Records; New Bedford Immigration and Ship Passenger Lists, 19 April 1902– 24 Nov. 1903 (T944, roll 1); Marilyn Halter, *Between Race and Ethnicity: Cape Verdean American Immigrants, 1860–1965* (Urbana: Univ. of Illinois Press, 1993).

18. *United States v. Grace.*

19. Ibid.

20. *New Bedford Standard-Times* cc, Oct. 31, 1926; *Baltimore Afro-American,* 5 March 1960; *Charlotte Observer,* 13 Jan. 1960. The *New Bedford Standard-Times* clippings collection, referred to hereafter as "NBST cc," serves as the morgue of three newspapers: the *New Bedford Times,* the *New Bedford Evening Standard,* and the *New Bedford Standard-Times.* The last paper was a result of the 1932 merger of the first two. The collection also includes articles from other newspapers with which the *New Bedford Standard-Times* had some affiliation, as well as documents that in-house reporters used for research. I was told that the dates stamped on each clipping reflect when the article was put in the collection, and therefore these are not always the precise dates of publication.

21. *Charlotte Observer* cc, 16 Jan. 1960.

22. NBST cc, telegram dated 4 Feb. 1960.

23. *United States v. Grace.*

24. Ibid.

25. *Charlotte News,* 13 Sept. 1936; Passenger and Crew Lists of Vessels Arriving at New York, 1897–1957, vol. 8011 (roll 3500).

26. "Sweet Daddy's Sugar," *Newsweek,* 15 Feb. 1960, 32; *Charlotte Observer* cc, 5 Sept. 1947; *Cleveland Call and Post,* 16 Jan. 1960; *Jet,* 10 May 1956, 23; *New Bedford Standard-Times,* 13 March 1958, repr. from *New York Herald Tribune,* n.d.; *Charlotte News,* 17 Aug. 1956, 8 Sept. 1941, 19 June 1959; *Baltimore Afro-American,* 27 Feb. 1960.

27. *Charlotte Observer* cc, 4 Feb. 1960; *New Bedford Standard-Times,* 18 Feb. 1933; *United States v. Grace.*

28. *Washington Post,* 9 March 1960; *Journal and Guide,* 31 July 1937; *New York Amsterdam News,* 26 March 1960.

29. *Washington Post,* 9 March 1960; *Charlotte News,* 17 Aug. 1956; *Charlotte Observer* cc, 5 Feb. 1960; *United States v. Grace.* Though Grace spoke about war on numerous occasions, there is no record of his addressing some of the most important social and political issues in his lifetime, such as the Great Migration, the Depression, and the civil rights movement. Grace's lack of direct commentary on large social issues was not atypical of African American Pentecostalism in the early part of the twentieth century.

30. NBST cc, 18 June 1924, 18 Sept, 1960; *Journal and Guide,* 9 Feb. 1935; *United States v. Grace; Charlotte News* cc, 10 Sept. 1949; "America's Richest Negro Minister," *Ebony,* Jan. 1952, 23; *Charlotte News,* 10 Sept. 1951.

31. *Charlotte Observer* cc, 18 Apr. 1951.

32. *Philadelphia Tribune,* 16 Jan. 1960; other examples include G. Norman Eddy, "Store-Front Religion," *Religion in Life* 28 (Winter 1958–59), 75; *Baltimore Afro-American,* 23 Jan. 1960, 27 Feb. 1960; *Charlotte News,* 19 June 1959, 10 Sept. 1949; *Jet,* 10 May, 1956, 23.

33. *Charlotte News,* 10 Sept. 1949.

34. *Washington Post,* 9 March 1960, 13 March 1960, 10 March 1960.

35. For example, see *Charlotte News,* 13 Sept. 1936.

36. Hunter, *Prophets and Profits,* 43.

37. *Washington Post,* 13 March 1960.

38. Ibid., 10 March 1960.

39. *New Bedford Standard-Times,* 27 July 1951.

40. Page 38 in this volume.

41. Arthur Huff Fauset, *Black Gods of the Metropolis: Negro Religious Cults of the Urban North* (Philadelphia: Univ. of Pennsylvania Press, 1944).

42. Additionally, the church continued to grow and develop as an institution beyond 1940, but the academic world did not make corresponding reassessments.

43. Eddy, "Store-Front Religion," 68–85. According to Lenwood Davis, Eddy also wrote an unpublished manuscript on "deviant religions" that included a section on the church; librarians at Boston University were unable to locate this manuscript. Lenwood G. Davis, comp., *Daddy Grace: An Annotated Bibliography* (New York: Greenwood Press, 1992).

44. Alexander Alland Jr., " 'Possession' in a Revivalistic Negro Church," *Journal for the Scientific Study of Religion* 1 (Spring 1962): 204–13.

45. John W. Robinson, "A Song, a Shout, and a Prayer," in *The Black Experience in Religion,* ed. C. Eric Lincoln, 213–35 (Garden City, NY: Anchor Books, 1974).

46. Arthur Carl Piepkorn, *Profiles in Belief,* vol. 3 (San Francisco: Harper and Row, 1977), 223–24.

47. John O. Hodges, "Charles Manuel 'Sweet Daddy' Grace," in *Twentieth-Century Shapers of American Popular Religion,* ed. Charles Lippy, 170–79 (New York: Greenwood Press, 1989).

48. Danielle Brune Sigler, "Daddy Grace: An Immigrant's Story," in *Immigrant Faiths: Transforming Religious Life in America,* ed. Karen I. Leonard et al., 67–78 (Walnut Creek, CA: AltaMira Press, 2005); Danielle Brune Sigler, "Beyond the Binary: Revisiting Father Divine, Daddy Grace, and Their Ministries," in *Race, Nation, and Religion in the Americas,* ed. Henry Goldschmidt and Elizabeth McAlister, 209–27 (New York: Oxford Univ. Press, 2004). Sigler is also the author of a dissertation on Grace, discussed below.

49. James Daniel Tyms, "A Study of Four Religious Cults Operating among Negroes" (master's thesis, Howard University, Washington, DC, 1938).

50. Chancellor Williams, "The Socio-Economic Significance of the Store-Front Church Movement in the United States Since 1920" (PhD dissertation, American University, Washington, DC, 1949).

51. Whiting, "United House." Whiting published a 1955 article based on his dissertation in the *Quarterly Review of Higher Education among Negroes.*

52. Jean E. Barker, "The Cape Verdean Immigrant Experience in Harwich, Massachusetts" (master's thesis, University of Massachusetts at Boston, 1993). I was not able to confirm all of Barker's findings independently.

53. Danielle E. Brune, "Sweet Daddy Grace: The Life and Times of a Modern Day Prophet" (PhD dissertation, University of Texas at Austin, 2002). Brune published her subsequent work under her married name, Sigler.

54. Catherine L. Albanese, *America: Religions and Religion,* 1st and 3rd eds. (Belmont, CA: Wadsworth Pub. Co., 1981, 1999). I do not mean to indicate that Albanese's work is insufficient overall; in fact, I consider her textbook one of the best in the field.

55. R. Marie Griffith, "Body Salvation: New Thought, Father Divine, and the Feast of Material Pleasures," *Religion and American Culture* 11, no. 2 (2001): 120.

56. Hans A. Baer and Merrill Singer, *African-American Religion in the Twentieth Century: Varieties of Protest and Accommodation* (Knoxville: Univ. of Tennessee Press, 1992). There were no changes to the section about Grace and the House of Prayer in the revised, 2002 edition of this book.

57. It is not completely clear why African American forms of religion are not readily explored within the NRM field. The answer may be related to the historical marginalization of African American people and the hegemony of whiteness and white subjects within scholarship. Specialists in African American religion, in efforts to reclaim untold history, are very willing to embrace and explore all forms of religion within their studies, and so African American

NRMs are often studied within this context. However, the answer may be less complicated, related to the fact that the NRM field is dominated by Caucasian scholars.

58. Gordon Langley Hall, *The Sawdust Trail: The Story of American Evangelism* (Philadelphia: Macrae Smith, 1964). Hall subsequently became a woman named Dawn Langley Simmons; some libraries have recatalogued Hall's books under this later name.

59. Hunter, *Prophets and Profits.*

60. *House of Prayer Quarterly* 12, no. 1 (1953). As a side note, the House of Prayer during Grace's years used only the King James Version of the Bible. Though scholars might find this version archaic, I have followed the church's lead on this point, and so all Biblical references are quoted from the King James Version.

61. *Baltimore Afro-American,* 23 Jan. 1960.

62. Payne, Wardell J., ed., *Directory of African American Religious Bodies,* 2nd ed. (Washington, DC: Howard Univ. Press, 1995), s.v. "United House of Prayer for All People, Church on the Rock of the Apostolic Faith, Inc."

63. My speculations are based on my own observations of active congregations on the East Coast, in combination with newspaper reports about church activity in the past fifteen years.

64. For example, consider this internal memo from a New Bedford newspaper: "NOTE: No mention is to be made, in any story about 'Bishop' Grace, of the fact that he at one time sold patent medicines on the Cape, or that he has been in court for any violations. This order comes from Mr. Lewin." NBST cc, 7 Oct. 1941.

65. More detailed information about newspaper sources can be found in the essay on sources.

66. I did not conduct such interviews for two reasons: first, a great many of the people I would want to hear from are deceased, and second, I received no response to my solicitations for the input of current House of Prayer leaders and members.

67. Two key volumes examining the theory of religious economy are Rodney Stark and Roger Finke, *Acts of Faith: Explaining the Human Side of Religion* (Berkeley and Los Angeles: Univ. of California Press, 2000), and Roger Finke and Rodney Stark, *The Churching of America, 1776–2005: Winners and Losers in Our Religious Economy* (New Brunswick, NJ: Rutgers Univ. Press, 2005).

68. Consider not only the content of news stories, but also the fact that stories about Grace and the church were rarely found on the Religion page and instead were lumped in with sensational news, often on the last page.

69. For a more extensive explication of this theory, see Stark and Finke, *Acts of Faith,* or Finke and Stark, *The Churching of America.*

70. Jones, *Black Messiahs,* 124–25.

NOTES TO CHAPTER 1

1. *New Bedford Evening Standard,* 8 Jan. 1922.

2. For much of the general Cape Verdean history on the following pages, including the section on race and class, I have synthesized and drawn on a number of sources to which I am indebted: Antonio Carreira, *The People of the Cape Verde Islands: Exploitation and Emigration* (Hamden, CT: Archon Books, 1982); Basil Davidson, *The Fortunate Isles: A Study of African Transformation* (Trenton, NJ: Africa World Press, 1989); Richard A. Lobban Jr., *Cape Verde: Crioulo Colony to Independent Nation* (Boulder, CO: Westview Press, 1995); Deirdre Meintel, *Race, Culture, and Portuguese Colonialism in Cabo Verde* (Syracuse, NY: Syracuse Univ. Press, 1984); Joao Monteiro, "The Church of the Nazarene in Cape Verde: A Religious Import in a Creole Society" (PhD dissertation, Drew University, Madison, NJ, 1997).

3. Baptism of all slaves who passed through Cape Verde was required by Portuguese law. Meintel, *Race, Culture,* 78.

4. According to Richard Lobban, slave movement from Cape Verde to New England was phased out in the late 1700s, but continued to Brazil until the early 1800s.

5. The structure of government, the division of land, and the patterns of slave ownership developed quite similarly in Lusophone Brazil. However, manumission was less frequent in Brazil, therefore power dynamics among African-descended peoples operated differently in both social and economic arenas. For more information on Portuguese colonization in Brazil, see Nancy Naro, *A Slave's Place, A Master's World: Fashioning Dependency in Rural Brazil* (New York: Continuum, 2000), and David Baronov, *The Abolition of Slavery in Brazil: The "Liberation" of Africans through the Emancipation of Capital* (Westport, CT: Greenwood Press, 2000).

6. Archibald Lyall, *Black and White Make Brown: An Account of a Journey to the Cape Verde Islands and Portuguese Guinea* (London: W. Heinemann, 1938), 140.

7. Records of the Dept. of State, Despatches from U.S. Consuls in Santiago, Cape Verde Islands, 1818–1898, *Appenso Ao "Boletim Official" Do Governo Da Provincia De Cabo Verde,* 1896 (RG-59), National Archives of the United States.

8. Augusto Casimiro, *Portugal Crioulo* (Lisbon: Edições Cosmos, 1940), 113. All references to Casimiro are my own translation.

9. Lyall, *Black and White,* 34, 150, 144–45; Meintel, *Race, Culture,* 21; Casimiro, *Portugal Crioulo,* 113.

10. Based on the retelling of this story in Lyall, *Black and White,* 142–43.

11. In the United States, natives of Brava are commonly referred to as "Bravas," though other terms, such as "Bravans" and "Bravenses," have also

been used. More generally, people of the islands have been called both "Cape Verdeans" and "Cape Verders."

12. K. David Patterson, "Epidemics, Famines, and Population in the Cape Verde Islands, 1580–1900." *International Journal of African Historical Studies* 21, no. 2 (1988): 293–98, 301–2; Meintel, *Race, Culture,* 2. Additionally, records of the Dept. of State imply that illness statistics may have gone underreported for the archipelago. For example, though there was a smallpox quarantine on St. Vincent in the summer of 1891, several consular agents inquired with their superior about whether their official reports should claim clean bills of health for the residents.

13. Patterson, "Epidemics," 299. Carreira points out that illnesses such as syphilis and tuberculosis became more prominent on Brava in the late 1800s, when emigrants began returning from the United States.

14. Patterson, "Epidemics," 291–95. However, even the nine thousand people of Brava were affected by the severe drought and famine from 1901 to 1904.

15. Meintel, *Race, Culture,* 17.

16. Ibid., 17, 26.

17. Lyall, *Black and White,* 141, 144; Casimiro, *Portugal Crioulo,* 92–94; George Finlay Simmons, "Sinbads of Science: Narrative of a Windjammer's Specimen-Collecting Voyage to the Sargasso Sea, to Senegambian Africa and among Islands of High Adventure in the South Atlantic," *National Geographic,* July 1927, 15.

18. Halter, *Between Race,* 45; Patterson, "Epidemics," 294–95. The immigration numbers represent only legal immigrants; it is certain that many more came clandestinely.

19. Lyall, *Black and White,* 141.

20. Quoted in ibid., 104. "Sodade" is the Crioulo spelling; in Portuguese it is "saudade."

21. Quoted in ibid., 105–6.

22. Ibid., 111.

23. Ibid., 149. According to Peter Manuel, *mornas* are often serious or sad poems written in the Crioulo language and set to music in an *aabb* melody pattern. For Mauel's explanation or more information, see: Richard Lobban and Marlene Lopes, *Historical Dictionary of the Republic of Cape Verde,* 3rd ed. (Metuchen, NJ: Scarecrow Press, 1995), 144; or Sherri Marcia Damon, "The Trombone in the Shout Band of the United House of Prayer for All People" (Doctor of Musical Arts dissertation, University of North Carolina at Greensboro, 1999), chapter 2.

24. The character Pedr is sometimes called Tubinh. For examples of these stories, see Elsie Clews Parsons, "Ten Folk-Tales from the Cape Verde Islands," *Journal of American Folk-Lore* 30 (April 1917): 230–38.

25. Monteiro, "Church of the Nazarene," 103–4; for example see Lyall, *Black and White*, 151.

26. Monteiro, "Church of the Nazarene," 108–9.

27. Ibid., 117–29.

28. Dierdre Meintel-Machado, "Language and Interethnic Relations in a Portuguese Colony," in *Ethnic Encounters: Identities and Contexts*, ed. George L. Hicks and Philip E. Leis, 49–62 (North Scituate, MA: Duxbury Press, 1977); Robert French, "A Perspective on Cape Verdean Crioulo," in *Spinner: People and Culture in Southeastern Massachusetts*, vol. 3 (New Bedford, MA: Spinner Publications, 1984); Pierre Bourdieu, *Language and Symbolic Power* (Cambridge, MA: Harvard Univ. Press, 1991).

29. Meintel-Machado, "Language," 60.

30. St. Clair Drake and Horace R. Cayton, *Black Metropolis: A Study of Negro Life in a Northern City*, vol. 2 (New York: Harcourt, Brace, 1945).

31. Monteiro, "Church of the Nazarene," 84.

32. Meintel, *Race, Culture*, 93–112.

33. Similarly, in the United States today the word "ghetto" is increasingly used as an adjective to refer to someone's class. Yet it also has racial nuances.

34. The exception to this would be *negro*, which is indeed considered insulting even as it might also be considered descriptive.

35. Davidson, *Fortunate Isles*, 30. Likewise, Meintel's anthropological research on Brava in the 1970s found 140 racial terms in use.

36. Belmira Nunes Lopes, *A Portuguese Colonial in America* (Pittsburgh: Latin American Literary Review, 1982), 4–5.

37. Judith A. Boss and Joseph D. Thomas, *New Bedford: A Pictorial History* (Norfolk, VA: Donning Publishers, 1983).

38. "Immigrants in New Bedford," 1911, New Bedford Free Public Library, New Bedford, MA.

39. Kingston William Heath, *The Patina of Place: The Cultural Weathering of a New England Industrial Landscape* (Knoxville: Univ. of Tennessee Press, 2001), 80–83; Marsha McCabe and Joseph D. Thomas, eds., *Portuguese Spinner: An American Story* (New Bedford, MA: Spinner Publications, 1998).

40. U.S. Bureau of the Census, 1900, Bristol County, Massachusetts (T-623, roll 638); "Immigrants in New Bedford," 5–8.

41. U.S. Census, 1900. The census did not identify Cape Verdeans in a way that distinguished them from people who were born in Portugal. However, it did specify each "Portuguese" person as being white or Black in color. Based on the work of historians who have examined the distinctly Portuguese area of New Bedford, it seems a safe assumption that most "Portuguese" people in this neighborhood, both white and Black, would have actually been from Cape Verde.

42. I was unable to locate his information in the ship records for this previ-

ous visit. It is possible that he came as a ship crew member, in which case a record is unlikely to exist. It is also possible he entered through a port other than New Bedford.

43. *Spinner,* vol. 4, 83.

44. New Bedford Immigration and Ship Passenger Lists, 19 April 1902–24 Nov. 1903 (T944, roll 1); *New Bedford and Fairhaven City Directory,* various years; U.S. Census, 1900; Sanborn Co. Fire Insurance Maps, City of New Bedford, 1888–1924. The ages of the da Graca children as listed here do not in all cases agree with the ages on their gravestones; for various reasons I defer to the ship manifests as being more likely to be correct. I was unable to locate any record of a previous visit to the United States by Marcelino; the possibility that this was his first trip is further supported by the fact that decades later the church was observing the anniversary of Grace's arrival to the United States on May 3rd, the arrival date of the *Luiza.*

45. Based on the more consistent recordings of the ages of their children, the most likely set of choices among these numbers is 48 for his father and 42 for his mother at the time of immigration in 1902, which meant his mother would have given birth to son Marcelino when she was 20 and to daughter Louise when she was 36.

46. An example of supporting information that corresponds with this is the fact that when Gertrude da Graca died, the property she owned at 242 Pleasant Street was divided five ways.

47. "Lewis Hine on the Cranberry Bogs," and Marilyn Halter, "Working the Cranberry Bogs: Cape Verdeans in Southeastern Massachusetts," both in *Spinner,* vol. 3.

48. "Immigrants in New Bedford," 17.

49. Sampled from the *New Bedford Evening Standard,* 10 Sept. 1904.

50. Sampled from the *New Bedford Morning Mercury,* 23 July 1904.

51. Interethnic tension was not limited to issues with Cape Verdeans. Relations among Azoreans, Madeirans, and continental Portuguese have also long been problematic. For a more recent exploration of this issue, see Stephen L. Cabral, *Tradition and Transformation: Portuguese Feasting in New Bedford* (New York: AMS Press, 1989).

52. *New Bedford Republican Standard,* 24 Dec. 1903.

53. Halter, *Between Race,* 148–49; *Churches of the Diocese of Fall River,* http://www.rootsweb.com/ussnei/FRdiocese.htm, 28 Jan. 2004.

54. NBST cc, 23 Aug. 1955; Author's visit to Pine Grove Cemetery, 2004.

55. NBST cc, 24 April 1963; Index to Passengers Arriving at New Bedford, 1 July 1902—18 Nov. 1954 (T522, roll 1). Elsewhere his Cape Verdean name has been given as Bonaventura and Braventura; I have no basis for determining which of these names is correct, and have chosen to use Benventura simply because it is the closest to "Benjamin," his American name.

56. Much of this has been written repeatedly in periodicals and books. Some of it is verifiable, other parts will always be questions. For examples, see Fauset, *Black Gods;* Robinson, "A Song"; Hodges, "Charles Manuel"; Hall, *The Sawdust Trail;* and *Baltimore Afro-American,* 2 Oct. 1926.

57. *New Bedford Evening Standard,* 8 Jan. 1922.

58. NBST cc, internal memo, Jan. 1923.

59. For an example of a "Black neighborhood" reference, see Margery Eagen, "Subtle Bigotry Halted Black Progress," *New Bedford Standard-Times,* 22 Feb. 1980.

60. The 1921 *City Directory* lists a barbershop run by Marcelino Manuel at 339 Kempton Street. Is this a striking coincidence, or is it the same man? There is no way to know.

61. For an in-depth analysis of the relationship of culture, economics, and the three-decker building, see Heath, *Patina of Place.*

62. Sanborn Maps; *City Directories;* U.S. Bureau of the Census, 1920, Bristol County, Massachusetts (T-625, roll 686); *New Bedford Evening Standard,* 17 Dec. 1921, 11 Feb. 1922; NBST cc, 8 Jan. 1922. For more on the concepts involved in a religious economy, see Stark and Finke, *Acts of Faith.*

63. *City Directories;* Sanborn Maps; NBST cc, 8 Jan. 1922, 24 Aug. 1922, internal memo, Jan. 1923, 17 June 1924, 15 June 1924; U.S. Census, 1920.

64. My study covers the early decades of House of Prayer history, and therefore beliefs discussed refer only to that time period. It is possible that theological developments have occurred in the decades since Grace's death.

65. Despite scholar Joao Monteiro's hints to the contrary, Grace would not have had much contact with the Pentecostal Mission of Brava because it arrived on the island just as he departed, and therefore the House of Prayer should not be considered a possible spin-off of the Church of the Nazarene. However, Grace may have been influenced by it to some degree, especially since he claimed to have stayed at a Pentecostal Mission in Egypt during his overseas trip in 1923–24.

66. I use the word "congregationalism" here not to suggest anything about the organizational structure of the church, which will be discussed in a later chapter, but to emphasize the relative theological autonomy held by House of Prayer ministers.

67. This brief history of Holiness, Pentecostals, and Nazarenes is drawn from the following sources: *Encyclopedia of the American Religious Experience,* ed. Charles H. Lippy and Peter W. Williams (New York: Scribner, 1988), s.v. "Pentecostalism" (by Grant Wacker) and s.v. "Holiness and Perfection" (by Jean Miller Schmidt); Stanley M. Horton, "The Pentecostal Perspective," in *Five Views on Sanctification,* 105–48 (Grand Rapids, MI: Zondervan, 1987); In-Gyeong Kim Lundell, *Bridging the Gaps: Contextualization among Korean Nazarene Churches in America* (New York: Peter Lang Publishing, 1995); Tim-

othy L. Smith, *Called unto Holiness* (Kansas City, MO: Nazarene Publishing House, 1962).

68. This is the same Protestant church that first went to Brava. For a number of years it was called the Pentecostal Church of the Nazarene, but because "Pentecostal" emerged as the primary label for tongues-speaking groups, it was dropped from the name in 1919.

69. Several specific House of Prayer beliefs, such as how members regarded Daddy Grace, will be discussed in detail in later chapters.

70. *New Bedford Evening Standard,* 8 Jan. 1922; for an example, see transcription of the *Grace Magazine* article on "The Day of Salvation" in Whiting, "United House," 67–69.

71. NBST cc, internal memo, Jan. 1923; Eddy, "Store-Front Religion," 74; Whiting, "United House," 62–63; Tyms, "A Study," 64–65.

72. *New Bedford Evening Standard,* 8 Jan. 1922.

73. Whiting, "United House," 74–75, 93–95, 114; Tyms, "A Study," 65–66; NBST cc, 8 Jan. 1922.

74. NBST cc, month unknown 1926, 27 Dec. 1927; Tyms, "A Study," 133–34.

75. *New Bedford Evening Standard,* 8 Jan. 1922. Punctuation added.

76. NBST cc, 17 June 1924. Decades later, many parts of Kempton Street were rebuilt, and the House of Prayer moved one block north to number 419. A second House of Prayer opened in June 1941 at the former Ahavath Achim Synagogue on Howland Street.

NOTES TO CHAPTER 2

1. NBST cc, internal memo, Jan. 1923, 27 Dec. 1927; Elizabeth S. Randolph, ed., *An African-American Album: The Black Experience in Charlotte and Mecklenburg County* (Charlotte, NC: Public Library of Charlotte and Mecklenburg County, 1992), 99; *Southcoast Today,* 21 Oct. 1996.

2. *Charlotte Observer* cc, 17 Jan. 1960; *Savannah Tribune,* 1 April 1926 and 22 April 1926; NBST cc, internal memo, Jan. 1923.

3. Enoch Walker's testimony is included in the files of *Mankind Homebuilders, Inc., v. the United House of Prayer for All People, Inc.,* Philadelphia Ct. of C.P., case file 3373 (March term 1960), microfilm reel AA-37. Walker claimed to be a "silent commission officer" of the House of Prayer, based on a contract about church leadership and money allegedly made between Grace and four men in the late 1920s or early 1930s. After Grace's death, Walker was the sole surviving member of this group. He claimed to have commissioned new officers for the corporation, and the new officers then filed suit to take legal control of House of Prayer assets; this case is discussed in chapter 6. Walker also later sued the church independently.

47. *Virginian-Pilot,* 13 Jan. 1960.

48. *Charlotte News,* 17 Aug. 1956.

49. NBST cc, 17 June 1924.

50. For examples, see Eddy, "Store-Front Religion," 76; and *Virginian-Pilot,* 13 Jan. 1960.

51. Letter dated 19 March 1959, untitled booklet of Grace letters, MALP Collection.

52. Williams, "Socio-Economic Significance," 125.

53. Poinsett, "Farewell," 30; Eddy, "Store-Front Religion," 78.

54. The House of Prayer is unique among African American churches in that, similar to Roman Catholicism, a single man presides over the entire organization.

55. NBST cc, date illegible, 1926.

56. For examples, see Eddy, "Store-Front Religion," 76, and *New Bedford Standard-Times,* 13 March 1958, repr. from *New York Herald Tribune,* n.d.

57. Untitled pamphlet, MALP Collection.

58. Hunter, *Prophets and Profits,* 72.

59. *Charlotte News,* 13 Sept. 1936; NBST cc, 17 July 1936.

60. For example, frequent urgings in the *House of Prayer Quarterly* suggested that readers should examine additional passages; see also Whiting, "United House," 125.

61. Whiting, "United House," 94–95.

62. The term "charisma" can be used in a variety of ways. In this instance I refer to the most technical religious studies definition, in which "charismata" means "supernatural spiritual gifts." Others have used the term "charismatic" to describe leaders of religious movements who feel God has bestowed upon them a special gift of wisdom, leadership, and/or power. A more colloquial usage, which I employ elsewhere in the text by referring to Grace as a "charismatic leader," is that he simply had attractive, indescribable qualities that drew people to him.

63. *Baltimore Afro-American,* 20 Feb. 1960.

64. NBST cc, internal memo, Jan. 1923; *Philadelphia Tribune,* 20 Aug. 1936.

65. Eddy, "Store-Front Religion," 74; Robinson, "A Song," 230.

66. Whiting, "United House," 62–63.

67. News of General Interest, *Grace Magazine,* Aug. 1948, 10.

68. While ideas about backsliding distinguish Pentecostalism from Holiness, there are gray areas in this distinction. Even Holiness recipients of "entire sanctification" must deliberately remain steadfast in faith and behavior. However, the suppression of one's sinful nature is believed to come more readily to those who have been entirely sanctified.

69. *New Bedford Standard-Times,* 18 Feb. 1933.

70. NBST cc, 17 July 1936; "By-Laws for the Auxiliaries of the United House of Prayer," MALP Collection.

71. Hodges, "Charles Manuel," 175; *Journal and Guide,* 14 July 1934, 4 Oct. 1930; NBST cc, 17 July 1936; Hunter, *Prophets and Profits,* 58–59, 76; Damon, "The Trombone," 59; *Charlotte Observer* cc, 17 Jan. 1960.

72. "By-Laws for the Auxiliaries of the United House of Prayer," MALP Collection.

73. *Charlotte Observer* cc, 8 Sept. 1947.

74. Music is an essential element of worship in most Holiness-derived churches. The centrality of music is therefore not what makes the House of Prayer unique, but rather, the advanced style of music. The House of Prayer was among a few progressive churches that welcomed into the worship arena instruments and styles normally considered secular. For more information on religious music in African American worship spaces of the early twentieth century, see Michael W. Harris, *The Rise of Gospel Blues: The Music of Thomas Andrew Dorsey in the Urban Church* (New York: Oxford Univ. Press, 1992), especially chapters 5 and 6, and Anthony Heilbut, *The Gospel Sound: Good News and Bad Times,* rev. ed. (New York: Limelight Editions, 1997).

75. Hymns differ from gospel songs in style, content, and function. For more information on this see James Sallee, *A History of Evangelistic Hymnody* (Grand Rapids, MI: Baker Book House, 1978). Grace hymnal found in Daddy Grace Collection, 1953–2000, Manuscript, Archives, and Rare Book Library, Emory University, Atlanta (hereafter cited as Grace/Emory Collection).

76. *Charlotte News,* 10 Sept. 1949; NBST cc, 8 Jan. 1922; *Charlotte News* cc, 7 Dec. 1982; *Savannah Tribune,* 6 Sept. 1928.

77. Damon, "The Trombone," 4, 26–27, 34–35, 40, 44, 52, 61; *The Music District,* VHS, directed by Susan Levitas (California Newsreel, 1995); *New York Daily News,* 7 Aug. 1999. The eighth chapter of Damon's dissertation provides a delineation of the musical elements of shout. Though Damon suggests that the Cape Verdean musical forms the *morna* and the *coladeira* were influential on shout, this seems unlikely since Grace himself was not especially involved in the creation of the church music, and there were few Cape Verdean church members. However, Damon demonstrates more effectively that there are some generalized African musical and dance influences on shout. See Damon, "The Trombone," chapter 3, and also Jonathan C. David, "On One Accord: Community, Musicality, and Spirit among the Singing and Praying Bands of Tidewater Maryland and Delaware" (PhD dissertation, University of Pennsylvania, Philadelphia, 1994), 113–14, 297–98.

78. Damon, "The Trombone," 18, 35–36. Trombones were present in House of Prayer music prior to Holland; for example, trombonist George Williams of Newport News, as mentioned in *Mankind v. United House of Prayer,* and the description of baptism in *Journal and Guide,* 10 Sept. 1938.

79. Damon, "The Trombone," 36–37; *Charlotte News* cc, 7 Dec. 1982.

80. *Charlotte Observer,* 3 Jan. 1990; a slightly variant version of this is reported in Damon, "The Trombone," 37–40.

81. Damon, "The Trombone," 40–42.

82. For more information on this point see ibid. 62—65, and *The Music District,* VHS.

83. Interviewed by Levitas in *The Music District,* VHS.

84. Eddy, "Store-Front Religion," 76–77; Whiting, "United House," 55, 75. The largest congregation in each region was referred to as the Mother House.

85. Untitled pamphlet, MALP Collection. Here the book is erroneously referred to as "Michael."

86. Hunter, *Prophets and Profits,* 63.

87. *Charlotte Observer* cc, 8 Sept. 1947; Robinson, "A Song," 228–29; *Washington Post,* 31 Aug. 1996, Hunter, *Prophets and Profits,* 39; WPA, *Drums and Shadows,* 47.

88. Williams, "Socio-Economic Significance," 135; *New Bedford Standard-Times,* 27 July 1951; Eddy, "Store-Front Religion," 76; Hunter, *Prophets and Profits,* 52; site visit report by Dorothy West, 21 Dec. 1938, WPA Federal Writers' Project Collection, Manuscript Division, Library of Congress, http://memory .loc.gov/wpa/; Robinson, "A Song," 229.

89. As observed by Williams, "Socio-Economic Significance," 124n10.

90. *Charlotte News,* 17 Feb. 1979; *Journal and Guide,* 7 April 1934.

91. Fauset Papers, box 4, folder 86.

92. Though specific sources are cited for details, my generalizations about services are informed by the numerous firsthand reports made over several decades by researchers in a variety of locations. To explain services, I have culled elements that remained consistent within these reports. For some examples of firsthand accounts, see Fauset, *Black Gods,* Whiting, "United House," and Williams, "Socio-Economic Significance."

93. *Charlotte News,* 18 Aug. 1956; *New Bedford Standard-Times,* 21 Oct. 1996; Williams, "Socio-Economic Significance," 137; Eddy, "Store-Front Religion," 76–77; site visit report by Dorothy West, 21 Dec. 1938, WPA Federal Writers' Project Collection; Fauset Papers, box 4, folder 86; Whiting, "United House," 76; *Baltimore Afro-American,* 20 Feb. 1960; Poinsett, "Farewell," 31.

94. Site visit report by Dorothy West, 21 Dec. 1938, WPA Federal Writers' Project Collection; Robinson, "A Song," 229; *Baltimore Afro-American,* 23 Jan. 1960. Whiting explained that the kinds of movement one could observe in the House of Prayer varied from place to place, with the exception of the very uniform marches. Whiting, "United House," 77–78.

95. *New Bedford Standard-Times,* 27 July 1951; Williams, "Socio-Economic Significance," 137; WPA, *Drums and Shadows,* 47–48; Poinsett, "Farewell," 26.

96. Williams, "Socio-Economic Significance," 126; *Baltimore Afro-American,* 27 Feb. 1960.

97. *House of Prayer Quarterly* 11, no. 3 (1952). Additionally, there is negative evidence for this interpretation of Grace's speaking: church publications made no effort to transcribe his sermons and at most excerpted a few sentences for reprint, and only three of Grace's sermons are known to have been recorded.

98. *Charlotte News,* 13 Sept. 1936, Williams, "Socio-Economic Significance," 137. The recordings of snippets of Grace's preaching are more than a quarter century apart and differ greatly in technological advancement. In fact, Grace's accent sounds more prominent at the end of his life than it did in 1926, and the later recording also demonstrates more tendencies of a non-native speaker of English, such as dropped articles. *Preachers and Congregations: Volume 4, 1924–1931,* two sermonettes recorded by Daddy Grace in 1926 (Vienna, Austria: Document Records, 1997); Daddy Grace, *The Last Sermon on the Mount: You Must Be Born Again,* sermon recorded in Los Angeles, 7 Jan. 1960 (Los Angeles: Aries Recording Co., 1960). The liner notes for a recording made at the Harlem House of Prayer in 1955, called *A Night with Daddy Grace,* erroneously claim that Grace is the speaker on that recording.

99. Williams, "Socio-Economic Significance," 138; WPA, *Drums and Shadows,* 50; Marcus H. Boulware, *The Oratory of Negro Leaders: 1900–1968* (Westport, CT: Negro Univ. Press, 1969), 209–10; Robinson, "A Song," 222.

100. Williams, "Socio-Economic Significance," 137; Eddy, "Store-Front Religion," 77; WPA, *Drums and Shadows,* 51.

101. Letter dated 23 Nov. 1959, untitled booklet of Grace letters, MALP Collection.

102. *House of Prayer Quarterly* 3, no. 3 (1944); *Baltimore Afro-American,* 23 Jan. 1960, 27 Feb. 1960; *Charlotte News,* 18 Aug. 1956.

103. In general, Grace's approach to faith healing was distinct from the wider practice only in his use of material objects to transmit healing power, and even this was not unique to the House of Prayer. For more information on the larger tradition of faith healing, see Nancy A. Hardesty, *Faith Cure: Divine Healing in the Holiness and Pentecostal Movements* (Peabody, MA: Hendrickson, 2003), and David Edwin Harrell, *All Things are Possible: The Healing and Charismatic Revivals in Modern America* (Bloomington: Indiana Univ. Press, 1975).

104. NBST cc, 27 Dec. 1927.

105. Williams, "Socio-Economic Significance," 128–29.

106. *Charlotte Observer,* 1 July 1926.

107. NBST cc, date missing, 1926.

108. His youngest sister, Louise, traveling with him, affirmed this as fact. NBST cc, 30 Nov. 1926; *Washington Post,* 7 March 1960.

109. Poinsett, "Farewell," 27.

110. Whiting, "United House," 151–54.

111. Testimonies, *Grace Magazine*, Aug. 1948, 8.

112. Ibid., Dec. 1941, 8.

113. Whiting, "United House," 71–72.

114. *Charlotte Observer,* 1 July 1926; *Savannah Tribune,* 15 April 1926; *Charlotte News,* 11 July 1926.

115. *Charlotte News,* 11 July 1926; *New Bedford Standard-Times,* 18 Sept. 1960.

116. Williams, "Socio-Economic Significance," 130; Site visit report by Dorothy West, 21 Dec. 1938, WPA Federal Writers' Project Collection.

117. Hodges, "Charles Manuel," 175; Graphic 1304, Graphics Collections, Gelman Library Special Collections, George Washington University, Washington, DC; Williams, "Socio-Economic Significance," 130.

118. Poinsett, "Farewell," 27.

119. Fauset Papers, box 4, folder 91; Grace/Emory Collection, folder 3.

120. It is unclear whether the healing cloth was a distinct item from the blessed handkerchiefs. Williams, "Socio-Economic Significance," 127; *Charlotte News,* 11 July 1926.

121. Hodges, "Charles Manuel," 175. The *Grace Magazine* is discussed in more detail in chapter 5 and in the essay on sources. The intense value of the magazine for members may be one of the reasons that it is so difficult to obtain today.

122. *House of Prayer Quarterly* 11, no. 2 (1952).

123. Testimonies, *Grace Magazine,* Dec. 1941, 6.

124. Whiting, "United House," 143; *Baltimore Afro-American,* 27 Feb. 1960.

125. *Savannah Tribune,* 29 April 1926.

126. NBST cc, 27 Dec. 1927.

127. *Savannah Tribune,* 29 April 1926. The perspective in the advertisements-cum-articles often changed midway through, and sometimes multiple times. This makes it particularly unclear whether Grace wrote the articles himself, co-wrote them with his manager, or merely approved someone else's copy.

128. Lillian Ashcraft Webb, *About My Father's Business: The Life of Elder Michaux* (Westport, CT: Greenwood Press, 1981), 160; *Charlotte News,* 17 Aug. 1956.

129. Quoted comments were made by Michael Mulvoy of St. Mark's Roman Catholic Church, Ethelred Brown of Harlem Unitarian Church, and Adam Clayton Powell Jr. of Abyssinian Baptist Church, respectively. *New York Amsterdam News,* 12 March 1938.

130. *Chicago Defender,* 6 Sept. 1947.

131. Ibid., 27 Sept. 1947.

132. Occasionally, Grace softened his approach and allowed access to researchers and interviewers, but these repeatedly resulted in negative assessments of the church. Examples of this include Whiting, "United House," and Fauset, *Black Gods.*

NOTES TO CHAPTER 3

1. Jane Carter Webb, *Newport News* (Charleston, SC: Arcadia Press, 2003), 8–9, 19, 37, 46, 49, 117; Charles F. Marsh, ed., *The Hampton Roads Communities in World War II* (Chapel Hill: Univ. of North Carolina Press, 1951), 10–15. Newport News did not officially incorporate as a city until the late nineteenth century. Its size constantly changed as it annexed various towns, and it increased dramatically when it absorbed Warwick County in 1958.

2. Earl Lewis, *In Their Own Interests: Race, Class, and Power in Twentieth-Century Norfolk, Virginia* (Berkeley and Los Angeles: Univ. of California Press, 1991), 30–33, 40–43, 68; Thomas C. Parramore, *Norfolk: The First Four Centuries* (Charlottesville: Univ. Press of Virginia, 1994), 271–95, 311–12; Norma C. Fields, "Blacks in Norfolk Virginia during the 1930s" (master's thesis, Old Dominion University, Norfolk, VA, 1979), 1; Amy Waters Yarsinske, *Norfolk's Church Street: Between Memory and Reality* (Charleston, SC: Arcadia Press, 1999), 7–10, 76–77; Henry Lewis Suggs, *P. B. Young, Newspaperman: Race, Politics, and Journalism in the New South, 1910–1962* (Charlottesville: Univ. Press of Virginia, 1988), 12–14.

3. NBST cc, 27 Dec. 1927; *Journal and Guide,* 22 Sept. 1928; Webb, *Newport News,* 61. This location was subsequently referred to as the Ivy Avenue House of Prayer. It is not clear whether Grace rebuilt in the same spot but put a new entrance around the corner on Ivy Avenue, or if the building simply acquired this name over time.

4. NBST cc, 27 Dec. 1927; Lewis, *In Their Own,* 151; *Journal and Guide,* 22 Sept. 1928, 9 Feb. 1935; *Grace Magazine,* Dec. 1940, 12; *Savannah Tribune,* 12 July 1928; Works Projects Administration, Virginia Writers' Program, *The Negro in Virginia* (New York: Hastings House, 1940), 256.

5. Religion, *Newsweek,* 19 Aug. 1955, 70; Pearl Bailey, *The Raw Pearl* (New York: Harcourt, Brace, and World, 1968), 8–9.

6. Bailey, *The Raw Pearl,* 8, 22, 162; untitled pamphlet, MALP Collection.

7. The article found 32 Baptist churches, 17 Methodist, 15 Holiness, and about two dozen others in Norfolk. *Journal and Guide,* 20 Dec. 1930.

8. Suggs, *P. B. Young,* 24–35, 47; *Journal and Guide,* 26 May 1934.

9. *Journal and Guide,* 7 April 1934, 26 May 1934, 9 Feb. 1935, 16 July 1938, 10 Sept. 1938; Fields, "Blacks in Norfolk," 8–12.

10. *Baltimore Afro-American,* 18 June 1949.

11. *Charlotte News,* 17 Aug. 1956.

12. "Churches. House of Prayer for People" [*sic*], file #1, photograph archives at the *Charlotte Observer.*

13. *Journal and Guide,* 9 June 1934; General News, *Grace Magazine,* Dec. 1940, 7; WPA, *Negro in Virginia,* 156–57. See also Grace's comments on membership numbers in *United States v. Grace.* In news reports over the years, Newport News was consistently one of the cities with the largest House of Prayer membership.

14. This proportion of the population can only be assumed because racial breakdowns were not made in census figures for cities with fewer than one hundred thousand people.

15. For examples, see Robinson, "A Song"; Tyms, "A Study"; and Sydney E. Ahlstrom, *A Religious History of the American People* (New Haven: Yale Univ. Press, 1972).

16. Such unsubstantiated assertions are not limited to the House of Prayer; assertions about Pentecostals in general have frequently presumed that they are deprived on both socio-economic and spiritual levels.

17. Tyms, "A Study," 59.

18. Clark, *Small Sects,* 122–23.

19. Eddy, "Store-Front Religion," 77–78.

20. Alland, "Possession," 205.

21. Specifically, six were from South Carolina, three were from North Carolina, five were from Virginia, two were from Florida, and two were from Georgia. Fourteen had previously been Baptists, two had been Methodists, and two had not been part of a church. Fauset Papers, box 4, folders 104 and 89.

22. I do not mean to suggest that Fauset's theory is without merit, but I do question the evidence on which it was based.

23. Whiting, "United House," 82–92.

24. Ibid., 82, 181, 236. The Rorschach test was the primary psychological evaluation used by Whiting.

25. Williams, "Socio-Economic Significance," 118–20.

26. Eddy, "Store-Front Religion," 77.

27. Whiting, "United House," 86–88, 96.

28. Ibid., 151–54, 187.

29. Stark and Finke, *Acts of Faith,* chapters 6 and 8. Additionally, being in high tension with the broader society, a quality which the House of Prayer exemplified, also leads to exclusivity and deep commitment.

30. Testimonies, *Grace Magazine,* Dec. 1952, 9.

31. Poinsett, "Farewell," 32.

32. Whiting, "United House," 187–88; Eddy, "Store-Front Religion," 78.

33. Stark and Finke, *Acts of Faith,* 118–23.

34. Whiting, "United House," 93–95, 159–65.

35. Stark and Finke borrow the term "satisficing" to discuss religion but are not the originators of the concept. For more on both the original idea and their interpretation, see *Acts of Faith,* 35–41.

36. Whiting, "United House," 125.

37. *New York Amsterdam News,* 6 Feb. 1960.

38. General News, *Grace Magazine,* Dec. 1952, 7. Eddy's work draws the same conclusion.

39. The El Dorado is discussed in more detail in chapter 4.

40. For one example, see General News, *Grace Magazine,* Dec. 1952, 7.

41. *Washington Post,* 6 March 1960.

42. Fauset, *Black Gods,* 26.

43. Fauset Papers, box 4, folder 87.

44. For examples, see: Robinson, "A Song," 218–19; Poinsett, "Farewell"; and Rufus Wells in the *Baltimore Afro-American,* 27 Feb. 1960.

45. Brune, "Sweet Daddy," 64–71, 170. Additionally, the full text of the quote indicates even more clearly that it was spoken by a member rather than Grace. Fauset included the full text in the appendix of his book, *Black Gods,* 112–13.

46. Testimonies, *Grace Magazine,* Dec. 1941, 8.

47. Eddy, "Store-Front Religion," 75.

48. *House of Prayer Quarterly* 11, no. 2 (1952).

49. Williams, "Socio-Economic Significance," 123–24. For additional examples, see Mitchell's explanation of the Noah story in "Thy Will Be Done in Earth," *Grace Magazine,* Dec. 1940, 11, and his interpretation of Paul's words in "The Alphabetical History of the House of Prayer from A to Z, b.c. 4003–1926," *Grace Magazine,* Dec. 1952, 4.

50. "Do Not Pass Judgment on a Man of What You Hear of Him, Come, See for Yourself," *Grace Magazine,* Aug. 1948, 3–5.

51. Williams, "Socio-Economic Significance," 133.

52. Author's name illegible, "The Gift of God," Grace Magazine, Dec. 1940, 4–5.

53. *House of Prayer Quarterly* 3, no. 3 (1944).

54. *House of Prayer Quarterly* 12, no. 3 (1953), and 3, no. 3 (1944).

55. *Virginian-Pilot,* 17 Jan. 1965.

56. NBST cc, date illegible, 1926; Poinsett, "Farewell," 27; "America's Richest Negro Minister," 23; letter postmarked 28 Nov. 1940, file on Marcelino Manuel Da Graca, Federal Bureau of Investigation of the United States Dept. of Justice.

57. NBST cc, 5 March 1938; *New York Amsterdam News,* 25 Jan. 1958.

58. Eddy, "Store-Front Religion," 75.

59. *Charlotte Observer,* 13 Jan. 1960.

60. Letter dated 18 Aug. 1955, *Grace Magazine,* n.d., 8, MALP Collection.

61. Letter dated 4 Dec. 1959, untitled booklet of Grace letters, MALP Collection.

62. *Charlotte News,* 17 Feb. 1979; *New Bedford Standard-Times,* 13 March 1958, repr. from *New York Herald Tribune,* n.d.; *Charlotte Observer* cc, 8 Sept. 1947. Curiously, a snapshot of Grace as a young man shows him holding a pipe in his mouth, so it appears he did not always eschew smoking. Graphics Collection 6, Gelman Library Special Collections, George Washington University, Washington, DC.

63. *Baltimore Afro-American,* 23 Jan. 1960.

64. Robinson, "A Song," 218; *Charlotte News,* 17 Aug. 1956. Singer Pearl Bailey recounted that the first time her father saw her perform was in the mid-1960s, because up to that point he refused to attend the theater due to religious belief. Shortly thereafter, he also took his first airplane trip. Bailey, *The Raw Pearl,* 165–67.

65. *Baltimore Afro-American,* 3 March 1934. It is not entirely clear what Grace was referring to in this statement. One could readily surmise that, since his Mann Act trial would begin soon, he expected bad press and wanted to prevent followers from reading it. However, the same article quotes Grace as commenting that, "These papers call me a 'Negro.' I am not a Negro, and no Negro in this country can do what I am doing." Therefore, it is possible the remark was due to bitterness about newspapers' misrepresenting him. Whatever the impetus for these particular comments, Grace's advice to followers regarding newspapers was by no means limited to this one occasion.

66. *Baltimore Afro-American,* 3 March 1934; NBST cc, July 17, 1936.

67. His concern with the American military situation during World War II was also heightened because one of his sons and several nephews served in the military. *Journal and Guide,* 31 July 1937; NBST cc, 12 Nov. 1942.

68. C. L. Jones, "One Man," *Grace Magazine,* Dec. 1941, 4–5.

69. *Journal and Guide,* 14 April 1945, 5 July 1947; *New Bedford Standard-Times,* 27 July 1951.

70. *Winston Salem Journal-Sentinel,* 4 May 1952; *Grace Magazine,* n.d., 8, MALP Collection.

71. *House of Prayer Quarterly* 3, no. 3 (1944).

72. *Charlotte News,* 13 Sept. 1936.

73. Letter dated 21 Jan. 1955, *Grace Magazine,* n.d., 7, MALP Collection.

74. *Charlotte News,* 13 Sept. 1936.

75. For examples, see *Journal and Guide,* 11 July 1936, and *United States v. Grace.* I have found no evidence that the topic of male homosexuality was ever raised in public.

76. Poinsett, "Farewell," 30; Site visit report by Dorothy West, 21 Dec. 1938, WPA Federal Writers' Project Collection; Fauset Papers, box 4 folder 86; *Charlotte News,* 13 Sept. 1936.

77. NBST cc, 28 Jan. 1960; *Journal and Guide,* 9 June 1934, 21 April 1934; Tyms, "A Study," 53–58; General News, *Grace Magazine,* Dec. 1940, 7; *United States v. Grace,* Government's Exhibit 5; *Washington Post,* 13 March 1960; *Grace Youth Gazette,* Grace/Emory Collection, folder 9; *Baltimore Afro-American,* 23 Jan. 1960.

78. Hodges, "Charles Manuel," 177; *Charlotte Observer* cc, 6 Sept. 1958.

79. *Journal and Guide,* 14 July 1934; Whiting, "United House," 202. According to Damon, women were originally allowed to play in bands and there were several that were all female, but at some point Grace made a rule that they were no longer permitted in them. Damon, "The Trombone," 35, 61. However, it is not clear if women were forbidden from all types of bands; for instance, *Grace Magazine* lists a female president, Inez Rivers, of the Tambourine Band in Augusta. *Grace Magazine,* Dec. 1940, 4.

80. If more issues of *Grace Magazine* become available for study, I suspect that a much clearer picture of women's theological contributions to the House of Prayer will be documented.

81. *House of Prayer Quarterly* 11, no. 2 (1952).

82. Ibid.

83. "Thy Will Be Done in Earth," *Grace Magazine,* Dec. 1940, 11.

84. *Southcoast Today,* 21 Oct. 1996.

85. Letter dated 22 June 1955, *Grace Magazine,* n.d., 7, MALP Collection.

86. "Ex-Soldier Lauds Sweet Daddy Grace," *Grace Magazine,* Aug. 1948, 12–13.

87. Laws that church members considered an imposition on religious freedom, such as those preventing interracial religious meetings or those which rendered House of Prayer services disturbing to the peace, would already have been excluded from those they respected.

88. All information in this section, except that which is specifically cited to other sources, is taken from the testimony of this trial as found in the case file at the National Archives. *United States v. Grace.*

89. On the birth certificate, introduced as Defendant's Exhibit B, his middle name is merely designated as "M."

90. It is possible that Grace's stance against lesbianism, mentioned earlier, was caused by or related to the case of Minnie Lee Campbell, but there is no evidence to substantiate this possibility.

91. Miss Wilks was expected to testify but fainted in the courtroom before she could be called.

92. However, Lewis's wife testified at the subsequent paternity trial. *Baltimore Afro-American,* 19 May 1934.

93. Fauset Papers, box 4, folders 86 and 87. See edited version in Fauset, *Black Gods,* 113–14.

94. This sentence was somewhat lenient, as the maximum penalty was five

years in prison and a five-thousand-dollar fine. *Journal and Guide*, 24 March 1934.

95. *Baltimore Afro-American*, 7 April 1934.

96. *Charlotte Observer*, 17 March 1934. The *Philadelphia Tribune* was extra colorful, describing Wilks as a "ghastly ghost out of a sex-crazed past," 22 March 1934. For other examples, see the following: *Journal and Guide*, 24 March 1934, 7 April 1934; *Baltimore Afro-American*, 3 March 1934, 24 March 1934, 7 April 1934; NBST cc, 16 March 1934.

97. *Baltimore Afro-American*, 10 March 1934.

98. Ibid.; *Journal and Guide*, 7 April 1934.

99. *Baltimore Afro-American*, 7 April 1934.

100. *Journal and Guide*, 31 March 1934. The Mann Act is commonly referred to as the white slave trade act.

101. *Journal and Guide*, 7 April 1934.

102. *Washington Tribune*, 29 March 1934; *Journal and Guide*, 7 April 1934.

103. *Journal and Guide*, 7 April 1934.

104. Ibid.

105. Ibid.

106. Ibid.

107. *Commissioner of Public Welfare of the City of New York v. Charles M. Grace*, 1935 NY App. Div. Lexis 8001; *Journal and Guide*, 19 May 1934.

108. *United States v. Grace.*

109. *Journal and Guide*, 19 May 1934.

110. See discussions of commitment process in Howard S. Becker, "Notes on the Concept of Commitment," *American Journal of Sociology* 66 (1960): 32–40, and in David R. Rudy and Arthur L. Greil, "Taking the Pledge: The Commitment Process in Alcoholics Anonymous," *Sociological Focus* 20 (Jan. 1987): 45–59. For analysis of more extreme instances of commitment to religious organizations in response to persecution, see Ian Reader, "Imagined Persecution," in *Millennialism, Persecution, and Violence*, ed. Catherine Wessinger, 158–82 (Syracuse, NY: Syracuse Univ. Press, 2000); and John R. Hall, *Gone From the Promised Land: Jonestown in American Cultural History* (New Brunswick, NJ: Transaction Books, 1987), especially chapter 10.

111. Becker's delineation of "side bets" in commitment theory gives validity to this concept. Becker, "Notes."

112. *Journal and Guide*, 9 June 1934.

113. Ibid., 9 Feb. 1935.

114. *Baltimore Afro-American*, 24 Aug. 1935.

115. NBST cc, 17 July 1936. From the time he started preaching until his death, legal entanglements were a constant in the bishop's life. However, whether this specific boast was true is not clear. Known cases he was involved in

during the mid-1930s include one for federal tax evasion, one for libel and slander, the Mann Act case, and the paternity case. Primarily Grace dwelled on his victories in the federal cases, but other typical problems included violations of local ordinances and every permutation of monetary dispute.

116. "Daddy Grace," *Life,* 1 Oct. 1945, 53.

NOTES TO CHAPTER 4

1. Tyms, "A Study," 52. His thesis, based on participant observation and interviews, compared factors affecting the growth of four African American religious groups, two of which were the House of Prayer and the Peace Mission. The following year, Raymond Julius Jones also evaluated both Grace and Divine in a Philosophy master's thesis at Howard. Jones's thesis, which was part anthropology and part philosophy, did not include any discussion of Daddy Grace beyond a passing reference to him in the first chapter, in which he asserted that Grace and Divine were alike, primarily because the function of the religions they had created was to "magnify the personality of the leader." The published version of Jones's work, modestly revised, included more information about Grace and the House of Prayer, but they still received far less attention than other groups Jones had studied. There is no indication of whether these students knew each other, and I was unable to locate records of which professor(s) advised them. Raymond Julius Jones, "A Comparative Study of Religious Cult Behavior among Negroes with Special Reference to Emotional Group Conditioning Factors," (master's thesis, Howard University, Washington, DC, 1939); Raymond Julius Jones, *A Comparative Study of Religious Cult Behavior among Negroes with Special Reference to Emotional Group Conditioning Factors* (Washington, DC: Howard Univ. Studies in the Social Sciences, 1939).

2. Fauset studied the following five groups via participant observation and interviews: Mt. Sinai Holy Church, the United House of Prayer for All People, the Church of God (Black Jews), Father Divine's Peace Mission, and the Moorish Science Temple of America. Fauset was familiar with Jones's work and viewed his scheme of categorization favorably. Fauset Papers, box 4, folder 86.

3. As Fauset phrases it, he compares them with "more orthodox evangelical Christian denominations." Fauset, *Black Gods,* 68.

4. Ibid., 26. As discussed in my second chapter, Fauset's understanding of how members regarded Grace was incorrect.

5. Ibid., 62, emphasis his.

6. These categories are not particularly useful because they group religions based on characteristics that are more superficial than substantive; for example, parallels between religious groups are drawn because of their location, or the leader's personality, and so forth. Today we recognize the need for much more nuanced categories of analysis.

7. Sweet, Olmstead, Gaustad, and Corbett are among the well-known American-religion historians who do not mention Grace in their texts.

8. Additionally, Father Divine is usually given far more space in the text than Grace.

9. Clark, *Small Sects,* 280, 224.

10. Winthrop S. Hudson, *Religion in America* (New York: Scribner's, 1965), 353.

11. Winthrop S. Hudson and John Corrigan, *Religion in America,* 5th ed. (Upper Saddle River, NJ: Prentice Hall, 1992), 339–40. All editions misname Grace's church, referring to it as the House of Prayer for All Nations.

12. Ahlstrom, *A Religious History,* 1061.

13. Albanese, *America,* 1st ed., 129.

14. Richard E. Wentz, *Religion in the New World: The Shaping of Religious Traditions in the United States* (Minneapolis: Fortress Press, 1990), 83; Peter W. Williams, *America's Religions: Traditions and Cultures* (1990; repr., Urbana, IL: Univ. of Chicago Press, 1998), 304, 228. For the 2002 edition, Williams added a comparison of the Peace Mission with Shakers and the Oneida community.

15. These particular quotes come from C. Eric Lincoln and Lawrence H. Mamiya, *The Black Church in the African American Experience* (Durham, NC: Duke Univ. Press, 1990), 121, 385.

16. Hans A. Baer and Merrill Singer, *African American Religion: Varieties of Protest and Accommodation,* 2nd ed. (Knoxville: Univ. of Tennessee Press, 2002).

17. The background of Father Divine and the Peace Mission has been discussed fully by numerous scholars, including Watts, Weisbrot, and Burnham, among others. Herein I draw primarily from the works of these three authors. Jill Watts, *God, Harlem U.S.A.* (Berkeley and Los Angeles: Univ. of California Press, 1992); Robert Weisbrot, *Father Divine and the Struggle for Racial Equality* (Urbana: Univ. of Illinois Press, 1983); Kenneth Burnham, *God Comes to America* (Boston: Lambeth Press, 1979).

18. It is possible that the year, and by extension the end of World War I, is more critical here than anything, because several other leaders also experienced important turning points in 1919. Examples include Marcus Garvey, founder of the Universal Negro Improvement Association, whose organization experienced dramatic increases in membership in 1919 and which "seemed to be on the verge of sweeping aside conservative civil rights organizations and absorbing like-minded ones," according to David L. Lewis, *When Harlem Was in Vogue* (New York: Knopf, 1981), 37, see also Jervis Anderson, *This Was Harlem: A Cultural Portrait, 1900–1950* (New York: Farrar, Straus, and Giroux, 1982), 121–27; Elder Lightfoot Solomon Michaux, future founder of the Church of God, who began a life devoted to ministry in September 1919 with a revival he

led with his wife in Newport News, according to Webb, *About My Father's Business,* 14–15; and Aimee Semple McPherson, who over the course of 1919 made an observable break from Pentecostal practices and came to what biographer Blumhofer called "a critical moment" in her religious leadership, Edith Blumhofer, *Aimee Semple McPherson: Everybody's Sister* (Grand Rapids, MI: Eerdmans, 1993), 145–49.

19. Grace's trip seemed to be a combination of proselytizing and personal spiritual development; Divine's goal was to increase his ministry, and though he was well received, only one person joined his fold. Brune, "Sweet Daddy," 81–83; Watts, *God, Harlem U.S.A.,* 57.

20. Grace's "divinity" has already been discussed in chapter 3; property issues will be discussed in more detail at the end of this chapter. The "divinity" of Father Divine has been discussed at length by other scholars, such as Weisbrot, *Father Divine,* 78–84, and Burnham, *God Comes,* 27–30.

21. Because the name "Peace Mission" did not emerge until the early 1930s, my use of it to describe them prior to that time is anachronistic.

22. He renamed himself Reverend Major Jealous Divine in approximately 1917, and followers subsequently began calling him Father Divine. Watts, *God, Harlem U.S.A.,* 27, 46–48.

23. More detailed explorations of Father Divine's theology can be found in: Griffith, "Body Salvation," 119–53; Watts, *God, Harlem U.S.A.,* 21–25, 57–60, 89–90; Burnham, *God Comes,* 24–30.

24. These monikers altered over the years. By the early 1940s, status was signified by membership in religious orders that developed within the Peace Mission.

25. Watts, *God, Harlem U.S.A.,* 21–25, 57–60; Griffith, "Body Salvation," 122–24. Because of this belief in the mental cause of illness, the Peace Mission is aligned with Mind Cure religions such as Christian Science, New Thought, and the Unity School; all of these are distinguished from Faith Cure religions such as Pentecostalism. For a concise introduction to New Thought, see chapter one of Charles S. Braden, *Spirits in Rebellion: The Rise and Development of New Thought* (Dallas: Southern Methodist Univ. Press, 1963); for more information on faith healing, see Hardesty, *Faith Cure.*

26. Griffith, "Body Salvation," 129–33; Watts, *God, Harlem U.S.A.,* 26–30. It is not clear precisely when and how the idea that Father Divine was God became part of their beliefs, though various incidents have been noted as contributing validity to the idea. Also, Peace Mission members never use words that signify race because they consider such racial categorizations to be human-made falsehoods.

27. Weisbrot, *Father Divine,* 22–23; Burnham, *God Comes,* 24–30; Watts, *God, Harlem U.S.A.,* 41–45.

28. Derivative words were loosely defined and not based on etymology. For

example, "Peace" was the greeting used instead of "Hello"; and the *Amsterdam News* was referred to as the "Amsterbless News."

29. Weisbrot, *Father Divine,* 71–72; Watts, *God, Harlem U.S.A.,* 64.

30. For example, any opportunity to hear Divine speak, even if only in a large public auditorium, was a sacred event for the faithful. Likewise, singing and testimonials were special even if not paired with a banquet or talk. The subjects of Divine's talks varied widely but might include a profession of his theological ideas, educational messages about government and citizenship, and commentary on the organization itself. In the 1930s, the great demand for Divine's attention meant that the times and locations of banquets became less predictable. By the 1940s banquets were rarely open to the public, though the public was welcome to Divine's speaking engagements or to attend member gatherings for singing or testimonials.

31. Such outsiders included their Sayville neighbors, journalists, and the public who read about them in newspapers and magazines.

32. For other engaging discussions of Harlem as a city separate from Manhattan, see John L. Jackson Jr., *Harlemworld: Doing Race and Class in Contemporary Black America* (Chicago: Univ. of Chicago Press, 2001), and Anderson, *This Was Harlem.*

33. Scholars demarcate the beginning and end of the Great Migration in various ways, and some suggest that its first waves began prior to 1900. Most agree that the peak occurred between 1915 and 1930.

34. Claude McKay, *Negro Metropolis* (New York: E. P. Dutton, 1940), 16–17; Gilbert Osofsky, *Harlem: The Making of a Ghetto* (New York: Harper and Row, 1963), 93.

35. Osofsky, *Harlem,* 138–40; Allon Schoener, ed., *Harlem on my Mind: Cultural Capital of Black America, 1900–1968,* updated ed. (New York: New Press, 1995).

36. McKay, *Negro Metropolis,* 89. Technically, Harlem was not a suburb. However it was far enough from Manhattan's business districts that its atmosphere was essentially small town rather than big city, and it is this aspect I refer to when calling it a "suburb."

37. Lewis, *When Harlem,* 25; Anderson, *This Was Harlem,* 49–52.

38. E. Franklin Frazier, "Negro Harlem: An Ecological Study," *American Journal of Sociology* 43, no. 1 (July 1937): 73; Lewis, *When Harlem,* 25.

39. Frazier, "Negro Harlem," 73, 76; Osofsky, *Harlem,* 109.

40. Slum Clearance Committee of New York, maps and charts (New York, 1934).

41. Osofsky, *Harlem,* 128–32; Ira De Augustine Reid, *The Negro Immigrant: His Background, Characteristics, and Social Adjustment, 1899–1937,* repr. ed. (New York: Arno Press, 1969), 12–13.

42. McKay, *Negro Metropolis,* 89–90. The Italian population, which was

east of Lexington Avenue between 96th and 125th Streets, gradually moved out and was replaced by a Latino population, hence today that area is referred to as Spanish Harlem.

43. *New York Daily News,* 31 Oct. 1929; Lewis, *When Harlem,* 209–10; Anderson, *This Was Harlem,* 174–75.

44. McKay, *Negro Metropolis,* 118; Lewis, *When Harlem,* 169–70.

45. Originally the Lafayette Theater was for whites only, but in 1914 it switched to an all-Black format. In addition to plays the Lafayette offered musical performances. Anderson, *This Was Harlem,* 110–12, 236; Schoener, *Harlem on My Mind,* 162.

46. Anderson, *This Was Harlem,* 237.

47. Osofsky, *Harlem,* 128.

48. Anderson, *This Was Harlem,* 45–47; Osofsky, *Harlem,* 138–40. Furthermore, a cluster of buildings had gone up very quickly when the subway line was extended to Harlem, and these tended to be of shoddy construction.

49. Osofsky, *Harlem,* 136–40.

50. Cheryl Lynn Greenberg, *"Or Does It Explode?" Black Harlem in the Great Depression* (New York: Oxford Univ. Press, 1991), 31–41.

51. Osofsky, *Harlem,* 120.

52. Greenberg, *"Or Does It,"* 18–31. One researcher, Samuel Lafferty, found evidence that some Harlem residents "pay as high as 94 per cent of their income for rent." Samuel Lafferty, "The Housing Problem of the Urban Negro," *Crisis* 44, no. 9 (1937): 269.

53. Greenberg, *"Or Does It,"* 42–47; see also descriptions of Depression conditions in Chicago in volume 2 of St. Clair Drake and Horace Cayton, *Black Metropolis: A Study of Negro Life in a Northern City,* rev. ed. (New York: Harper and Row, 1962).

54. Greenberg, *"Or Does It,"* especially chapters 2 and 5.

55. Although it was no longer Divine's headquarters, the Peace Mission kept the residence in Sayville and still maintains it today. Watts, *God, Harlem U.S.A.,* 62–74, 86–87.

56. Extensions, also referred to as "Heavens," were new Peace Mission locations. Many of the Peace Missions that started without Divine's direct involvement were racially segregated. Watts, *God, Harlem U.S.A.,* 74, 104, 123–24, 144–46; Weisbrot, *Father Divine,* 65–67; *New Day,* 30 July 1936. The last source referred to here, the *New Day,* was a weekly house organ of the Peace Mission Movement that began publication in 1936. Each issue printed the text of Divine's recent speaking engagements. Dates given for the *New Day,* therefore, indicate when the speech was published rather than when it was delivered.

57. Divine never kept records of membership, but Watts estimates that by late 1933 Father Divine had approximately fifty thousand followers; this number includes both live-in members and highly interested dabblers. Weisbrot has

a thoughtful discussion of the various methods for tabulating membership, and he comes to a similar conclusion. Watts, *God, Harlem U.S.A.*, 112, 160–61; Weisbrot, *Father Divine*, 68–71.

58. Hubert Kelley, "Heaven Incorporated," *American Magazine*, Jan. 1936; Watts, *God, Harlem U.S.A.*, 106–7; Weisbrot, *Father Divine*, 74.

59. See, for example, Edwin T. Buehrer, "Harlem's God," *Christian Century*, 11 Dec. 1935. A thorough discussion of this point is found in St. Clair McKelway and A. J. Liebling, "Who Is This King of Glory?" part 3, *New Yorker*, 27 June 1936.

60. I am not claiming originality in dispelling this myth. This information is clearly explained in many of the better academic explorations of Divine, including Watts, *God, Harlem U.S.A.*, Weisbrot, *Father Divine*, and Burnham, *God Comes*.

61. Burnham emphasizes that Peninniah's savings paid for the house, despite both names' being on the deed. Burnham, *God Comes*, 5, 9; McKelway and Liebling, "Who Is," part 1, 13 June 1936; Robert Allerton Parker, *Incredible Messiah* (Boston: Little, Brown, 1937), 278–79.

62. Some properties were owned by a handful of members, while others had several hundred names on the deed. McKelway and Liebling, "Who Is," part 3; Watts, *God, Harlem U.S.A.*, 102–4, 124, 130, 137; *New York Times*, 25 April 1937, 13 May 1937, 11 Sept. 1965.

63. The cars were mostly second- and thirdhand donations; used buses had been purchased by member John Lamb; and the airplane was procured by member Hubert Julian, a pilot. Parker, *Incredible Messiah*, 225–26, 275, 285–86; Watts, *God, Harlem U.S.A.*, 117–18.

64. Father Divine's teachings on economics have been published in many places, including Weisbrot, *Father Divine*, chapters 4 and 6; Watts, *God, Harlem U.S.A.*, especially chapter 6; Burnham, *God Comes*, chapters 6 and 7; and the Peace Mission brochure entitled *What We Believe*.

65. Watts, *God, Harlem U.S.A.*, 106.

66. The fact that the Peace Mission was still an unregistered, unincorporated body made certain questions of donations and taxes relatively easy to avoid for Divine, who was legally attached to nothing and was not formally employed.

67. *New York Times*, 15 May 1937; Watts, *God, Harlem U.S.A.*, 152–53.

68. Watts, *God, Harlem U.S.A.*, 152–54; *New York Times*, 25 April 1937.

69. Watts, *God, Harlem U.S.A.*, 155, 165–66; *New York Times*, 13 May 1937.

70. *New York Times*, 16 May 1937, 19 May 1937.

71. Watts, *God, Harlem U.S.A.*, 144–50.

72. *New York Times*, 18 June 1937, 19 June 1937.

73. *New York Times*, 26 April 1937, 25 Nov. 1937; *Philadelphia Tribune*, 13 Jan. 1938.

74. Watts, *God, Harlem U.S.A.*, 151–52, 157; Religion, *Time*, 3 May 1937.

75. Lauretta Bender and Zuleika Yarrell, "Psychoses among Followers of Father Divine," *Journal of Nervous and Mental Disease* 87 (April 1938): 418–49; Hadley Cantril and Muzafer Sherif, "The Kingdom of Father Divine," *Journal of Abnormal and Social Psychology* 33, no. 2 (1938): 147–67.

76. Watts, *God, Harlem U.S.A.*, 151, 160.

77. Ibid., 155.

78. Frazier, "Negro Harlem," 87–88.

79. Parker, *Incredible Messiah*, 109.

80. Ibid., 109; *New York Times*, 2 Feb. 1938.

81. Parker, *Incredible Messiah*, 109.

82. Frazier, "Negro Harlem," 78–79.

83. The southern side of the block, which included the building in question, was part of a swath of land razed in the late 1940s as an extension of "slum clearance." Today a high-rise housing project stands in its place.

84. Rogall's name is sometimes spelled "Rogell." According to McKelway and Liebling, the real name of Blessed Purin Heart was Lena Brinson. *New York Times*, 22 Feb. 1938; *Washington Post*, 8 March 1960; McKelway and Liebling, "Who Is," part 2.

85. Parker, *Incredible Messiah*, 108. Parker used the term "tapestry brick" in quotation marks; however, because tapestry brick is a technical term rather than a colloquialism, quotation marks are unnecessary.

86. Parker, *Incredible Messiah*, 110.

87. Ottley reported that 20 West 115th Street had formerly been a Turkish bathhouse; however, I believe he confused the building with a Peace Mission on 126th Street. Parker, *Incredible Messiah*, 108–10; *New York Age*, 26 Feb. 1938; Roi Ottley, *'New World A-Coming': Inside Black America* (Boston: Houghton Mifflin, 1943), 91.

88. *New York Times*, 22 Feb. 1938.

89. *New York Age*, 26 Feb. 1938, 12 March 1938; *New York Times*, 21 Feb. 1938, 22 Feb. 1938; *Journal and Guide*, 12 March 1938; *Washington Post*, 8 March 1960.

90. Peace Mission secretary John Lamb, however, initially said that Grace was deliberately trying to undermine Father Divine. *New York Times*, 12 Feb. 1938, capitalization in the original; *Journal and Guide*, 26 Feb. 1938.

91. *New York Times*, 21 Feb. 1938.

92. As recounted by Paul Benzaquin in the *Boston Globe*, 9 Feb. 1960.

93. *New York Times*, 22 Feb. 1938.

94. *New York Age*, 26 Feb. 1938.

95. Ibid., 7 May 1938.

96. Ibid., 26 Feb. 1938.

97. *New York Amsterdam News*, 26 Feb. 1938, 5 March 1938.

98. Ibid., 12 March 1938.

99. Ibid., 23 April 1938, 7 May 1938.

100. *New York Times,* 4 March 1938; *New York Age,* 12 March 1938.

101. *New York Amsterdam News,* 26 March 1938.

102. *New York Times,* 2 June 1938; *New York Amsterdam News,* 4 June 1938.

103. *New York Amsterdam News,* 4 June 1938.

104. *New York Times,* 13 June 1938.

105. Ibid., 21 Feb. 1938, 22 Feb. 1938.

106. It is unclear whether Divine was referring to a real building, as no property resembling his description came into Peace Mission hands after that. *New Day,* 2 June 1938.

107. Ibid.

108. Ibid., 9 June 1938.

109. The Madison Avenue building was the former home and office space of a doctor and was purchased by Peace Mission members in August. Creating an assembly space in this building required substantial renovation. Survey of *New Day,* 1936–39; *New Day,* 2 June 1938, 26 Jan. 1939; *New York Times,* 4 Aug. 1938.

110. *New York Times,* 13 June 1938; *New York Amsterdam News,* 11 June 1938.

111. Jim Haskins, *James Van DerZee: Picture Takin' Man* (Trenton: Africa World Press, 1991), 105–6, 141–42.

112. *Charlotte Observer,* 5 Sept. 1947.

113. More specifically, beginning in 1940 the Peace Mission incorporated as several separate but affiliated religious corporations, including the Unity Mission, the Circle Mission, the Palace Mission, the Nazareth Mission, and the Peace Center Church and Home. It is unclear how many of these corporations remain functioning today. Burnham, *God Comes,* 73–75; Watts, *God, Harlem U.S.A.,* 160–63.

114. *Baltimore Afro-American,* 18 June 1949; Burnham, *God Comes,* 141–49.

115. Based on references in the *Philadelphia Tribune,* it is evident that Grace's Philadelphia House of Prayer has been located in the same spot since at least 1936; however, property records show that he did not buy the land until 1955. The cornerstone of the building itself is dated 1932.

116. Today, of these six specific properties, all three Houses of Prayer remain in operation, while only the Broad Street hotel remains of the former Peace Missions. Some information for this section is based on property transfer paperwork recorded by the Bureau of Engineering, Surveys and Zoning for the City of Philadelphia; files are located at both the Philadelphia Department of

Records and the City Archives. Other information has been culled from the *Grace Magazine* and *New Day*.

117. *Charlotte News,* 17 Aug. 1956.

118. *New York Amsterdam News,* 1 June 1957; *Charlotte Observer* cc, 26 May 1957.

119. *New York Times,* 27 May 1957; People, *Newsweek,* June 10, 1957; NBST cc, 2 June 1957. According to Peeks in *Long Struggle,* 253, after Divine's public appearance Grace clarified his statement by commenting: "A lot of people are dead, but they just haven't been buried yet."

120. People, *Newsweek,* 10 June 1957.

121. For examples, see: *Baltimore Afro-American,* 18 June 1949; *Pittsburgh Courier,* 17 Sept. 1949; "America's Richest Negro Minister."

122. However, by that time Grace's New Bedford following was quite small, and certainly not in need of an additional building. NBST cc, 27 April 1941.

123. Ibid., 15 April 1943, 17 April 1943.

124. Ibid., 3 Aug. 1947; *New York Amsterdam News,* 16 Jan. 1960; *New York Times,* 17 Dec. 1995. It was also reported, with some fanfare, that Adam Clayton Powell Jr. had wanted to acquire the 125th Street property; *Baltimore Afro-American,* 9 Aug. 1947.

125. *Charlotte Observer,* 10 June 1953; NBST cc, 30 July 1953, 26 Nov. 1953.

126. *Pittsburgh Courier,* 29 Nov. 1958. Jones had moved out earlier that year after being arrested for "gross indecency," according to J. Gordon Melton, ed., *Encyclopedia of American Religions,* 2nd ed. (Detroit: Gale, 1987), 302.

127. *New York Amsterdam News,* 16 Jan. 1960; *Washington Post,* 8 March 1960.

128. *Pittsburgh Courier,* 15 March 1958.

129. Steven Ruttenbaum, *Mansions in the Clouds: The Skyscraper Palazzi of Emery Roth* (New York: Balsam Press, 1986), 133, 136–44; *Pittsburgh Courier,* 16 May 1953.

130. For examples, see Eddy, "Store-Front Religion," 76; *Washington Post,* 21 Jan. 1960.

131. NBST cc, 15 March 1960; *New York Amsterdam News,* 9 Sept. 1961.

NOTES TO CHAPTER 5

1. *New Bedford Standard-Times,* 12 Jan. 1985; see also *Charlotte Observer,* 5 Sept. 1947 and *Charlotte News,* 16 Aug. 1956.

2. *Charlotte Observer,* 23 June 1970.

3. John R. Rogers and Amy T. Rogers, *Charlotte: Its Historic Neighborhoods* (Charleston, SC: Arcadia, 1996), 7, 63, 86–88; Thomas W. Hanchett,

Sorting Out the New South City: Race, Class, and Urban Development in Charlotte, 1875–1975 (Chapel Hill: Univ. North Carolina Press, 1998), 3–4, 116–17.

4. Hanchett, *Sorting Out*, 129–34, 202.

5. Randolph, *An African-American Album*, 21, 76–77; Vermelle Diamond Ely, Grace Hoey Drain, and Amy Rogers, *Charlotte, North Carolina* (Charleston, SC: Arcadia, 2001), 37; *The Brooklyn Story* (n.p.: Afro-American Cultural and Service Center, 1978), 4–5; Rogers and Rogers, *Charlotte*, 30.

6. Rogers and Rogers, *Charlotte*, 39; *Charlotte News*, 7 Feb. 1937, 8 Feb. 1937.

7. *Charlotte News*, 16 Aug. 1956; *Charlotte Observer*, 5 Sept. 1947.

8. *Charlotte Observer*, 12 Dec. 1963; *Charlotte News*, 16 Sept. 1982, 13 Sept. 1936; *Charlotte News* cc, 22 Sept. 1983.

9. Rogers and Rogers, *Charlotte*, 38; Rose Leary Love, *Plum Thickets and Field Daisies* (Charlotte, NC: Public Library of Charlotte and Mecklenburg County, 1996), 4, 8–9, 14, 59.

10. *Charlotte Observer* cc, 12 Dec. 1963; *Charlotte News*, 16 Aug. 1956.

11. Less than a decade after its completion, a compelling newspaper quote described a Grace guardsman exuberantly explaining the interior of the McDowell Street House of Prayer as he "pointed with pride to the imposing building which towered incongruously over run-down homes in the area." *Baltimore Afro-American*, 13 Feb. 1960.

12. Depending on which decade it was and which term was deemed more politically acceptable at a given time, the process of razing Brooklyn was labeled "slum clearance," "blight removal," or "urban renewal." Hanchett, *Sorting Out*, 227–50; Pat Watters, *Charlotte*, special report by the Southern Regional Council, (Atlanta: Southern Regional Council, 1964), 2.

13. Generalizations about Grace's annual travel schedule are based on a timeline I have pieced together that tracks as many of Grace's geographic movements as possible for the years 1920 to 1960.

14. "The Grace Flag March," *Grace Magazine*, Aug. 1948, 5.

15. News of General Interest, *Grace Magazine*, Aug. 1948, 9–10. This quote is reminiscent of the opening lines of one of Dr. Tross's books: "I write of this thing called religion—this thing around me, beneath me, above me, and within me—the energy of my mind, my heart, my will," J. S. N. Tross, *This Thing Called Religion* (Charlotte, NC: n.p., 1934), xv.

16. It was named this because "Emmanuel" means "God with us" in Greek. *Charlotte Observer*, 27 June 1961.

17. *Charlotte Observer* cc, 13 Jan. 1960; *Charlotte News* cc, 12 Jan. 1960; *Charlotte News*, 17 Aug. 1956.

18. "General Council Laws of the United House of Prayer for All People," no. 14, (n.p., n.d.), MALP Collection. This version of the "General Council

Laws" remained in effect throughout Grace's bishopric. There is no date on the booklet, but Albert Whiting also appears to have used the same version of the laws and he dated them as 1938. The laws were amended after Grace's death.

19. Casimiro, *Portugal Crioulo*, chapters 8, 10.

20. Meintel, *Race, Culture*, 117–21, 143; Halter, *Between Race*, 154–55; Lobban and Lopes, *Historical Dictionary*, 195–98.

21. Halter, *Between Race*, 154–55; Meintel, *Race, Culture*, 117–21.

22. As explained in the *House of Prayer Quarterly* 3, no. 3 (1944): "Convocation is the oldest feast in the world, which was set up for a Pass over by God him self [*sic*], and he delivered it unto Moses and Moses delivered it unto the people that it should be kept through all generations."

23. "General Council Laws," no. 19, MALP Collection.

24. Ibid., nos. 42, 40.

25. *Charlotte Observer*, 12 Sept. 1949.

26. *New York Daily News*, 7 Aug. 1999; *Baltimore Afro-American*, 24 Aug. 1935; *Washington Post*, 1 Sept. 1978.

27. As quoted by the Associated Press, 6 Oct. 1998.

28. *Washington Post*, 1 Sept. 1978.

29. *New York Times*, 7 Aug. 2000.

30. *Baltimore Afro-American*, 24 Aug. 1935; *Charlotte Observer*, 8 Oct. 1990; "The Fourteenth Annual Holy Convocation at Newport News, VA," *Grace Magazine*, Dec. 1941, 3; Williams, "Socio-Economic Significance," 139; *Charlotte News*, 8 Sept. 1941. Interestingly, Greenwood mentions that the Black "better class" had long looked down upon public baptisms because they were an embarrassment to the community, with references going as far back as 1883. See Janette Thomas Greenwood, *Bittersweet Legacy: The Black and White "Better Classes" in Charlotte, 1850–1910* (Chapel Hill: Univ. of North Carolina Press, 1994), 85, 269n23.

31. *New Bedford Standard-Times*, 17 Jan. 1960 (repr. of 1953 article); *Charlotte Observer*, 3 Oct. 1977; *Charlotte Observer* cc, 5 Sept. 1947, 12 Sept. 1947.

32. *Charlotte Observer* cc, 12 Sept. 1966.

33. This specific quote is from a pool baptism conducted by Bishop McCollough, *Charlotte Observer*, 8 Oct. 1990. However, Grace and his successors have usually prayed something akin to this at the start of all baptisms. Indeed, both the pledge and the prayer were quite similar when I attended a fire-hose baptism led by Bishop Madison in August 2004.

34. Associated Press, 9 Oct. 1998. Mayor Richard Lee of New Haven, Connecticut recalled that one time the hose was not adjusted properly, and when Daddy Grace turned on the water the force knocked everyone over. *Washington Post*, 8 March 1960.

35. *Pittsburgh Courier*, 19 Aug. 1944; *Philadelphia Tribune*, 16 Aug. 1952.

36. Associated Press, 6 Oct. 1998.

37. Today, fire-hose baptisms are rarely done outside of New York City and Buffalo. *New York Times*, 7 Aug. 2000; *New York Daily News*, 7 Aug. 1999.

38. Philadelphia convocation booklet, Aug. 1955, Grace/Emory Collection. Capitalization in the original.

39. *Charlotte News*, 8 Sept. 1941, 8 Sept. 1952; *Charlotte Observer* cc, 8 Sept. 1947; *Charlotte Observer*, 12 Sept. 1949, 10 Sept. 1956. Church estimates of parade attendance were always higher; for example, in 1949 police estimated 35,000 while the church said it was closer to 70,000.

40. *Charlotte News*, 17 Aug. 1956.

41. "Convocation in Augusta," *Grace Magazine*, Dec. 1940, 4.

42. Letter dated 15 June 1959, untitled booklet of Grace letters, MALP Collection.

43. *Charlotte Observer* cc, 5 Sept. 1947; *Charlotte News*, 8 Sept. 1941. The House of Prayer has a tradition of demonstrating respect for elders by shielding them from the sun with an umbrella, and young men are often pictured holding one over the bishop.

44. *Charlotte Observer* cc, 8 Sept. 1947; *New Bedford Standard-Times*, 17 Jan. 1960 (repr. of 1953 article); *Charlotte Observer*, 12 Sept. 1949, 14 Sept. 1959; *Charlotte News*, 8 Sept. 1941, 17 Aug. 1956.

45. *Charlotte Observer*, 9 Sept. 1957.

46. *Charlotte Observer* cc, 18 Aug. 1984.

47. *Charlotte Observer* cc, 8 Sept. 1947, 6 Feb. 1957, 5 Sept. 1947; *New Bedford Standard-Times*, 17 Jan. 1960 (repr. of 1953 article); *Charlotte News*, 8 Sept. 1941, 8 Sept. 1952. In other places, especially South Carolina, local police did not always appreciate the House of Prayer parade security men nor the fact that they openly carried guns.

48. "General Council Laws," nos. 13, 53, 54.

49. *Journal and Guide*, 11 July 1936; Williams, "Socio-Economic Significance," 138; *New York Amsterdam News*, 28 July 1956; Fauset, *Black Gods*, 26; Fauset Papers, box 4, folder 86; "General Council Laws," no. 50. Elder Ernest Mitchell was Convocation King so many times that they created a new title for him, "Champion King." *Charlotte Observer* cc, 3 Feb. 1960.

50. "General Council Laws," no. 40.

51. For example, one reader wrote in response to a picture of one of these events: "This is to condemn your newspaper for printing . . . the picture of those [sic] bunch of idiots having a money barbecue. . . . That issue set Negro journalism back fifty years." *Philadelphia Tribune*, 31 May 1960. *Washington Post*, 11 March 1960; *Boston Globe*, 8 Feb. 1960; *Philadelphia Tribune*, 28 May 1960.

52. *Charlotte Observer*, 3 Jan. 1990.

53. *Charlotte News* cc, 10 Sept. 1949.

54. *W. M. Taylor v. C. M. Grace,* 1936 S.C. of Virginia, Lexis 174.

55. *Charlotte News,* 10 Sept. 1949; *New York Amsterdam News,* 20 Feb. 1960.

56. *Charlotte News,* 17 Aug. 1956; *Journal and Guide,* 9 Feb. 1935; Miles Mark Fisher, "Negroes Get Religion," *Opportunity* 14, no. 5 (May 1936): 149; Williams, "Socio-Economic Significance," 125–26.

57. "General Council Laws," no. 9. This particular rule may have been inspired by the Mann Act case accusations.

58. Williams, "Socio-Economic Significance," 126, 129; Whiting, "United House," 55; "General Council Laws," nos. 18, 17.

59. Whiting, "United House," 199–200; "General Council Laws," nos. 10, 11, 12, 30, 38.

60. "General Council Laws," nos. 3, 4, 5.

61. Whiting, "United House," 199; *Charlotte News* cc, 8 Feb. 1960. I was able to confirm that Mitchell ran the *Grace Magazine* from 1940 to 1952, but it is very likely that he was at its helm for several years on either side of this timeframe.

62. Individual members were also given some responsibility to manage their own accounts. For example, the *Grace Magazine* of August 1948 reminded members: "Be sure that your Book is checked up that in case of death there will be no hold up of your claim." *Washington Post,* 10 March 1960; *Family Aid Association of the United House of Prayer for All People v. the United States,* 1941 U.S. Ct. Cl., Lexis 134; Tyms, "A Study," 56–57.

63. Fauset, *Black Gods,* 26, 89.

64. *Charlotte News,* 16 Sept. 1982.

65. For example, see *Taylor v. Grace.*

66. *Charlotte Observer* cc, 3 Feb. 1960. As suggested in chapter 3, Grace most likely ended this practice after some of these donations were raised as "evidence" by those making accusations of paternity against him.

67. NBST cc, 4 Jan. 1958, 18 Sept. 1960, 2 Feb. 1960; *New York Amsterdam News,* 30 Jan. 1960.

68. *New York Amsterdam News,* 13 Feb. 1960.

69. NBST cc, 22 July 1947, 19 July 1947.

70. *Grace Magazine,* Aug. 1948, 11–12.

71. NBST cc, 4 Jan. 1958, 8 Dec. 1951, 4 May 1953, 13 Jan. 1960.

72. In 1952 Marcelino, who had taken an assumed name, began serving a two-to-ten-year sentence for robbery at an Illinois prison. Ibid., 18 Sept. 1960.

73. Ibid., 23 Aug. 1955.

74. *Charlotte Observer,* 31 March 1971; Jean Alexander Nourse, *Weeping Willow African Methodist Episcopal Zion Church: A History* (Charlotte, NC: AME Zion Church, 1995), 109–10. The list of Tross's achievements is extensive and cannot be described in full here.

75. Tate was a cofounder of the Afro-American Mutual Insurance Company and the Mecklenburg Investment Company; Grier was a funeral services proprietor; Alexander was a businessman who later became a state senator; Blake was the first principal of West Charlotte High School. Randolph, *African-American Album*, 94.

76. Greenwood, *Bittersweet Legacy*, 6. Greenwood argues that because in the early twentieth century African Americans had very little economic and/or political power in Charlotte, it is inappropriate to refer to an elite, middle, and low class among them. Hence she uses the term "better class," a term Charlotte residents used themselves at least as early as the 1870s, to distinguish those who were respected and influential among Black residents. Though not precisely the same kind of social division, it bears similarity to Evelyn Brooks Higginbotham's term "politics of respectability," explained in her book *Righteous Discontent: The Women's Movement in the Black Baptist Church, 1880–1920* (Cambridge, MA: Harvard Univ. Press, 1993).

77. Watters, *Charlotte*, 39; Greenwood, *Bittersweet Legacy*, 239, 85.

78. Nourse, *Weeping Willow*, 109.

79. *Charlotte Observer*, 31 March 1977.

80. *Charlotte News*, 16 March 1960; Watters, *Charlotte*, 4. Charlotte's public businesses were officially desegregated in 1963.

81. *Charlotte Observer*, 31 March 1977; Dan L. Morrill, *Historic Charlotte: An Illustrated History of Charlotte and Mecklenburg County* (n.p.: Historical Publishing Network, 2001), 90.

82. Watters, *Charlotte*, 20, 33–34.

83. Nourse, *Weeping Willow*, 30–33.

84. *Washington Post*, 8 March 1960.

85. Ibid., 10 March 1960.

86. *Charlotte Observer* cc, 17 Jan. 1960. There are several indications that Tross is the unnamed man being quoted in this article. After Grace's death Tross was quoted several times in the *Washington Post* series written by Phil Casey, who described him as Grace's good friend and "a doctor of philosophy and pastor of a conservative Negro church in Charlotte." Likewise, the *Charlotte Observer* interviewed a local but unnamed friend of Grace, describing him as "a learned and widely respected Negro minister of an established faith." I believe the man quoted in the *Observer* is the same one quoted in the *Post* because Grace's circle of friends was quite small, and because it is unlikely that he had more than one close friend in Charlotte who both held a doctorate and was a conservative Black pastor.

87. *Charlotte Observer* cc, 17 Jan. 1960.

88. Ibid., 31 March 1977, 9 Dec. 1947; *Baltimore Afro-American*, 18 Jun. 1949; NBST cc, 9 Dec. 1948.

89. J. S. Nathaniel Tross, introduction to *The Anthology of Zion Method-*

ism, by William Henry Davenport (Charolotte, NC: AME Zion Publishing House, 1925), also published online by Academic Affairs Library at the University of North Carolina at Chapel Hill, http://docsouth.unc.edu/church/davenport/davenport.html, accessed in 2005.

90. Based on several issues of the *House of Prayer Quarterly,* Gelman Library Special Collections, George Washington University. Over time the preface statement was reworded slightly. There is no indication of who selected the Biblical passages nor of who authored the Main Thought. Based on issues from the 1940s and 1950s it appears that the Main Thought was written and edited by as few as two people, as its tone and approach is quite consistent. William Toland was the only person listed in all available issues as being involved in its production. After Grace's death the *Quarterly* was renamed the *McCollough Sunday School Lesson Book,* and its content was slightly amended. My thanks goes to Rachael Swierzewski for assistance with research on the *Quarterly.*

91. Nourse, *Weeping Willow,* 30–32, 109.

NOTES TO CHAPTER 6

1. *New York Amsterdam News,* 30 Jan. 1960. The papers suggested Grace had recorded his own eulogy, which was not the case.

2. Grace, *Last Sermon on the Mount.*

3. NBST cc, 21 Jan. 1960; *Journal and Guide,* 16 Jan. 1960, 23 Jan. 1960; *Baltimore Afro-American,* 23 Jan. 1960; Poinsett, "Farewell"; *New York Amsterdam News,* 23 Jan. 1960.

4. *Baltimore Afro-American,* 23 Jan. 1960.

5. NBST cc, 24 Jan. 1960; NBST cc, photograph files; *New Bedford Standard-Times,* 12 Jan. 1985.

6. *Journal and Guide,* 23 Jan. 1960; NBST cc, 21 Jan. 1960.

7. *Washington Post,* 21 Jan. 1960.

8. NBST cc, 21 Jan. 1960; *Philadelphia Evening Bulletin,* 21 Jan. 1960, 22 Jan. 1960.

9. *Philadelphia Evening Bulletin,* 22 Jan. 1960; *New York Times,* 23 Jan. 1960.

10. NBST cc, 23 Jan. 1960, 24 Jan. 1960; *New York Amsterdam News,* 30 Jan. 1960; NBST cc, photograph files.

11. *New York Amsterdam News,* 30 Jan. 1960.

12. NBST cc, 15 Jan. 1960, 28 Jan. 1962, 29 Oct. 1964.

13. Jennie received money because she maintained that divorce records containing her signature had been falsified, and that all along she had thought she was still married to Grace. It is not clear why Irene received money but Marcelino did not, though it may be because the decisions came from courts in different states. *New York Amsterdam News,* 6 Feb. 1960; *Washington Post,* 2 Feb.

1960; NBST cc, 13 Jan. 1960, 3 March 1960, 12 March 1960, 22 March 1960, 19 July 1961, 29 Sept. 1962, 18 Jan. 1965.

14. NBST cc, 26 July 1963.

15. Ibid., 5 July 1962.

16. *New York Amsterdam News,* 13 Feb. 1960.

17. NBST cc, 20 March 1960. The school board ultimately purchased the property in 1962 for market value less back taxes.

18. *New York Times,* 2 Feb. 1960, 3 June 1961.

19. NBST cc, 17 June 1961; *New York Amsterdam News,* 6 Feb. 1960. The executors originally named were Grace's niece Marie Miller and his former doctor, Ernesto Balla.

20. NBST cc, 17 July 1961, document from Massachusetts Probate Court; *Mankind v. United House of Prayer,* microfilm reel AA-37. C.P. 3373 contains over 550 microfilmed pages, not especially in order, of documents related to *Mankind v. United House of Prayer.* Such related documents include partial records from cases in other jurisdictions, including the following identifiable ones: *McClure et al. v. McCollough et al.,* C.A. 2971-60 (U.S. Dist. Ct. of the District of Columbia); *The United House of Prayer for All People of the Church on the Rock of the Apostolic Faith v. The United House of Prayer for All People, Inc.,* C.A. 2627-59 (Sup. Ct. of NJ, Chancery Div., Essex Cty.); [title unknown], C.A. 2149-60 (U.S. Dist. Ct. of the District of Columbia). Unless cited to other specific sources, all of the information related to legal cases in this chapter, including quotes from documents, is based on the records in C.P. 3373.

21. *Philadelphia Tribune,* 23 Jan. 1960; NBST cc, 21 Jan. 1960; *Baltimore Afro-American,* 23 Jan. 1960.

22. *New York Amsterdam News,* 23 Jan. 1960, 30 Jan. 1960.

23. *New York Amsterdam News,* 20 Feb. 1960.

24. *Philadelphia Tribune,* 16 Jan. 1960, 23 Jan. 1960.

25. *Journal and Guide,* 7 July 1945.

26. *Baltimore Afro-American,* 23 Jan. 1960; *Pittsburgh Courier,* 13 Feb. 1960.

27. Hodges, "Charles Manuel," 176.

28. They later said that their opposition was not only to procedural violations but also to the man himself, because he claimed to be the reincarnation of Daddy Grace. *Washington Post,* 10 June 1960; *New York Times,* 3 Oct. 1961; *New York Amsterdam News,* 1 Feb. 1964.

29. Judge Hart was quoted in numerous articles as well as in the case files describing the state of the church's financial affairs as "chaotic confusion."

30. Bryant first made national news three years earlier when he was appointed to the Committee on Admissions and Grievances of the District Court in Washington. *Pittsburgh Courier,* 29 Nov. 1958; *Washington Post,* 15 April 1976.

31. NBST cc, 5 Jan. 1962.

32. At that time, Hart did not follow through with the charge because he did not wish to "make a martyr" of McCollough when the election for a new bishop was still pending. After the legally sanctioned election, Hart dismissed the charge "with prejudice."

33. The majority of the remaining votes were cast for Henry Price of Harlem, according to the *Philadelphia Evening Bulletin,* 9 April 1962. The quoted material is itself quoted in the court case files; it is not clear, but its original source seems to be the church bylaws.

34. *Baltimore Afro-American,* 8 Sept. 1962.

35. A single church called True Grace Memorial first incorporated in Pennsylvania in June 1961, but the break became a more significant action when several dismissed elders joined in in 1962. *Lawson et al., v. United House of Prayer for All People of the Church on the Rock of the Apostolic Faith,* 1966 U.S. Dist. Ct. for the Eastern Dist. of Pennsylvania, Lexis 7785; NBST cc, 19 Aug. 1962; J. Gordon Melton, ed., *Encyclopedia of American Religions,* 1st ed. (Wilmington, NC: McGrath Publishing, 1978), 302–3; Piepkorn, *Profiles in Belief,* 224–25.

36. All property accountings are from *McClure v. McCollough.* Despite repeated reports of the church's owning a coffee plantation in Brazil, there is no evidence in the property records of any foreign real estate other than in Cuba. Perhaps this property was sold sometime earlier, but it is also possible that the property was a complete fabrication.

37. *New York Amsterdam News,* 12 March 1960, 9 Sept. 1961; NBST cc, 15 March 1960.

38. Mankind's stockholders were Walton, at fifty-two shares, and Katie Smith and Ira Lovett, who had twenty-four shares each. In the fall of 1960, Charles Wragg became the president of Mankind.

39. This was a new church insomuch as the courts ruled it had no affiliation with Daddy Grace's House of Prayer. However, from day one the "members" involved in the lawsuit consistently asserted that they were in fact the true heirs of Grace's leadership, and that McCollough had usurped their role.

40. Most of the contract focuses on payment and how it would be made, rather than what tasks Mankind was supposed to complete. One portion, a statement by Enoch Walker, tangentially outlines why it was that this church claimed to be the true church once founded by Grace.

41. The signs specified that "pursuant to Title 14:2–7 of New Jersey Revised Statutes," they were "protect[ing] the interests and the assets of this church" by not allowing trespassers who might seek to take any property.

42. The liquidating trustees included Charles Wragg, Erma Griffin, Enoch Walker, and James Walton. Griffin, Walker and Walton also happened to be trustees of the church; Wragg was president of Mankind.

43. *Philadelphia Evening Bulletin,* 8 Dec. 1964, 30 Aug. 1966.

44. Elsewhere, Walton's wife's name has been given as Doris Walton; it is not clear from the record whether this is the same woman, or if he had more than one wife.

45. It is unclear what became of this suit, but the last known record shows it was still in litigation in April 1973.

46. NBST cc, 10 July 1973, 21 Nov. 1973.

47. Hebrews 4:16, as quoted to an interviewer from the *New York Amsterdam News,* 13 Feb. 1960. Examples of baiting include reporters' commenting that an "air of uncertainty" permeated the churches, as written in the *Baltimore Afro-American,* 23 Jan. 1960; or that Grace's "flock shifts aimlessly without a leader," as written in the *Boston Daily Globe,* 7 Feb. 1960.

48. Simeon Booker, Washington Notebook, *Ebony,* Feb. 1981, 25.

49. *Washington Post,* 19 Sept. 1985; NBST cc, 21 Jan. 1960; *Who's Who in the World,* 8th ed., s.v. "Walter McCollough"; *Boston Globe,* 7 Feb. 1960; Payne, *Directory of African American Religious Bodies,* s.v. "United House of Prayer for All People, Church on the Rock of the Apostolic Faith, Inc."; *Philadelphia Tribune,* 23 Jan. 1960.

50. *New York Amsterdam News,* 13 Feb. 1960; Hunter, *Prophets and Profits,* 56.

51. Graphic 1305, Gelman Library Special Collections, George Washington University; *Washington Post,* 29 May 1977; NBST cc, 21 Jan. 1963; "Who Started Shout? 'Daddy Grace' and The United House of Prayer for All People," *arts.community* 2, no. 4 (1997), http://arts.endow.gov/Community/Features24/Babb5.html.

52. *Charlotte Observer,* 19 Sept. 1990; Associated Press, 12 Oct. 1998. Harlem is one of the few places where fire-hose baptisms have continued. Though there is no longer a House of Prayer located at 20 W. 115th Street, every August the baptism takes place there.

53. *Washington Post,* 1 Sept. 1978.

54. *New Bedford Standard-Times,* 21 Oct. 1996; Robinson, "A Song," 230–31; *Charlotte Observer,* 29 Sept. 1990; *Washington Post,* 23 March 1991.

55. *Washington Post,* 14 April 1996, 19 Sept. 1985; *Who's Who in the World,* 8th ed., s.v. "Walter McCollough"; Robinson, "A Song," 233. Most likely the ministerial program was housed by the local House of Prayer in Richmond. I have not been able to find any information that suggests it still exists.

56. *Washington Post,* 19 Sept. 1985; *Charlotte Observer,* 29 Sept. 1990, 10 Oct. 1988; *McCollough Magazine,* n.d., 17, Grace/Emory Collection; Robinson, "A Song," 231–33.

57. *Washington Post,* 25 Aug. 1974.

58. *Washington Post,* 19 Sept. 1985, 23 March 1991.

59. *Washington Post,* 25 Aug. 1974, 23 March 1991; *Who's Who in the World,* 8th ed., s.v. "Walter McCollough."

60. Robinson, "A Song," 232–33.

61. *New York Times,* 17 Dec. 1995. McCollough died after a long period of deteriorating health, in some places recorded as heart failure and in other places as cancer. Comments from his son also suggest that he was suffering from Alzheimer's disease.

62. *Charlotte Observer,* 23 March 1991; *Washington Post,* 14 April 1996, 26 May 1996; *New York Times,* 17 Dec. 1995; *Cutter v. Madison,* et al, Lexis 2012 (U.S. Dist. Ct. for the District of Columbia, 1992). Clara, called Saint Madame by followers, had been very involved in organizing church programs during McCollough's reign. After his death, she felt ostracized from the church and from her former leadership roles.

63. *Washington Times,* 13 May 1992; *Washington Post,* 14 April 1996. Devoted followers still visit the empty tomb at Lincoln Cemetery and leave flowers in McCollough's honor.

64. *Washington Post,* 14 April 1996; *Charlotte Observer,* 23 March 1991.

65. John Mangin, "Gods of the Metropolis: The Rise and Decline of the Black Independent Church," *The Next American City* 1, no. 3 (2003), 19–23; Payne, *Directory of African American Religious Bodies,* s.v. "United House of Prayer for All People, Church on the Rock of the Apostolic Faith, Inc."; *New York Times,* 17 Dec. 1995; *Charlotte Observer,* 23 March 1991; Andrew Beaujon, "God's Trombones," *Richmond Style Weekly,* 26 May 2004, http://StyleWeekly.com/article.asp?idarticle=8465. Although auxiliaries begun under Grace's aegis certainly had the effect of keeping people too busy with church to get into trouble, it was McCollough who made an effort to organize these bands as a deliberate attempt to keep youth involved in the church, and Madison has not dropped this from his purview. Some bands have now taken the new bishop's name, such as the Madison Sunrisers and Madison's Lively Stones.

66. *New York Times,* 17 Dec. 1995.

67. Ibid., 10 Dec. 1995, 17 Dec. 1995. The Harlem House of Prayer was normally located upstairs from the fire-ravaged stores, but had temporarily moved to a location on 116th Street while the sanctuary underwent renovations. The fire caused a setback in their construction progress and the space did not reopen until 1997.

68. For more on this definitional framework see Rodney Stark and William Sims Bainbridge, *The Future of Religion: Secularization, Revival, and Cult Formation* (Berkeley and Los Angeles: Univ. of California Press, 1985).

69. For more on this definitional framework, see the introductory essay by J. Gordon Melton in *When Prophets Die: The Postcharismatic Fate of New Religious Movements,* ed. Timothy Miller, 1–12 (Albany: State Univ. of New York Press, 1991).

70. Baer and Singer, *African American Religion,* 55.

71. Baer and Singer are particularly interested in delineating sectarian categories, and so much of their very intriguing work is focused on these distinctions. Just as NRM scholars find the word "cult" problematic, there is little agreement about the meaning of the term "storefront" among specialists of African American religion. Baer and Singer use it to refer to small churches formed in the North by southern migrants as one measure against urban bewilderment. In contrast, Arthur Paris has argued that despite its preponderance, the only consistent thing this term describes is the physical space a religious group uses. The word "storefront," he argues, says nothing about theology, behavior, membership, community involvement, affluence, and so forth, yet it does tend to have negative connotations. Arthur Paris, *Black Pentecostalism: Southern Religion in an Urban World* (Amherst: Univ. of Massachusetts Press, 1982).

72. I am not suggesting scholars need to agree on a single framework. Conundrums of how to define and categorize exist in many, many fields of study, and ultimately, there is no harm in having multiple ways to measure things as long as we are conscious of what distinctions are being made in any given definition.

73. One particularly important factor that affects how a group is perceived is region. Consider, as an example, Mormons. The acceptance of the Latter Day Saint Church as being mainline religion varies from region to region, both in and outside of the United States. Depending on where one is, Mormons might be closer to a "religion" or to a "cult" in public opinion.

74. For recent examples of this debate, see the article series in *Nova Religio,* Perspectives, 8, nos. 1–3 (2004–5).

75. Eileen Barker, "What Are We Studying?" *Nova Religio* 8, no. 1 (2004): 99. Barker has raised this issue elsewhere, for example in her edited volume *New Religious Movements: A Perspective for Understanding Society* (New York: Edwin Mellen Press, 1982).

76. Though I am focusing here on groups falling within a Christian framework, these generic categories are by no means limited to Christianity. The Nation of Islam, for example, is a religious body that has demonstrated considerable movement on this spectrum over the years.

77. J. Milton Yinger, *The Scientific Study of Religion* (New York: Macmillan, 1970), 266.

78. I would prefer that a new, more distinct term be found for this in-between place, most especially because Yinger's use implied that established sects inherently move toward the legitimacy of denominationalism and away from sectarian status, whereas I believe that groups in this middle ground can move in either direction. I defer to the precedent of Yinger's term because he is the only person I am aware of who has considered this in-between category significant enough to name.

79. Yinger, *Scientific Study,* 266–67. Yinger classified most Pentecostals into a sect subcategory called "avoidance sects," primarily because their focus is otherworldy.

80. Max Weber, *The Theory of Social and Economic Organization,* trans. and ed. A. M. Henderson and Talcott Parsons (New York: Free Press, 1947), 358–73.

81. Additionally, George Chryssides has argued that because Weber did not distinguish between types of charisma nor types of charismatic leadership, his ideas are unwieldy for analyzing the many different types of NRMs. See: George Chryssides, "Unrecognized Charisma? A Study of Four Charismatic Leaders," conference paper, international conference organized by CESNUR (Center for Studies on New Religions) and INFORM (Information Network Focus on Religious Movements), London, April 2001, available online at http://www.cesnur.org/2001/london2001/chryssides.htm, accessed in 2005.

82. Miller, *When Prophets Die,* vii.

83. One could also consider some of these groups, such as the Shakers and the Mormons, as following the trajectory of the "revitalization process" as described in Anthony Wallace, "Revitalization Movements," *American Anthropologist* 58, no. 2 (1958), 264–81. However, the process undergone by the House of Prayer does not readily fit Wallace's schema.

NOTES TO THE CONCLUSION

1. In the list of comparisons, I do not mean to suggest that these men offer(ed) similar theologies; rather, it is their dramatic, stylistic approach to preaching and religious leadership that is comparable.

2. It took me a very long time to realize that Campbell's story was, in fact, important for understanding the House of Prayer; but the story of Louvenia Royster is not, unless her version of events is actually true. In a 1957–58 case that became quite public, Royster sued Grace, claiming they were married in 1923 when he went by the name John Royster and that he deserted her sometime thereafter. The judge found in favor of Grace after evidence showed he had been abroad when Mrs. Royster's marriage took place. For an excellent examination of this case, see Brune, "Sweet Daddy."

3. Wallace Best, in the context of discussing Reverend Clarence Cobbs, offers interesting insights about perceptions of homosexuality during that era. Wallace Best, *Passionately Human, No Less Divine: Religion and Culture in Black Chicago, 1915–1952* (Princeton, NJ: Princeton Univ. Press, 2005).

4. For examples of these varying approaches, see James R. Goff, *Fields White unto Harvest: Charles F. Parham and the Missionary Origins of Pentecostalism* (Fayetteville: Univ. of Arkansas Press, 1988); Walter J. Hollenweger, "The Black Roots of Pentecostalism," in *Pentecostals after a Century,* ed. Allan

H. Anderson and Walter J. Hollenweger, 33–44 (Sheffield, UK: Sheffield Academic Press, 1999); Allan H. Anderson, *An Introduction to Pentecostalism* (Cambridge, UK: Cambridge Univ. Press, 2004); and Grant Wacker, *Heaven Below: Early Pentecostals and American Culture* (Cambridge, MA: Harvard Univ. Press, 2001).

5. Vinson Synan, *The Holiness-Pentecostal Tradition: Charismatic Movements in the Twentieth Century* (Grand Rapids, MI: Eerdmans, 1997), 177.

6. Ibid., 176–77. However, Synan appears to agree with the exclusion of the House of Prayer from the Pentecostal tradition.

7. For more on this point, see Iain MacRobert, *The Black Roots and White Racism of Early Pentecostalism in the USA* (Basingstoke, UK: Macmillan Press, 1988), including the excellent foreword by Walter J. Hollenweger.

8. Synan, *The Holiness-Pentecostal Tradition*, 177.

9. Hardesty, *Faith Cure*, 119. She refers to this as the Charles Finney model.

10. Ibid., 119–26.

11. Ibid., 126.

12. Synan, *The Holiness-Pentecostal Tradition*, 195–203; Hardesty, *Faith Cure*, 114.

Bibliography

DOCUMENTS, SPECIAL COLLECTIONS, AND
MIXED-MEDIA SOURCES

Claude A. Barnett Papers. Microfilm. Frederick, MD: University Publications of America, 1986.

"Despatches from US Consuls in Santiago, Cape Verde Islands, 1818–1898." U.S. Department of State, National Archives of the United States, College Park, MD.

Arthur Huff Fauset Papers, 1855–1983. Rare Book and Manuscript Library, University of Pennsylvania, Philadelphia.

Da Graca, Marcelino Manuel. Federal Bureau of Investigation files, U.S. Department of Justice, Washington, DC.

Grace, Daddy. *The Last Sermon on the Mount: You Must Be Born Again.* LP. Los Angeles: Aries Recording Co., 1960.

Daddy Grace Collection, 1953–2000. Manuscript, Archives, and Rare Book Library, Emory University, Atlanta.

Graphics Collections. Gelman Library Special Collections, George Washington University, Washington, DC.

"Immigrants in New Bedford." 1911. New Bedford Free Public Library, New Bedford, MA.

"Index to Passengers Arriving at New Bedford, July 1, 1902–Nov. 18, 1954." New Bedford Free Public Library, New Bedford, MA.

"Inward Passenger Lists, New Bedford, Massachusetts, 1823–1899." New Bedford Free Public Library, New Bedford, MA.

Miscellaneous American Letters and Papers Collection. Manuscripts, Archives, and Rare Books Division of the Schomburg Center for Research on Black Culture, New York Public Library, New York.

The Music District. VHS. Dir. Susan Levitas. California Newsreel, 1995.

New Bedford Death Records. New Bedford Free Public Library, New Bedford, MA.

New Bedford Immigration and Ship Passenger Lists, April 19, 1902–Nov. 24, 1903. New Bedford Free Public Library, New Bedford, MA.

Newspaper clippings collection and photograph collection. *Charlotte Observer.* Charlotte, NC.

Newspaper clippings collection and photograph collection. *New Bedford Standard-Times.* New Bedford, MA.

"Passenger and Crew Lists of Vessels Arriving at New York, 1897–1957." Vol. 8011. National Archives of the United States, Washington, DC.

Preachers and Congregations: Volume 4, 1924–1931. CD. Vienna, Austria: Document Records, 1997.

Sanborn Co. Fire Insurance Maps, City of New Bedford, 1888–1924. New Bedford Free Public Library, New Bedford, MA.

Slum Clearance Committee of New York. Maps and charts. New York, 1934. Harvard University Library, Cambridge, MA.

United States Bureau of the Census. Bristol County, Massachusetts, 1900 and 1920. New Bedford Free Public Library, New Bedford, MA.

WPA Federal Writers' Project Collection. Manuscript Division, Library of Congress, http://memory.loc.gov/wpa/.

COURT RECORDS

Commissioner of Public Welfare of the City of New York v. Charles M. Grace. 1935 N.Y. App. Div., Lexis 8001.

Horace L. Cutter, Sr., et al., v. S.C. Madison and the United House of Prayer for All People, Church on the Rock of the Apostolic Faith. 1992 U.S. Dist., Lexis 2012.

Family Aid Association of the United House of Prayer for All People v. the United States. 1941 U.S. Ct. Cl., Lexis 134.

Lawson et al. v. United House of Prayer for All People of the Church on the Rock of the Apostolic Faith. 1966 U.S. Dist. Ct. Eastern Dist. of Pennsylvania, Lexis 7785.

Mankind Homebuilders, Inc., v. the United House of Prayer for All People, Inc. March term 1960 Phila. Ct. of C.P. 3373, Philadelphia Office of the Prothonotary, Older Records Division.

State v. C. M. Grace. 1928 S.C. of North Carolina, Lexis 349.

W. M. Taylor v. C. M. Grace. 1936 S.C. of Virginia, Lexis 174.

United States v. Charles M. Grace. 1934 2nd Cir. Ct. App. 13440, National Archives of the United States, New York City.

PERIODICALS

Baltimore Afro-American
Boston Globe
Charlotte News

Charlotte Observer
Chicago Defender
Cleveland Call and Post
Ebony
Grace Magazine
House of Prayer Quarterly
Jet
New Bedford Evening Standard
New Bedford Morning Mercury
New Bedford Republican Standard
New Bedford Standard-Times
New Bedford Times
New Day
Newsweek
New York Age
New York Amsterdam News
New York Daily News
New York Times
Norfolk Journal and Guide
Philadelphia Evening Bulletin
Philadelphia Tribune
Pittsburgh Courier
Savannah Tribune
Southcoast Today
Tchuba Newsletter
Time Magazine
Virginian-Pilot
Washington Evening Star
Washington Post
Washington Post and Times Herald
Washington Times
Washington Tribune
Winston Salem Journal-Sentinel

BOOKS, ARTICLES, DISSERTATIONS, AND THESES

Ahlstrom, Sydney E. *A Religious History of the American People.* New Haven: Yale Univ. Press, 1972.

Albanese, Catherine L. *America: Religions and Religion.* 1st and 3rd eds. Belmont, CA: Wadsworth, 1981, 1999.

Alland, Alexander. " 'Possession' in a Revivalistic Negro Church." *Journal for the Scientific Study of Religion* 1 (Spring 1962): 204–13.

"America's Richest Negro Minister." *Ebony*, Jan. 1952: 17–23.

Anderson, Allan H. *An Introduction to Pentecostalism*. Cambridge, UK: Cambridge Univ. Press, 2004.

Anderson, Allan H., and Walter J. Hollenweger, eds. *Pentecostals after a Century*. Sheffield, UK: Sheffield Academic Press, 1999.

Anderson, Jervis. *This Was Harlem: A Cultural Portrait, 1900–1950*. New York: Farrar, Straus, and Giroux, 1982.

Baer, Hans A., and Merrill Singer. *African American Religion: Varieties of Protest and Accommodation*. 2nd ed. Knoxville: Univ. of Tennessee Press, 2002.

———. *African-American Religion in the Twentieth Century: Varieties of Protest and Accommodation*. Knoxville: Univ. of Tennessee Press, 1992.

Bailey, Pearl. *The Raw Pearl*. New York: Harcourt, Brace, and World, 1968.

Barker, Eileen. "What Are We Studying?" *Nova Religio* 8, no. 1 (2004): 88–102.

Barker, Jean E. "The Cape Verdean Immigrant Experience in Harwich, Massachusetts." Master's thesis, University of Massachusetts at Boston, 1993.

Baronov, David. *The Abolition of Slavery in Brazil: The "Liberation" of Africans through the Emancipation of Capital*. Westport, CT: Greenwood Press, 2000.

Becker, Howard S. "Notes on the Concept of Commitment." *American Journal of Sociology* 66 (1960): 32–40.

Bender, Lauretta, and Zuleika Yarrell. "Psychoses among Followers of Father Divine." *Journal of Nervous and Mental Disease* 87 (April 1938): 418–49.

Best, Wallace. *Passionately Human, No Less Divine: Religion and Culture in Black Chicago, 1915–1952*. Princeton, NJ: Princeton Univ. Press, 2005.

Beuhrer, Edwin T. "Harlem's God." *Christian Century*, Dec. 11, 1935: 1590–93.

Blumhofer, Edith. *Aimee Semple McPherson: Everybody's Sister*. Grand Rapids, MI: Eerdmans, 1993.

Boss, Judith A., and Joseph D. Thomas. *New Bedford: A Pictorial History*. Norfolk, VA: Donning Publishers, 1983.

Boulware, Marcus H. *The Oratory of Negro Leaders: 1900–1968*. Westport, CT: Negro Univ. Press, 1969.

Bourdieu, Pierre. *Language and Symbolic Power*. Cambridge, MA: Harvard Univ. Press, 1991.

Braden, Charles S. *Spirits in Rebellion: The Rise and Development of New Thought*. Dallas: Southern Methodist Univ. Press, 1963.

The Brooklyn Story. N.p.: Afro-American Cultural and Service Center, 1978.

Brune, Danielle E. "Sweet Daddy Grace: The Life and Times of a Modern Day Prophet." PhD dissertation, University of Texas at Austin, 2002.

Burnham, Kenneth E. *God Comes to America*. Boston: Lambeth Press, 1979.

Cabral, Stephen L. *Tradition and Transformation: Portuguese Feasting in New Bedford*. New York: AMS Press, 1989.

Cantril, Hadley and Muzafer Sherif. "The Kingdom of Father Divine." *Journal of Abnormal and Social Psychology* 33, no. 2 (1938): 147–67.

Carreira, Antonio. *The People of the Cape Verde Islands: Exploitation and Emigration.* Hamden, CT: Archon Books, 1982.

Casimiro, Augusto. *Portugal Crioulo.* Lisbon: Edicões Cosmos, 1940.

Chryssides, George. "Unrecognized Charisma? A Study of Four Charismatic Leaders." Conference paper, international conference organized by CESNUR (Center for Studies on New Religions) and INFORM (Information Network Focus on Religious Movements), London, April 2001. Available online at http://www.cesnur.org/2001/london2001/chryssides.htm. Accessed in 2005.

"Churches of the Diocese of Fall River." *Rootsweb.* http://www.rootsweb.com/ussnei/FRdiocese.htm, Jan. 28, 2004.

Clark, Elmer T. *Small Sects in America.* 1st and 2nd eds. ed. Nashville: Cokesbury Press, 1937/New York: Abingdon-Cokesbury Press, 1949.

"Daddy Grace." *Life,* Oct. 1, 1945: 51–58.

Dallam, Marie W. "By Daddy Grace Only: Bishop Grace and the Foundational Years of the United House of Prayer." PhD dissertation, Temple University, Philadelphia, 2006.

Damon, Sherri Marcia. "The Trombone in the Shout Band of the United House of Prayer for All People." Doctor of Musical Arts dissertation, University of North Carolina at Greensboro, 1999.

David, Jonathan C. "On One Accord: Community, Musicality, and Spirit among the Singing and Praying Bands of Tidewater Maryland and Delaware." PhD dissertation, University of Pennsylvania, Philadelphia, 1994.

Davidson, Basil. *The Fortunate Isles: A Study of African Transformation.* Trenton: Africa World Press, 1989.

Davis, Lenwood G., comp. *Daddy Grace: An Annotated Bibliography.* New York: Greenwood Press, 1992.

Drake, St. Clair, and Horace R. Cayton. *Black Metropolis: A Study of Negro Life in a Northern City.* 1st and rev. eds. New York: Harcourt, Brace, 1945/New York: Harper and Row, 1962.

Eddy, G. Norman. "Store-Front Religion." *Religion in Life* 28 (Winter 1958–59): 68–85.

Ely, Vermelle Diamond, Grace Hoey Drain, and Amy Rogers. *Charlotte, North Carolina.* Charleston, SC: Arcadia, 2001.

Fauset, Arthur Huff. *Black Gods of the Metropolis: Negro Religious Cults of the Urban North.* Philadelphia: Univ. of Pennsylvania Press, 1944.

Fields, Norma C. "Blacks in Norfolk Virginia during the 1930s." Master's thesis, Old Dominion University, Norfolk, VA, 1979.

Finke, Roger, and Rodney Stark. *The Churching of America, 1776–2005: Winners and Losers in Our Religious Economy.* New Brunswick, NJ: Rutgers Univ. Press, 2005.

Fisher, Miles Mark. "Negroes Get Religion," *Opportunity* 14, no. 5 (May 1936): 147–50.

Frazier, E. Franklin. "Negro Harlem: An Ecological Study." *American Journal of Sociology* 43, no. 1 (July 1937): 72–88.

Glassner, Barry. "Cape Verdeans: The People without a Race." *Sepia,* Nov. 1975: 65–69.

Goff, James R. *Fields White unto Harvest: Charles F. Parham and the Missionary Origins of Pentecostalism.* Fayetteville: Univ. of Arkansas Press, 1988.

Greenberg, Cheryl Lynn. *"Or Does It Explode?" Black Harlem in the Great Depression.* New York: Oxford Univ. Press, 1991.

Greenwood, Janette Thomas. *Bittersweet Legacy: The Black and White "Better Classes" in Charlotte, 1850–1910.* Chapel Hill: Univ. of North Carolina Press, 1994.

Griffith, R. Marie. "Body Salvation: New Thought, Father Divine, and the Feast of Material Pleasures." *Religion and American Culture* 11, no. 2 (2001): 119–53.

Hall, Gordon Langley. *The Sawdust Trail: The Story of American Evangelism.* Philadelphia: Macrae Smith, 1964.

Hall, John R. *Gone from the Promised Land: Jonestown in American Cultural History.* New Brunswick, NJ: Transaction Books, 1987.

Halter, Marilyn. *Between Race and Ethnicity: Cape Verdean American Immigrants, 1860–1965.* Urbana: Univ. of Illinois Press, 1993.

Hanchett, Thomas W. *Sorting Out the New South City: Race, Class, and Urban Development in Charlotte, 1875–1975.* Chapel Hill: Univ. of North Carolina Press, 1998.

Hardesty, Nancy A. *Faith Cure: Divine Healing in the Holiness and Pentecostal Movements.* Peabody, MA: Hendrickson, 2003.

Harrell, David Edwin. *All Things Are Possible: The Healing and Charismatic Revivals in Modern America.* Bloomington: Indiana Univ. Press, 1975.

Harris, Michael W. *The Rise of Gospel Blues: The Music of Thomas Andrew Dorsey in the Urban Church.* New York: Oxford Univ. Press, 1992.

Haskins, Jim. *James Van DerZee: Picture Takin' Man.* Trenton: Africa World Press, 1991.

Heath, Kingston William. *The Patina of Place: The Cultural Weathering of a New England Industrial Landscape.* Knoxville: Univ. of Tennessee Press, 2001.

Heilbut, Anthony. *The Gospel Sound: Good News and Bad Times.* Rev. ed. New York: Limelight Editions, 1997.

Higginbotham, Evelyn Brooks. *Righteous Discontent: The Women's Movement in the Black Baptist Church, 1880–1920.* Cambridge, MA: Harvard Univ. Press, 1993.

Hodges, John O. "Charles Manuel 'Sweet Daddy' Grace." In *Twentieth-Cen-*

tury Shapers of American Popular Religion, edited by Charles Lippy, 170–79. New York: Greenwood Press, 1989.

Horton, Stanley M. "The Pentecostal Perspective." In *Five Views on Sanctification,* 103–35. Grand Rapids, MI: Zondervan, 1987.

Hudson, Winthrop S. *Religion in America.* New York: Scribner's, 1965.

Hudson, Winthrop S., and John Corrigan. *Religion in America.* 5th ed. Upper Saddle River, NJ: Prentice Hall, 1992.

Hunter, Paul. *Prophets and Profits: What's to Be Learned from Daddy Grace and Others Like Him.* New York: Revelation Books, 1996.

Jackson, John L., Jr. *Harlemworld: Doing Race and Class in Contemporary Black America.* Chicago: Univ. of Chicago Press, 2001.

Jones, Raymond Julius. "A Comparative Study of Religious Cult Behavior among Negroes with Special Reference to Emotional Group Conditioning Factors." Master's thesis, Howard University, Washington, DC, 1939.

——. *A Comparative Study of Religious Cult Behavior among Negroes with Special Reference to Emotional Group Conditioning Factors.* Washington, DC: Graduate School for the Division of the Social Sciences, Howard Univ., 1939.

Jones, Wilson Jeremiah. *Black Messiahs and Uncle Toms: Social and Literary Manipulations of a Religious Myth.* Rev. ed. University Park: Pennsylvania State Univ. Press, 1993.

Kelley, Hubert. "Heaven Incorporated." *American Magazine,* Jan. 1936: 40–41, 106–8.

LaFarge, John. "The Incredible Daddy Grace." *America,* April 2, 1960: 5.

Lafferty, Samuel. "The Housing Problem of the Urban Negro." *Crisis* 44, no. 9 (1937): 268–74.

Lewis, David L. *When Harlem Was in Vogue.* New York: Knopf, 1981.

Lewis, Earl. *In Their Own Interests: Race, Class, and Power in Twentieth-Century Norfolk, Virginia.* Berkeley and Los Angeles: Univ. of California Press, 1991.

Lincoln, C. Eric, and Lawrence H. Mamiya. *The Black Church in the African American Experience.* Durham, NC: Duke Univ. Press, 1990.

Lobban, Richard A., Jr. *Cape Verde: Crioulo Colony to Independent Nation.* Boulder, CO: Westview Press, 1995.

Lobban, Richard, and Marlene Lopes. *Historical Dictionary of the Republic of Cape Verde.* 3rd ed. Metuchen, NJ: Scarecrow Press, 1995.

Lopes, Belmira Nunes. *A Portuguese Colonial in America.* Pittsburgh: Latin American Literary Review, 1982.

Love, Rose Leary. *Plum Thickets and Field Daisies.* Charlotte, NC: Public Library of Charlotte and Mecklenburg County, 1996.

Lundell, In-Gyeong Kim. *Bridging the Gaps: Contextualization among Korean Nazarene Churches in America.* New York: Peter Lang Publishing, 1995.

Lyall, Archibald. *Black and White Make Brown: An Account of a Journey to the Cape Verde Islands and Portuguese Guinea.* London: W. Heinemann, 1938.

MacRobert, Iain. *The Black Roots and White Racism of Early Pentecostalism in the USA.* Basingstoke, UK: Macmillan Press, 1988.

Mangin, John. "Gods of the Metropolis: The Rise and Decline of the Black Independent Church." *Next American City* 1, no. 3 (2003): 19–23.

Marsh, Charles F., ed. *The Hampton Roads Communities in World War II.* Chapel Hill: Univ. of North Carolina Press, 1951.

McCabe, Marsha, and Joseph D. Thomas, eds. *Portuguese Spinner: An American Story.* New Bedford, MA: Spinner Publications, 1998.

McKay, Claude. *Negro Metropolis.* New York: E. P. Dutton, 1940.

McKelway, St. Clair, and A. J. Liebling, "Who Is This King of Glory?" *New Yorker,* part 1, June 13, 1936: 21–28; part 2, June 20, 1936: 22–28; part 3, June 27, 1936: 22–32.

Meintel, Deirdre. *Race, Culture, and Portuguese Colonialism in Cabo Verde.* Syracuse, NY: Syracuse Univ. Press, 1984.

Meintel-Machado, Dierdre. "Cape Verdean Americans." In *Hidden Minorities: The Persistence of Ethnicity in American Life,* edited by Joan H. Rollins, 233–56. Washington, DC: Univ. Press of America, 1981.

———. "Language and Interethnic Relations in a Portuguese Colony." In *Ethnic Encounters: Identities and Contexts,* edited by George L. Hicks and Philip E. Leis, 49–62. North Scituate, MA: Duxbury Press, 1977.

Melton, J. Gordon, ed. *Encyclopedia of American Religions.* 1st and 2nd eds. Wilmington, NC: McGrath Publishing, 1978/Detroit: Gale, 1987.

Miller, Timothy, ed. *When Prophets Die: The Postcharismatic Fate of New Religious Movements.* Albany: State Univ. of New York Press, 1991.

Monteiro, Joao. "The Church of the Nazarene in Cape Verde: A Religious Import in a Creole Society." PhD dissertation, Drew University, Madison, NJ, 1997.

Morrill, Dan L. *Historic Charlotte: An Illustrated History of Charlotte and Mecklenburg County.* N.p.: Historical Publishing Network, 2001.

Naro, Nancy. *A Slave's Place, A Master's World: Fashioning Dependency in Rural Brazil.* New York: Continuum, 2000.

New Bedford and Fairhaven City Directory. Boston: W. A. Greenough and Co., various years.

Nourse, Jean Alexander. *Weeping Willow African Methodist Episcopal Zion Church: A History.* Charlotte, NC: AME Zion Church, 1995.

Osofsky, Gilbert. *Harlem: The Making of a Ghetto.* New York: Harper and Row, 1963.

Ottley, Roi. *"New World A-Coming": Inside Black America.* Boston: Houghton Mifflin, 1943.

Paris, Arthur. *Black Pentecostalism: Southern Religion in an Urban World.* Amherst: Univ. of Massachusetts Press, 1982.

Parker, Robert Allerton. *Incredible Messiah.* Boston: Little, Brown, 1937.

Parramore, Thomas C. *Norfolk: The First Four Centuries.* Charlottesville: Univ. Press of Virginia, 1994.

Parsons, Elsie Clews. "Ten Folk-Tales from the Cape Verde Islands." *Journal of American Folk-Lore* 30 (April 1917): 230–38.

Patterson, K. David. "Epidemics, Famines, and Population in the Cape Verde Islands, 1580–1900." *International Journal of African Historical Studies* 21, no. 2 (1988): 291–313.

Payne, Wardell J., ed. *Directory of African American Religious Bodies.* 2nd ed. Washington, DC: Howard Univ. Press, 1995.

Peeks, Edward. *The Long Struggle for Black Power.* New York: Scribner's, 1971.

Piepkorn, Arthur Carl. *Profiles in Belief.* Vol. 3. San Francisco: Harper and Row, 1977.

Poinsett, Alex. "Farewell to Daddy Grace." *Ebony,* April 1960: 25–34.

Randolph, Elizabeth S., ed. *An African-American Album: The Black Experience in Charlotte and Mecklenburg County.* Charlotte, NC: Public Library of Charlotte and Mecklenburg County, 1992.

Reader, Ian. "Imagined Persecution." In *Millennialism, Persecution, and Violence,* edited by Catherine Wessinger, 158–82. Syracuse, NY: Syracuse Univ. Press, 2000.

Reid, Ira De Augustine. *The Negro Immigrant: His Background, Characteristics, and Social Adjustment, 1899–1937.* Reprint ed. New York: Arno Press, 1969.

Robinson, John W. "A Song, a Shout, and a Prayer." In *The Black Experience in Religion,* edited by C. Eric Lincoln, 213–35. Garden City, NY: Anchor Books, 1974.

Rogers, John R., and Amy T. Rogers. *Charlotte: Its Historic Neighborhoods.* Charleston, SC: Arcadia, 1996.

Rudy, David R., and Arthur L. Greil. "Taking the Pledge: The Commitment Process in Alcoholics Anonymous." *Sociological Focus* 20 (Jan. 1987): 45–59.

Ruttenbaum, Steven. *Mansions in the Clouds: The Skyscraper Palazzi of Emery Roth.* New York: Balsam Press, 1986.

Sallee, James. *A History of Evangelistic Hymnody.* Grand Rapids, MI: Baker Book House, 1978.

Schoener, Allon, ed. *Harlem on My Mind: Cultural Capital of Black America, 1900–1968.* Updated ed. New York: New Press, 1995.

Sigler, Danielle Brune. "Beyond the Binary: Revisiting Father Divine, Daddy Grace, and Their Ministries." In *Race, Nation, and Religion in the Americas,* edited by Henry Goldschmidt and Elizabeth McAlister, 209–27. New York: Oxford Univ. Press, 2004.

Sigler, Danielle Brune. "Daddy Grace: An Immigrant's Story." In *Immigrant Faiths: Transforming Religious Life in America,* edited by Karen I. Leonard et al., 67–78. Walnut Creek, CA: AltaMira Press, 2005.

Simmons, George Finlay. "Sinbads of Science: Narrative of a Windjammer's Specimen-Collecting Voyage to the Sargasso Sea, to Senegambian Africa, and among Islands of High Adventure in the South Atlantic." *National Geographic,* July 1927: 1–75.

Smith, Timothy L. *Called unto Holiness.* Kansas City, MO: Nazarene Publishing House, 1962.

Spinner: People and Culture in Southeastern Massachusetts. Vols. 1–4. New Bedford, MA: Spinner Publications, 1981–88.

Stark, Rodney, and William Sims Bainbridge. *The Future of Religion: Secularization, Revival, and Cult Formation.* Berkeley and Los Angeles: Univ. of California Press, 1985.

Stark, Rodney, and Roger Finke. *Acts of Faith: Explaining the Human Side of Religion.* Berkeley and Los Angeles: Univ. of California Press, 2000.

Suggs, Henry Lewis. *P. B. Young, Newspaperman: Race, Politics, and Journalism in the New South, 1910–1962.* Charlottesville: Univ. Press of Virginia, 1988.

Synan, Vinson. *The Holiness-Pentecostal Tradition: Charismatic Movements in the Twentieth Century.* Grand Rapids, MI: Eerdmans, 1997.

Tross, J. S. Nathaniel. Introduction to *The Anthology of Zion Methodism,* by William Henry Davenport. Charlotte, NC: AME Zion Publishing House, 1925. Also published online by Academic Affairs Library at the University of North Carolina at Chapel Hill, http://docsouth.unc.edu/church/davenport/davenport.html. Accessed in 2005.

———. *This Thing Called Religion.* Charlotte, NC: n.p., 1934.

Tyms, James Daniel. "A Study of Four Religious Cults Operating among Negroes." Master's thesis, Howard University, Washington, DC, 1938.

Wacker, Grant. *Heaven Below: Early Pentecostals and American Culture.* Cambridge, MA: Harvard Univ. Press, 2001.

Wallace, Anthony. "Revitalization Movements." *American Anthropologist* 58, no. 2 (1958): 264–81.

Watters, Pat. *Charlotte.* Special report by the Southern Regional Council. Atlanta: Southern Regional Council , 1964.

Watts, Jill. *God, Harlem U.S.A.* Berkeley and Los Angeles: Univ. of California Press, 1992.

Webb, Jane Carter. *Newport News.* Charleston, SC: Arcadia Press, 2003.

Webb, Lillian Ashcraft. *About My Father's Business: The Life of Elder Michaux.* Westport, CT: Greenwood Press, 1981.

Weber, Max. *The Theory of Social and Economic Organization*. Translated and edited by A. M. Henderson and Talcott Parsons. New York: Free Press, 1947.

Weisbrot, Robert. *Father Divine and the Struggle for Racial Equality*. Urbana: Univ. of Illinois Press, 1983.

Wentz, Richard E. *Religion in the New World: The Shaping of Religious Traditions in the United States*. Minneapolis: Fortress Press, 1990.

Whiting, Albert N. "The United House of Prayer for All People: A Case Study of a Charismatic Sect." PhD dissertation, American University, Washington, DC, 1952.

"Who Started Shout? 'Daddy Grace' and the United House of Prayer for All People." *Arts.community* 2, no. 4 (1997), http://arts.endow.gov/Community/Features24/Babb5.html. Accessed in 1998.

Williams, Chancellor. "The Socio-Economic Significance of the Store-Front Church Movement in the United States since 1920." PhD dissertation, American University, Washington, DC, 1949.

Williams, Peter W. *America's Religions: Traditions and Cultures*. 1990; reprint ed. Urbana: Univ. of Illinois Press, 1998.

Works Progress Administration (WPA), Federal Writers' Project in Georgia, Augusta Unit. *Augusta*. American Guide Series. Augusta: Tidwell Printing Supply, 1938.

———, Savannah Unit. *Savannah*. American Guide Series. Savannah: Review Printing Co., 1937.

Works Projects Administration (WPA), Georgia Writers' Project, Savannah Unit. *Drums and Shadows: Survival Studies among the Georgia Coastal Negroes*. Reprint ed. Spartanburg, SC: Reprint Co., 1974.

———, Virginia Writers' Program. *The Negro in Virginia*. New York: Hastings House, 1940.

Yarsinske, Amy Waters. *Norfolk's Church Street: Between Memory and Reality*. Charleston, SC: Arcadia Press, 1999.

Yinger, J. Milton. *The Scientific Study of Religion*. New York: Macmillan, 1970.

Index

About the Author

Marie W. Dallam completed her doctorate in American Religion at Temple University. Her research interests include New Religious Movements, African American Religious History, and Religion in Popular Culture. She lives in Philadelphia.